Fighting for Time

1969-70

The Vietnam Experience

Fighting for Time

by Samuel Lipsman, Edward Doyle,
and the editors of Boston Publishing Company

Boston Publishing Company/Boston, MA

Boston Publishing Company

President and Publisher: Robert J. George
Vice President: Richard S. Perkins, Jr.
Editor-in-Chief: Robert Manning
Managing Editor: Paul Dreyfus

Senior Writers:
Clark Dougan, Edward Doyle, Samuel
  Lipsman, Terrence Maitland, Stephen Weiss
Senior Picture Editor: Julene Fischer

Staff Writer: David Fulghum
Researchers:
Kerstin Gorham (Chief), Michael T. Casey,
  Susan Freinkel, Denis Kennedy, Carole
  Rulnick, Ted Steinberg

Picture Editors: Wendy Johnson, Lanng
  Tamura
Assistant Picture Editor: Kathleen A. Reidy
Picture Researchers:
Nancy Katz Colman, Nana Elisabeth Stern,
  Shirley L. Green (Washington, D.C.), Kate
  Lewin (Paris), Jane T. Merritt
Picture Department Assistants: Suzanne
  Spencer, Kathryn Steeves

Historical Consultants:
Vincent H. Demma, Lee Ewing, Ernest May
Picture Consultant: Ngo Vinh Long

Production Editor: Patricia Leal Welch
Assistant Editor: Karen E. English
Editorial Production:
Pamela George, Elizabeth Hamilton, Joan
  Kenney, Jeffrey L. Seglin

Design: Designworks, Sally Bindari

Marketing Director: Jeanne C. Gibson
Business Staff: Darlene Keefe, Amy P. Wilson

About the editors and authors

Editor-in-Chief *Robert Manning*, a long-time journalist, has previously been editor-in-chief of the *Atlantic Monthly* magazine and its press. He served as assistant secretary of state for public affairs under Presidents John F. Kennedy and Lyndon B. Johnson. He has also been a fellow at the Institute of Politics at the John F. Kennedy School of Government at Harvard University.

Authors: *Samuel Lipsman*, a former Fulbright Scholar, received his M.A. and M.Phil. in history at Yale. *Edward Doyle*, a historian, received his masters degree at the University of Notre Dame and his Ph.D. at Harvard University. Mr. Lipsman and Mr. Doyle have coauthored other volumes in *The Vietnam Experience*, including *Setting the Stage* and *America Takes Over*.
Historical Consultants: *Vincent H. Demma*, a historian with the U.S. Army Center of Military History, is currently working on the center's history of the Vietnam conflict. *Lee Ewing*, editor of *Army Times*, served two years in Vietnam as a combat intelligence officer with the U.S. Military Assistance Command, Vietnam (MACV) and the 101st Airborne Division. *Ernest May* is Charles Warren Professor of History at Harvard University.

Picture Consultant: *Ngo Vinh Long* is a social historian specializing in China and Vietnam. Born in Vietnam, he returned there most recently in 1980. His books include *Before the Revolution: The Vietnamese Peasants Under the French* and *Report From a Vietnamese Village*.

Cover Photo:

During the U.S. incursion into Cambodia of May-June 1970, men of the 11th Armored Cavalry Regiment watch as an enemy rocket-propelled grenade explodes near their tank.

Library of Congress Catalog Card Number: 83-72005

ISBN: 0-939526-07-7

10 9 8 7 6
5 4 3 2

Contents

The Tortuous Road to Peace

His left hand resting on an old family Bible, his right hand raised in the air, swearing to "preserve, protect and defend the Constitution," on January 20, 1969, Richard Milhous Nixon became the thirty-seventh president of the United States. The inauguration, perhaps more than the election, was the true celebration of American democracy. The joining of both former and future presidents on the dais, the presence of the chief justice of the United States as presiding officer, and the oath of office itself all emphasized continuity rather than interruption in the transition between administrations. And so, on January 20, 1969, along with Lyndon Johnson's Air Force-1 jet and Lyndon Johnson's presidential yacht and Lyndon Johnson's White House, Richard Nixon inherited Lyndon Johnson's undeclared, presidential war.

Not that he wanted to. Elected to office on November 5, claiming to have a "secret plan to end the war," Nixon well knew that his political future

could hinge on preventing Johnson's war from becoming Nixon's war. To achieve that goal, planning could not be delayed until January 20. Many of the most important decisions of his term in office would have to be made during the ten-week transition period between the election and the inauguration. More than any other factor, the men he chose to be his senior foreign policy advisers would determine how Richard Nixon would handle the legacy of Lyndon Johnson's war.

Transitions

Far away from network telecasts, the men of the 9th Marines heard about Richard Nixon's election in their home at Vandegrift combat base in the far northwestern corner of Quang Tri Province. Although separated by 12,000 miles, Captain David F. Winecoff, commander of Hotel Company, 2d Battalion, 9th Marines, 3d Marine Division, like his commander in chief-elect, faced a trying transition period of his own during December and January.

In mid-December, the one-year tour of duty for a full one-third of his company ended, "most of them fire team leaders and every squad leader." Fortunately, his battalion commander gave him an opportunity to prepare his new soldiers' transition. Hotel Company was assigned security duty at Fire Support Base Cates, where "the people who were going to have to run the squads and fire team leaders got some training in." Captain Winecoff liked to create a "family environment" within his company. Remembering his own experience attending three different high schools in three years, he believed it "a real duty to think the new men were in culture shock . . . and would have a hard time dealing with where they were." The two weeks at Cates gave him an opportunity to orient his new men to the reality of combat in Vietnam.

At the end of December Winecoff's entire battalion received an unusual treat, three days of R & R in the village of Cua Viet, located on the ocean, just south of the DMZ. "It was a picnic environment," Winecoff observed. "My strongest memory was going barefoot in a swimming suit with a T-shirt on." But Winecoff interrupted his company's three days of swimming, movies, and USO shows with a special class of his own. Aware of his men's inexperience and mindful that his own military schooling had not updated ambush tactics since the Korean War, Winecoff organized his own informal ambush class. "Right there at Cua Viet," he recalls, "I thought it was that important." A few weeks later, history would vindicate his decision.

On January 2, the 2d Battalion, 9th Marines, returned to combat for Operation Dawson River South. But Company H had only one contact with the enemy during the sixteen-

---

Preceding page. Transition. Lyndon Baines Johnson passes the responsibilities of office to Richard Milhous Nixon on January 20, 1969.

day operation. Just as well. "This was a real good shakedown cruise," Winecoff thought. "We found a lot of gear, we got practice on spot reporting, the new squad leaders got practice leading squads. . . . We got a lot of bugs shaken out." On January 19, the men returned to Vandegrift. The next day was Richard Nixon's inauguration.

★　　★　　★　　★

Well before that event, Richard Nixon flew to Key Biscayne, Florida, on the day after his election for a post-campaign rest. Staying at the home of Florida senator George Smathers, Nixon spent a quiet week with intimate friends. On Saturday another old friend, one-time running mate Henry Cabot Lodge, arrived for consultations. Little was said to the press except that the president-elect had "special assignments" in mind for Lodge. Eight weeks later Nixon announced that Lodge would be his chief negotiator at the Paris peace talks.

Nixon spent the next two weeks shuttling between Key Biscayne and New York, ending up in New York on Thursday, November 21. Now established at the Hotel Pierre, an exclusive luxury hotel on Fifth Avenue, Nixon awaited some of his most important visitors.

Early on Monday afternoon, November 25, an unlikely figure stepped out from a black limousine that regularly brought dignitaries to the Pierre. A senior professor in Harvard University's Department of Government, a contributor to that prestigious bastion of "Eastern liberalism," the Council on Foreign Relations, a protégé of New York governor Nelson Rockefeller, Henry Kissinger seemed to be a figure more likely to emerge out of the "best and brightest" of John Kennedy's New Frontier than from Richard Nixon's New Federalism. His ambitions disappointed when Rockefeller was denied the Republican presidential nomination, Kissinger now found himself with a second chance to reach the upper levels of national power.

His discussion with Nixon was a remarkable one for transition period politics. Not so much the substance of foreign policy, but its theories and methods were the topic of conversation. The two men, so outwardly different, had each found a kindred spirit. The one from his study of history, the other from his temperament and practical experience, agreed that the formulation of foreign policy must be tightly controlled and centrally directed. The influence of the career bureaucrats must be neutralized. Careful timing and utmost secrecy were the true friends of the statesman and diplomat. Their discussion was invigorating, even engrossing. So much so, that after Kissinger left his hotel room Nixon suddenly remembered that he had failed to offer Kissinger a job. But one week later Nixon and Kissinger met again, this time before the national press, to announce that Dr. Henry Kissinger would be the president's assistant for national security affairs. The *New York Times* duly endorsed the selection on its editorial page. The only discomfort expressed by James Reston was that it was "odd" that the national security ad-

The CH-46 Sea Knight added greatly to the marines' mobility after 1968. Here the command post of the 5th Marines, 1st Marine Division, is resupplied by one of the giant helicopters.

viser should be appointed before either the secretary of state or defense. "This may lead to some friction," the *Times's* major political columnist noted.

In the next few weeks Nixon announced other important appointments. In mid-December he presented his entire cabinet to the American public. Melvin Laird, a congressman from Wisconsin, would become secretary of defense, and William Rogers, attorney general in the Eisenhower administration, secretary of state. With his new foreign policy team in place, Nixon began to meet more formally with his advisers. On December 28, he requested that a full review of America's Vietnam policy be ready by Inauguration Day. After spending New Year's Day at the Rose Bowl, Nixon rounded out his foreign policy appointments, naming Elliot Richardson undersecretary of state while returning Ellsworth Bunker as ambassador in Saigon.

With the bulk of his appointments made, Nixon turned his attention to his inaugural address, breaking his routine to view the Super Bowl on January 12. That week he endorsed the compromise seating arrangement worked out by the Johnson administration at Paris, which gave promise of breaking the stalemate in negotiations. On Sunday, January 19, he flew to Washington and conferred with Kissinger and Lodge. The next day he would take the oath of office and assume the burden of the presidency.

Addressing the nation and his "fellow citizens of the world community," Richard Nixon delivered his inaugural address entitled, "Forward Together." "We are caught," he exclaimed, "in war, wanting peace. We're torn by division, wanting unity. We see around us empty lives, wanting fulfillment." The *New York Times* labeled his talk "a promise to search for peace." "The greatest honor history can bestow is the title of peacemaker," the new president stated. "This honor now beckons America." It was an honor that America deeply desired. But the fine print was there as well: "I know that peace does not come through wishing for it—that there is no substitute for days and even years of patient and prolonged diplomacy." For the one-half million American servicemen fighting in Vietnam those "days and years of patient and prolonged diplomacy" meant more war. On January 20, 1969, even as President Nixon addressed the nation on his promise of peace, Captain Winecoff's Hotel Company, 2d Battalion, 9th Marines, prepared for Operation Dewey Canyon.

The marines' new look

All along the DMZ one could see the change. For 1969, the marines had adopted a new look. Trading in their standard olive drab uniforms, the combat troops of the 3d Marine Division now displayed new camouflage utilities of shaded yellows and greens. Even the buttoned fly had been replaced by a modern zipper. "That ought to keep out the leeches," one corporal observed approvingly.

Less visible, but of far greater importance, was the new tactical look that some army and marine commanders were showing. Under Lieutenant General William B. Rosson's leadership as Provisional Corps commander, the army's 1st Cavalry (Airmobile) and 101st Airborne (Airmobile) divisions had gradually increased their mobility and the breadth of their operations, penetrating areas heretofore avoided by American ground troops. As for the marines, by late 1969 a sharp division of responsibility had emerged between the divisions in I Corps. The 1st Division, headquartered along the coast near Da Nang, continued to fight the guerrilla struggle in that heavily populated region. The 3d Division, stretched out along the DMZ, was fighting a quasiconventional war against NVA regulars in the sparsely populated hills of northern South Vietnam. Just as the border clashes of late 1967 and 1968 were ending, the 3d Division received a new commander, a man destined to become one of the most respected marine generals of the war, a Medal of Honor winner in Korea and a decisive leader, Major General Raymond A. Davis.

Davis arrived in June. He immediately set out to provide his division with an airmobility that heretofore had eluded the marines but had long characterized such army divisions as the 1st Air Cav and the 101st Airborne. Davis had come at a propitious moment. The 3d had been plagued throughout 1967 and much of 1968 by a lack of helicopters. They also had experienced severe mechanical problems with the large CH-46 helicopters required to move vast numbers of troops and heavy weapons. But Davis found that "our resources were finally fully generated. We had all new 46s which gave much better lift capability and the gunships were coming in, in serious numbers."

The new helicopters were an essential prerequisite. But perhaps more important were changes in Saigon. Davis took over the 3d Division almost immediately after General Creighton Abrams had replaced William Westmoreland as MACV commander. In his previous assignment as deputy commander of Provisional Corps in I Corps, Davis had watched, with a dismay shared by many marines, the reinforcement of troops along the DMZ ordered by Westmoreland. Westmoreland, Davis said, "was trying to maintain control of these outlying areas with fixed positions. He was determined to keep up forces out there in somewhat of a blocking position, although the forces were so immobile they did little blocking." Abrams was less intent on maintaining these positions and gave quick approval to Davis's decision to redeploy many of the troops based along the DMZ. "There is no question that the Abrams approach was different," Davis concluded.

Seizing the opportunity, Davis made uncharacteristically rapid changes:

I had always moved into new jobs on an idea of not trying to disturb things too quickly, but when I arrived at Dong Ha [Third Division headquarters], I determined that we were not going to try to fight that kind of war. It took me three hours to assemble

PFC Albert O. Covington, Cpl. Lester L. Reardon, and Cpl. James B. Taylor (right to left), all of the 3d Reconnaissance Battalion, carry NVA antiaircraft guns removed from an enemy ammunitions cache discovered while on patrol.

people and reduce those battalion positions down to company positions. It was that much of a concern of mine that we had our force immobilized in all those positions.

By reducing the DMZ "strong-points" from battalion to company size, Davis was able to free the troops he required to carry out his airmobile tactics.

In his capacity as deputy commander of Prov Corp under General Rosson, Davis was able to experiment with what General Westmoreland had in mind when he established the command in northern I Corps: a cross-fertilization of army and marine practices. When he was given command of the 3d Division, Davis found the opportunity to spread Rosson's tactics to the marines and add his own touches. Davis did not improvise new tactics; he agreed that his were "very similar" to those employed by the army airmobile divisions. Rather he combined them in a new manner to create his own distinctive concept of operations. Davis described his concept as "more extensive, more broad-based, a heavier commitment for a longer period."

He began with a more extensive reconnaissance and intelligence plan. Davis had a great deal of prior experience as an intelligence analyst, which gave him a head start in sifting through the "wheel-barrels full" of information gleaned from "line crosses, agents, double agents, electronic sources and communications intercept sources." But rather than rely heavily on his own judgment, Davis employed an "extensive reconnaissance effort—little four-man teams—throughout the mountains." Organizing sixty recon teams, Davis ordered that twenty of them be in the field at all times. The major innovation, according to Davis, of his reconnaissance effort was that "the whole basis was stealth." Unlike the common practice under "reconnaissance in force" and "long-range reconnaissance patrols," no effort was made to engage the enemy or call in reinforcements if the enemy was found.

Davis made this change because he designed his operations not so much to pin down and destroy enemy forces as to disrupt and destroy their logistics system. Since supplies were less "mobile" than enemy troops, he could afford to wait before acting on intelligence, with confidence that the supply caches would still be where they had been originally found. Davis was pleased with the results: He felt that his division had been able to "ferret out" the enemy's logistical system in its area of operations.

Even with this extensive reconnaissance effort, Davis believed that operations had to unfold slowly. His operations were, in his opinion, "more deliberate, methodical and prolonged, even though, in some cases, bolder . . ."

than previous army and marine efforts. The entire area of operations had to be thoroughly searched. If a logistical depot was found in one location, it was likely that others were near it. Always there was the danger that enemy troops might be nearby. Above all, Davis relied on more extensive foot patrolling than did army airmobile units.

There is a saying that the marines use helicopters as "ships"—to get *to* the battlefield—while the army uses helicopters as "horses"—to move *around* the battlefield. Davis's concept of operations bore this distinction out. Under Davis's use of airmobility, the marines would advance slowly into the mountains with CH-46 helicopters first bringing artillery and ground troops to establish firebases on the edges of the operational area. These bases were constructed to provide overlapping "artillery fans," a common practice, so that none of the area was beyond the reach of artillery protection from at least one firebase. From there marine rifle squads, even entire battalions, would march on foot to search the area thoroughly, slowly moving to the edge of artillery protection. Then a second phase would follow, including the construction of new firebases and permitting a deeper penetration of the operational area. Slowly, methodically, largely on foot, but never beyond the protection of artillery fans, additional phases could be carried out until the entire operational area had been searched for enemy logistical bases.

Of all of the 3d Marine operations under Davis's command, none achieved such great success—or generated so much controversy—as Dewey Canyon, initiated on Inauguration Day, 1969. The operation was preceded by the usual careful on-the-ground intelligence provided by recon teams. Division intelligence concluded that the enemy was initiating a large logistical build-up in its Base Area 611, which straddled the Vietnamese-Laotian border just north of the A Shau Valley and south of the Da Krong River. North Vietnamese Army engineers were reopening a number of major infiltration routes and vehicular traffic experienced a "dramatic surge." The number of trucks sighted along the major routes doubled in early January, reaching more than 1,000 a day at times. Enemy forces identified in the area included elements of the 6th NVA Regiment, 9th NVA Regiment, 65th Artillery Regiment, and the 83d Engineer Regiment—all support and replacement units rather than regular combat troops. More than three-quarters of the base area was believed to lie in Laos, along Route 922. This route later joined Route 548 to provide easy access for the NVA into the Da Nang-Hue coastal region. Mindful of the experiences of just one year earlier, Davis feared that the logistical build-up in Base Area 611 was a prelude to another Tet attack on the coastal cities. In a major departure from most earlier American efforts, the target of Dewey Canyon was enemy logistics, not enemy forces. "There was no [enemy combat] force down there," said Davis. "We knew that. Our primary target was to go in and ferret out this system—without any thought that there was a major force down there."

When the men of Captain David Winecoff's Company H returned to Vandegrift combat base on January 19, they found the 9th Marines already deeply involved in preparing for Dewey Canyon (see map, page 18). "There were all sorts of secret labels on everything. They were trying to keep the troops from knowing what was going on until we were actually in the area of operation." Winecoff's suspicion that this was going to be something special was confirmed by his intelligence briefing: "This was the first operation where we really felt good about the intelligence we had . . . down to the infantry company level."

Responsibility for the careful planning of the operation belonged to the commander of the 9th Marines, Colonel Robert H. Barrow. Barrow confronted some unique problems, including "the location, which was inhospitable: mountainous jungle terrain . . . very close proximity to Laos, which was a sanctuary, of course. It was a great distance from any support base, necessitating a rather significant helicopter support operation because the numbers of people involved were substantial." Above all, Barrow confronted poor weather conditions, which seriously hampered helicopter operations.

The 9th Marines on the move

Employing General Davis's tactical innovations, Barrow began the operation on January 20 by reopening two previously used marine fire support bases, Shiloh and Tun Tavern. Using them as a jumping-off point, Barrow ordered his 2d Battalion into the northernmost portion of the area of operations two days later to establish a new FSB, Razor. Captain Winecoff's Company H was assigned the task of clearing the triple-canopied high ground to establish Razor. He quickly faced the problems of inexperienced troops. "We immediately proceeded to bust about 50 to 60 percent of our axes before we found a few people that knew how to swing an ax." But with the help of the battalion engineers, the FSB was completed on schedule, permitting a rapid build-up of forces. Within two days over 1,500 marines, forty-six tons of cargo, and a battery of 105MM howitzers were in place on Razor.

Proceeding according to plan, another battalion, this time the 3/9, began construction of another FSB, Cunningham, about six kilometers farther south. With five firebases, including the previously opened FSB Henderson now offering overlapping artillery support, the 9th Marines initiated Phase II on January 24. The 2d and 3d battalions led off, the 2/9 on the far west near the Laotian border and the 3/9 on the eastern flank. Their objective was to search the area thoroughly and to construct an additional FSB, Erskine, another five kilometers to the south. When the 1st Battalion was inserted into the middle area, between the 2d and 3d, the marines proceeded southward in three columns, each two to three kilometers apart.

The principal territorial objective of the marines was Co Ka Leuye, Hill 1,175, a small promontory near the southern edge of the operational area. Captain Daniel A. Hitzelburger's Company G, 2d Battalion, drew the assignment of searching the hill. Confronted by slopes averaging up to seventy-five degrees, the company experienced difficult going. Hitzelburger's men had negotiated 500 meters on their first day on the hill, experiencing only a brief skirmish with a few NVA soldiers. Late that day an obstacle appeared—bad weather. The ever-present drizzle and fog were followed by heavy rains, turning the red Vietnamese earth to mush. Still, Company G achieved its objective.

To the enemy, bad weather was an ally, for it grounded most American air attacks and reconnaissance flights. On February 2, the NVA began shelling FSB Cunningham with large 122MM cannons positioned in Laos. One direct hit on the artillery battery's fire direction center killed five marines.

The bad weather continued on February 3, the fourth consecutive day, and Colonel Barrow was now faced with a difficult question. Was the regiment overextended?

Should the operation be canceled? Razor and Cunningham were well stocked with rations and small-arms ammunition, but artillery ammunition was running low, and bad weather precluded any reliable resupply. Barrow decided to bide his time. He ordered his battalions to pull in and remain close to the FSBs where they could be easily supported. Following these orders, Company G began a descent from Hill 1,175 on February 5.

As the marines began retracing their steps, the point squad spotted three NVA soldiers. Hitzelburger sent out a small patrol to check the area more thoroughly. Suddenly, his men were ambushed. A stream of enemy fire halted both the 2d and 3d platoons. Hitzelburger ordered his 1st Platoon to swing through a ravine in order to attack the enemy's left flank, thus enabling the 3d Platoon to break through enemy fire and eventually consolidate the company's position. Five marines were killed and eighteen wounded in the ambush. During the battle Lance Corporal Thomas P. Noonan, Jr., rescued a seriously wounded fellow marine before being mortally wounded himself. He was posthumously awarded the Medal of Honor.

Razor is operational. The 105MM howitzers of newly constructed Fire Support Base Razor fire toward Laos during Operation Dewey Canyon.

A casualty of Dewey Canyon. Marine Corporal Fred E. Kelso of Company L, 2/9 Marines, gets a light after sustaining a wound when his company was attacked by NVA sappers at FSB Cunningham.

The following day a relief company of the 2/9 met up with Company G. After a treacherous descent in which the wounded were lowered by rope down the face of the steep cliff, Company G arrived at LZ Dallas on February 8. Battalion commander Lieutenant Colonel George C. Fox immediately went to visit the company. "They were smiling and laughing. Their clothes were torn, and in some cases completely off of them, but they were ready for a fight," he later noted.

Nearly two weeks of bad weather cost the regiment its momentum and permitted the enemy to gauge more accurately the marines' intention. When the weather broke on February 10, Colonel Barrow occupied FSB Erskine in force and moved his command post from Razor to Cunningham, setting the stage for the final phase of the operation.

Phase III

Early on February 11, the 3d Battalion crossed the Da Krong River, followed by the 1/9 and 2/9 the next morn-

ing. Continuing the plan interrupted by poor weather, the 3d Battalion operated on the eastern flank, the 2d on the far west near the Laotian border, with the 1st holding the middle ground. Each battalion made immediate contact with the enemy, with the 1st thwarting a planned NVA raid on FSB Erskine. With the help of the overlapping artillery fires, the 1/9 claimed twenty-five enemy KIAs.

The heaviest fighting of the operation took place from February 18 to February 22, in the sector of the 1st Battalion. On the morning of the eighteenth, Companies A and C met heavy resistance near the Laotian border, but each claimed thirty enemy dead that day. Two days later, Company C pressed its attack against a heavily fortified NVA hilltop bunker. Relying primarily on air strikes and napalm drops within 500 meters of friendly positions, Company C was able to take the hill. They found a bonanza, capturing two Soviet-made 122MM field guns, the largest yet captured in the war. One of them was put proudly on display at the marine base in Quantico, Virginia.

The capture of the two heavy guns and the subsequent

withdrawal of the enemy force across the border into Laos underscored a problem that had threatened Dewey Canyon from the very beginning. General Davis's recon teams had discovered substantial caches of enemy supplies in the craters left by American bombs—a convenient storage space for the NVA. Davis assumed that the craters on the Laotian side of the border would be equally well stocked. As early as February 2, Davis had requested that his men be permitted to cross the border, arguing that "a raid by a force of two battalions could be launched quickly and effectively to cut [Route] 922 and moving rapidly back to the east to destroy artillery forces and other forces and installations which threaten us." Prevailing rules of engagement permitted such cross-border activity only "in exercise of the right of self-defense against enemy attacks." Davis later acknowledged that this would have been "purely a logistics hunt. . . . This would have been an overt invasion and I could understand why the politicians would be nervous." In the end, Davis's first request was shelved.

But two-and-one-half weeks later the situation changed, especially for the men in Captain Winecoff's Company H of the 2/9. On February 20, they found themselves sitting on a ridge directly overlooking Route 922 in Laos. The men watched as a stream of tracked vehicles passed within their view. Captain Winecoff later described his company's mood:

The company, of course, was talking about "Let's get down on that road and do some ambushing." I don't think they really thought that they were going to let us go over into Laos.

Winecoff reported the enemy movements, and artillery and air strikes attempted to pinpoint the enemy locations, but it was "difficult to zero in on movement" and the strikes were unable to knock out the moving convoys.

At that moment senior marine officers were considering more drastic action. Apprised of the situation, Lieutenant General Robert E. Cushman, commander of III MAF, forwarded to General Abrams at MACV headquarters in Saigon a request for permission to mount a limited raid into the heart of enemy Base Area 611, up to five kilometers inside the Laotian border.

Colonel Barrow, from his vantage point at FSB Cunningham, did not feel that he could wait for a reply.

It was becoming increasingly critical to what we were doing. The combination of what I would characterize as military necessity and opportunity came at the same time. We were a matter of a few hundred yards from this road. And the trucks are using this thing, and they're probably resupplying. I personally immediately saw the opportunity to do something. I'm protecting my forces. U.S. Marine casualties and all these sorts of things are tied up in it. The political implications of going into Laos are pretty unimportant to me at that point. So I said, "Do it!"

Fearing a fatal delay if he awaited permission to cross the border, Barrow did not inform his immediate superiors. "Now there was a little chicanery, or whatever else you want to call it," he later admitted. Assuming personal responsibility for his orders, Barrow ordered Captain Winecoff to cross the border and establish an ambush site along Route 922. Recognizing that he might well be placing his career in jeopardy, Barrow recalled thinking that he was "willing to pay whatever price as a consequence. But it was the right thing to do. I don't regret having done it a damn bit."

Early on the afternoon of February 21, Captain Winecoff received Barrow's secret order, taking "almost an hour to decode it." Captain Winecoff recalled his reactions:

This was a little bit of a shock because I had one platoon that was extremely tired that I hadn't had on a patrolling mission that day and I had the other two platoons which were pretty tired out on patrol. And to take a company out on patrol that night when it meant night movement and with the specific instruction to be back in Vietnam at 0630 the next morning is kind of a hard order to digest.

Winecoff responded with a message seeking a twenty-four-hour delay. The reply left little room for doubt: "Go ahead with the mission . . . there's very good reasons for this mission which we can't go into now, but it's vital that you get down and interdict Route 922 tonight."

Having wasted more than two hours with the messages, Winecoff found himself pressed for time. Both the lack of time and of suitable terrain prohibited what good leadership required: a well-planned rehearsal. He and his men would have to hope that they had learned their lesson well during "ambush class" at Cua Viet.

Across the border

Around four-thirty in the afternoon, Winecoff and his men began the descent down a small trail where the company rendezvoused with his 2d Platoon. At six, he briefed his company:

I spent a lot of time emphasizing the fact that we had to keep individuals closed up and how easy it was in the dark to think the person ahead of you had stopped, [and it] didn't take but a few feet for him to move out of hearing range. . . . I emphasized, also, repeatedly, that in an ambush, nine-tenths of them are not successful because the ambush is prematurely set off.

He informed the company that he alone would trigger the ambush by detonating a claymore mine. Just after dark, Winecoff moved his men toward the ambush site. The sound of a small running stream muffled their noise. Around ten, he sent out a small recon team to scout the actual site. In their absence, a small convoy of NVA trucks crept by along the road, but the ambush was not yet set. Moving the company as close as twenty-five meters off the road, Winecoff kept his men in a tight line rather than establishing a perimeter that might reveal their location. Shortly after 1:00 A.M., a single NVA soldier appeared, walking down the road, shooting his AK47. Winecoff decided that he "didn't want to bag one NVA soldier" and passed the word "to let this dude walk through the killing zone." Similarly, he let a single truck pass. Remembering that his orders stated that "there were good reasons for this ambush," Winecoff was hoping for a bigger catch.

Finally, at about two-thirty, he heard the sound of trucks approaching the ambush site. Moving very cautiously, the first vehicle rounded the bend into the killing zone, but Winecoff waited for a second vehicle to approach. The two lead vehicles both turned off their lights, but when a third set of lights appeared, Winecoff detonated the claymore. After a delay that "seemed like half a minute" but was probably only a few seconds, his men opened fire. "We probably fired the ambush a little bit longer than we needed to but everybody had been waiting a long time and the excitement was keen."

Fearing that an enemy force might respond to the sound of the explosions, Winecoff took time only for a quick search of the killing zone. Still, he determined that all three trucks and their loads of enemy small arms and ammunition had been destroyed. He then ordered a "left face," and his company retraced their steps. The damage may not have been extensive, but the enemy received notice that their Laotian sanctuaries would not serve as a safe haven in this operation.

His company's exhaustion forced Winecoff to give the men two hours rest on Laotian territory before returning to Vietnam after seven the following morning. By evening, they were back up on the ridge line overlooking the border. "The company was quite happy," Winecoff remembered. "We received a real good resupply that night. It had beer on it and everything we'd been looking forward to, that marines always look forward to."

While Winecoff's men rested, 3d Marine Division headquarters began a flurry of activity. Headquarters had learned of the ambush only by monitoring the radio traffic of the 9th Marines. The divisional chief of staff, Colonel Martin J. Sexton, decided to inform III MAF but not MACV until a full report could be written. General Davis was in Hong Kong at the time, visiting his son, a marine lieutenant and casualty of earlier fighting in Dewey Canyon. In the meantime, Abrams had sent his reply to the marine request of February 20 to cross the border. The answer was, "no." Only SOG forces would be permitted to operate in Laos. Tailoring their response to the existing rules of engagement, the marines informed Abrams that the ambush had been conducted in self-defense.

Was it truly self-defense? Barrow acknowledged that opportunity as well as necessity played a role in his decision to order the ambush but pointed out that the 122MM NVA guns formed a permanent threat to his men. His ambush was designed to signal the enemy that the marines would pursue them if they tried to move the guns out of range of American artillery but in a place where they would still be capable of hurting his forces. Was the ambush ordered for the "self-preservation of units" as the rules of engagement required? Barrow answered, "self-preservation? No, I'm not even going to suggest that that act preserved, but it was in the context of self-preservation." Colonel Barrow was later promoted to general and eventually became commandant of the U.S. Marine Corps.

The strongest vote of confidence Barrow received came from Abrams himself. When apprised of the purpose of the ambush, Abrams reversed his earlier position and authorized a full battalion of the 9th Marines to enter Laos for the purpose of destroying the threat posed by the 122s. Abrams requested only that there be "no public discussion" of the foray across the border and informed the American ambassador in Laos, William Sullivan, only after the operation was underway.

Within hours, Captain Winecoff received new orders "to move my whole company back down onto the bloomin' Route 922." Only a half hour earlier the company had been resupplied; now they would have to leave the supplies behind to be passed on to another company to their rear. But, "of course not the beer," Winecoff pointed out. "We consumed that."

This time Winecoff's men were not alone. The entire 2/9 moved down along Route 922 while the 1/9 and the 3/9 waited along the ridge line keeping the road within gun sight. The plan called for the 2d Battalion to act as the hammer, pushing the enemy into the anvil of the other two battalions. On February 24, Company H sprang another ambush, killing eight NVA soldiers. The next day, they themselves were ambushed but finally stormed through the enemy line. The marines suffered three dead in the engagement. During the fighting, Corporal William D. Morgan "in a daring dash, directed enemy fire away from two wounded companions, assisting in their rescue." Morgan was killed but was awarded a posthumous Medal of Honor for his bravery.

For a full week, the battalion remained in Laos. NVA resistance faded, but tons of supplies and thousands of rounds of ammunition were captured. While in Laos, the marines lost eight men, all officially reported dead "near Quang Tri Province, South Vietnam."

By early March, the 9th Marines had completed the offensive portion of Operation Dewey Canyon. After the 2d Battalion returned from Laos on March 3, the regiment began the slow process of liquidating the operation. Because of bad weather, the extraction of units was delayed and not until March 18 were all the marines back at Vandegrift combat base, thus officially ending the operation.

In all, the marines lost 130 men in the operation and suffered an additional 920 casualties. They counted 1,617 enemy dead, but more important was the disruption of enemy logistical planning. The marines captured sixteen artillery pieces, seventy-three antiaircraft guns, hundreds of smaller weapons, nearly a million rounds of ammunition, and more than 220,000 pounds of rice. According to the official marine historian of the operation, "The Marine strike into the Da Krong Valley disrupted the organizational apparatus of Base Area 611, effectively blocking the enemy's ability to strike out at civilian and military targets to the east. Attempts to rebuild this base and reorder disrupted supply lines would be long and arduous."

But as the army had found out three years earlier in attempting to wipe out the enemy base areas in War Zones C and D, it was one thing to push the enemy out of a base area, another to keep them out. Less than two months after the conclusion of Operation Dewey Canyon, Base Area 611 was the objective of another American operation, Apache Snow. This time it was the 101st Airborne Division that headed into the A Shau Valley, just south of the operational area of Dewey Canyon. The result was the most notorious battle in America's seven years' war.

Apache Snow

The A Shau Valley was not unknown terrain to the 101st Airborne Division, equipped since late 1968 with sufficient helicopters to qualify as a fully "airmobile" division. In the spring of 1968, the 101st had participated in the first American entry into the A Shau since 1966. The valley, shaped like a thirty-mile-long natural funnel, consists of rolling terrain covered by eight-foot-high elephant grass. The valley is protected by a rim of triple-canopied hills. At its very western edge, straddling the Laotian border, lay enemy Base Area 611, the old objective of Operation Dewey Canyon.

Within days after the completion of that marine operation, intelligence sources reported the movement of three NVA regiments back into Base Area 611. Aerial reconnaissance reported intensive building activity on the roads leading from Laos into South Vietnam. Other intelligence gained from prisoners revealed that the 9th NVA Regiment was already on the move toward Hue. All signs showed a repetition of the behavior the enemy had followed before attacking Hue in 1968. Rather than wait until the enemy struck in the populous coastal region, the 101st Airborne directed the 3d Brigade, augmented by a battalion from the 1st ARVN Division, to initiate Operation Apache Snow. The operation was conceived by XXIV Corps to block any further eastward movement by the enemy.

The operation began early on the morning of May 10 as sixty-five UH-1H helicopters carried the assault troops into five preselected landing zones. The three organic battalions of 3d Brigade of the 101st—1st Battalion, 506th Infantry; 3d Battalion, 187th Infantry; and 2d Battalion, 501st Infantry—were joined by the 4th Battalion, 1st ARVN Regiment. As each battalion landed, they broke into company-size units, each with targets to search for the enemy or enemy supplies. Little contact was made.

The experience of the 3d Battalion, 187th Infantry, was similar to the others. Lieutenant Colonel Weldon Honey-cutt sent his Company A to the northwest, Company C to the southwest, and Company D to the southeast toward Hill 937, a massif on the Laotian border. Company B had been held as a battalion reserve and did not join the operation until late in the afternoon. When it did, Company D had already secured the ridge line leading up to Hill 937 from the north. As they marched to join Company D, Company B made the first contact with the enemy in the operation, receiving small-arms fire supported by two rocket-propelled grenade launchers (RPGs). The enemy quickly vanished at the onset of return fire.

On the morning of May 11, each company continued its assigned mission, except that Company D now stayed in reserve while Company B continued moving up the ridge toward Hill 937. Following the small mountain trails, the company began to receive fire, first from a single sniper but then from a larger, well-dug-in enemy force. Despite the support of air strikes and artillery, Company B suffered several casualties and was forced to withdraw. Searching the area, the company found evidence of a sophisticated telephone network and documents that identified the enemy on Hill 937 as part of the 29th NVA Regiment. For the first time Honeycutt and 3d Brigade commander, Colonel Joseph B. Conmy, Jr., realized that they had found a sizable enemy force. "It became apparent," Conmy remembers, "that there was more there than we had bumped into elsewhere in the A Shau."

There was nothing special about Hill 937. The Vietnamese called it Dong Ap Bia. In the words of an army historian, it was "as a particular piece of terrain of no tactical significance. However, the fact that the enemy force was located there was of prime significance. . . . And so, the battle of Dong Ap Bia ensued." But it was the men of the 101st Airborne who gave the battle the painfully descriptive name by which it would be remembered in America: the battle of Hamburger Hill.

Hamburger Hill

On the morning of May 12, Colonel Honeycutt decided to commit all four companies of the 3/187, with Company A serving as a reserve force, and the battle began in earnest (see map, page 18). Company C moved to link up with Company B, which received enemy fire throughout the day. Company D was sent to approach the hill from the northeast. Company B prepared a new landing zone near its position to aid in the evacuation of the mounting casualties. Air strikes and artillery relentlessly pounded enemy positions throughout the day and night. The following day Companies B and C, fighting abreast, attempted a coordinated assault on the hill. Within thirty minutes they came under heavy fire and thirty-three men were wounded and four killed before the day ended. That night AC-47 gunships made their first appearance on the scene to fire at enemy positions throughout the darkness.

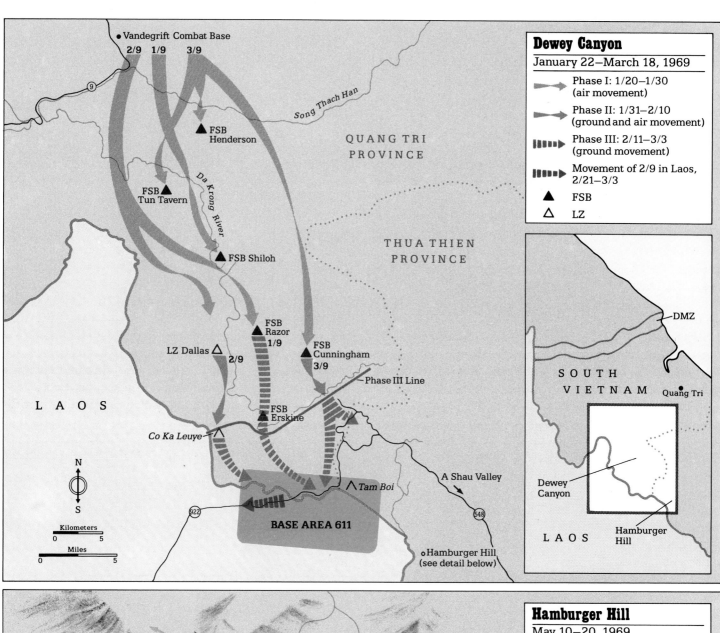

Dewey Canyon

January 22–March 18, 1969

→ Phase I: 1/20–1/30 (air movement)

→ Phase II: 1/31–2/10 (ground and air movement)

▸▸▸ Phase III: 2/11–3/3 (ground movement)

▸▸▸ Movement of 2/9 in Laos, 2/21–3/3

▲ FSB

△ LZ

Vandegrift Combat Base
2/9 1/9 3/9

Song Thach Han

▲ FSB Henderson

QUANG TRI PROVINCE

Da Krong River

▲ FSB Tun Tavern

▲ FSB Shiloh

THUA THIEN PROVINCE

▲ FSB Razor 1/9

LZ Dallas △ 2/9

▲ FSB Cunningham 3/9

Phase III Line

LAOS

▲ FSB Erskine

Co Ka Leuye △

N
S

Tam Boi ∧

A Shau Valley

922

BASE AREA 611

548

Hamburger Hill (see detail below)

Kilometers
0   5

Miles
0   5

DMZ

SOUTH VIETNAM

Quang Tri

Dewey Canyon

LAOS

Hamburger Hill

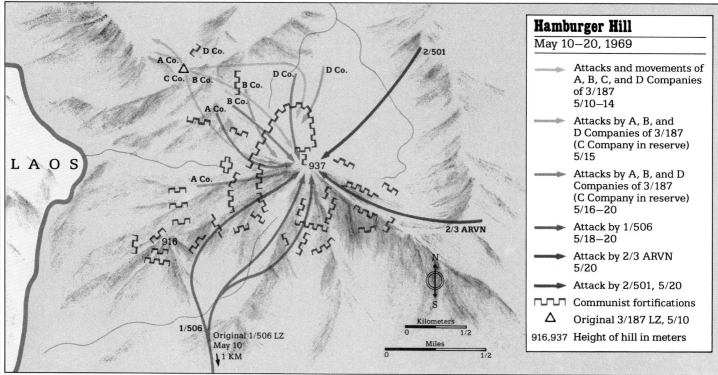

Hamburger Hill

May 10–20, 1969

→ Attacks and movements of A, B, C, and D Companies of 3/187 5/10–14

▸ Attacks by A, B, and D Companies of 3/187 (C Company in reserve) 5/15

→ Attacks by A, B, and D Companies of 3/187 (C Company in reserve) 5/16–20

→ Attack by 1/506 5/18–20

→ Attack by 2/3 ARVN 5/20

→ Attack by 2/501, 5/20

⊓⊔⊓⊔ Communist fortifications

△ Original 3/187 LZ, 5/10

916,937 Height of hill in meters

LAOS

A Co.   D Co.
C Co.   B Co.   D Co.   D Co.

2/501

B Co.
B Co.
A Co.

937

A Co.

2/3 ARVN

916

N
S

1/506

Original 1/506 LZ May 10
↓ 1 KM

Kilometers
0   1/2

Miles
0   1/2

On May 14 all three companies, approaching from three directions, attempted to push the enemy off Hamburger Hill. With Company B moving from the west, C from a more northwestwardly approach, and D from the north, the battalion confronted immediate enemy resistance. By 9:30 A.M., Company B had reached an intermediate objective, a small ridge line, but Company C reported that heavy fire would force it back. To avoid isolating Company B, Honeycutt ordered both B and C to withdraw to a defensible position. Honeycutt now estimated enemy troop strength at between two companies and a battalion. He replaced Company C with Company A, whose men were rested, and planned a major assault for the following day before the enemy could reinforce its position. In addition, Conmy ordered another battalion, the 1/506 commanded by Lieutenant Colonel James Bowers, to Hill 937 to augment the 3/187. The major objective of the battalion was to cut off Hill 937 from the west. Conmy explained, "We realized that the western border of that hill was close to the Laotian border. We figured that they must be resupplying and bringing people in from that side."

That night, the enemy emplaced claymores throughout the approaches to their bunkers. The following morning the men of the 3/187 were hard hit by the mines. Still, Companies A and B continued to advance to about 150 meters from the crest of the hill until a U.S. rocket gunship inadvertently fired on Company B, forcing the company to halt in order to evacuate the wounded. Although Company A continued to advance, Honeycutt did not want to expose a single unit and ordered both to pull back to a defensive position. That afternoon, Honeycutt's battalion headquarters was hit by enemy RPGs that wounded Colonel Honeycutt—his third wound of the operation—and his operations chief. Both refused evacuation. Meanwhile, the 1/506 was moving toward Hill 937, slowed by the rugged terrain and high elephant grass. Brigade command decided to postpone any renewed assault on the hill until the 1/506 was in place.

On May 16, the companies of the 3/187 held defensive positions, making few contacts with the enemy. The 1/506, on the other hand, met increased enemy resistance, and it slugged its way slowly up the hill. A new assault was postponed until May 18, the seventh day of the battle. Plans were set for 1/506 to launch the main attack from the southwest, while the 3/187 supported them. CS tear gas was brought in to augment the heavy air and artillery support. The men all received heavy flak jackets to reduce casualties, although the extreme heat made wearing them almost unbearable.

On the morning of May 18, the two full battalions launched their assault. As the 3/187 inched up the hill, enemy fire increased. Automatic weapons, RPGs, and claymore mines all inflicted heavy casualties. Company B was fired on from three directions. Still, the attack progressed, reaching almost the top of the hill, when the enemy set off a series of mines and grenades within its own perimeter.

The effectiveness of a full week's artillery and air strikes now turned against the American soldiers. U.S. firepower had denuded the once lushly vegetated hill. When torrential rains arrived on the afternoon of the eighteenth, the bald hill turned into a mud slide and the men kept skidding back down the hill. Already having suffered fourteen dead and sixty-four wounded that day, the 3/187 was ordered to pull back. The men, who by then had christened Dong Ap Bia "Hamburger Hill," now began to complain openly, particularly about Honeycutt. "That damned Blackjack [Honeycutt's code name] won't stop until he kills every damn one of us," one wounded soldier snapped to a reporter who was covering the battle.

The same conditions of heavy enemy fire and mud also slowed the 1/506, but at nightfall it had been able to form a defensive perimeter about a kilometer from the hilltop.

A difficult decision now confronted division commander Major General Melvin Zais, who had carefully followed the action, often from his personal helicopter-borne "observation deck." He faced the choice of committing additional troops to the battle or turning his back on Hill 937. His decision was to reinforce with two additional battalions, his own 2d Battalion, 501st Infantry, and the 2d ARVN Battalion, 3d Infantry, now made available to him.

According to Conmy, there was never any doubt in his mind or Honeycutt's that the enemy should be pursued on Hamburger Hill. "We had a handle on something pretty hot," he stated. "We realized that we hadn't encountered a great deal of opposition previously . . . and we must have hit something pretty important. Looking the terrain over, it was the predominant feature in that end of the A Shau Valley." Conmy also believed that the bunker system on the hilltop served as an NVA regimental command post. It was an opportunity too good and too important to walk away from. "In the year I spent over there, in continuous operations, I can only think of three occasions where I got the enemy cut off where he couldn't go anywhere," Conmy explained. "If I backed away the distance necessary to launch a B-52 strike he would disappear in the dark of the night and attack us somewhere else."

During the night of May 18 and the next day, the commanders developed plans for a four-battalion assault on May 20. The two new battalions were helilifted into the combat area, 2/501 to the northeast and the 2/3 ARVN Battalion to the east-southeast, while the 3/187 was augmented by Companies A and D of the 2/506. Only the 1/506 attempted to move up the hill, slowly edging its way to within 200 meters of the top by nightfall. On the morning of May 20, all four battalions began a coordinated assault on the hill.

Most of the enemy's force had now been spent. They permitted the 3/187, advancing three companies abreast,

A wounded paratrooper of the 101st Airborne winces in pain while awaiting evacuation from Dong Ap Bia.

A trooper comforts a seriously wounded buddy on the day before the 101st Airborne took the hill.

Two medics help a wounded paratrooper from the 101st Airborne Division through a blinding rainstorm during the height of the battle for Hamburger Hill, May 19, 1969.

to approach the top of the hill before opening fire. With the help of supporting artillery and mortar fire, the battalion was able to continue its advance. Shortly before noon, the first company from the 3/187 reached the crest. Even then the enemy continued to fight until every bunker was destroyed. The 1/506 followed to the top, joining the 3/187 after sporadic enemy resistance. The other two battalions reached the summit with little trouble. Shortly after noon the battle, in its ninth full day, was over. Enemy resistance disintegrated; those not killed or captured fled the area. The western portion of the perimeter established by the surrounding American forces was not closed until the final assault and the few surviving enemy soldiers were able to slip through toward the Laotian border. During the final assault, not a single American was killed.

After the hill was taken a landing zone was constructed to facilitate the search of the area. Captured documents proved that the hill was indeed a regimental command post. One week later the hill was abandoned, as was common practice during the war. As General Zais put it, "This is not a war of hills. That hill had no military value whatsoever." Near the landing zone, however, one soldier posted a memorial to the battle, a cardboard sign bearing the scrawled message, "Hamburger Hill. Was it worth it?"

Was it worth it?

The battle for Hamburger Hill almost immediately became a source of controversy in the United States. The press widely reported Senator Edward Kennedy's comment that the battle was "senseless and irresponsible." Much of the criticism was directed at General Zais's decision to take the hill, seemingly at all cost.

Defending his decision, Zais responded that the enemy had suffered 630 KIAs, compared to 56 American deaths, better than a 10 to 1 ratio. Hamburger Hill was destined to become the last American battle in which victory would be determined by "body count."

Other critics, including senior officers, wondered why infantry tactics and frontal assaults had been used rather than B-52 strikes. One colonel suggested, "We can get ourselves into another Korean War situation if we keep losing men on hills that don't have to be taken today or tomorrow. What's wrong with cordoning off a place and pounding the hell out of it?" Conmy had an answer: "In my experience with B-52 strikes, the enemy—I don't know how—seemed to sense their coming. With us being all around the hill and then withdrawing to a safe distance to permit a B-52 strike, it would have signalled to the enemy that something like a B-52 strike was coming and I think they would have withdrawn and we would have lost contact with them."

Ultimately, such questions of tactics can be answered only by the commanders actually in the field. Even Zais's critics acknowledged that. Nor did anyone doubt the bravery of the infantrymen who eventually did take the hill. The brigade won the Presidential Unit Citation. Colonel Conmy spoke with affection and admiration for his men: "No matter how tough the job is, the American soldier gets the job done. He might hate the hell out of it, but he never quits. . . . In Hamburger Hill, they might have grumbled, but my God, they were there when the chips were down! They eventually went up that hill and took it!"

But bravery and tactics aside, the battle at Hamburger Hill raised still other questions. The *New York Times* said after the battle, "The public is certainly entitled to raise questions about the current aggressive posture of the United States military in South Vietnam." The real question was, once again, what was American strategy in South Vietnam? Most press reports ignored that side of Senator Kennedy's criticism: "President Nixon has told us, without question, that we seek no military victory, that we seek only peace. How then can we justify sending our boys against a hill a dozen times?"

General Zais argued that his orders directed him to find and destroy the enemy wherever he might be. "We found the enemy on Hill 937 and that's where we fought him," he told reporters. Such tactics were clearly in order when General Westmoreland conducted a war of attrition. The question remained, however, whether this strategy was still in effect. Many of the new administration's highest officials considered the war of attrition discredited. Henry Kissinger was a firm critic, while Richard Nixon realized that attrition could not result in "military victory." General Abrams's staff was in the final stages of preparing a new strategy to guide the American military, but Conmy recalls, "I was vaguely aware that there was some talk back in Washington . . . that it was time to get out. But, I hadn't really seen any moves that indicated that we were actually going to do it. As far as I was concerned, the job was still to try to win the thing. We had nothing concrete to prove that anything was going to change."

And yet, some generals had already foreseen a new tactical thrust. General Davis's tactics in virtually the same operational area were designed not so much to meet the enemy head on as to disrupt his logistical system. General Abrams, while defending Zais's actions at Dong Ap Bia, nevertheless told reporters "Since the beginning of last fall, all our operations have been designed to get into the enemy's system. Once you start working in the system that he required to prepare his offensive operations, you can cause him to postpone his operations."

The American military now had two concepts of offensive operations before it. The one, emphasizing search and destroy operations designed to lead to the attrition of enemy fighting forces, was typified by the assault on Hamburger Hill. The other, developed by such officers as marine General Raymond Davis and army Lieutenant Generals William Rosson and Richard Stilwell took a more indirect approach and attempted to disrupt enemy logistics and lines of communications, thus preempting offensive operations. Which concept of operations would achieve prominence under the new administration of Richard Nixon?

Of all those with a stake in the battle of Hamburger Hill, perhaps the least vocal was the new commander in chief. In the four months since the inauguration, he had permitted military policy in Vietnam to drift. After the battle, one general in Saigon complained, "In terms of guidance from Washington, we have received nothing new except to hurry up." Lyndon Johnson's final orders to maintain "maximum pressure" on the enemy remained the only guiding principle to commanders in the field. If nothing else, Hamburger Hill proved that the American fighting men in Vietnam, no less than the public at home, could afford to wait no longer for Richard Nixon's decision.

Frustration

Peace was the theme of Richard Nixon's inauguration. For his swearing in the president-elect even had the Bible opened to Isaiah 2:4: "Nation shall not lift up sword against nation, neither shall they learn war anymore." Throughout the presidential campaign the public had signaled to the candidates its desire for peace and Nixon had won with his pledge to satisfy that desire. Now he confronted the problem of determining exactly what his mandate for ending the war meant. What kind of peace did Americans want? Answering that question was no easy task, for public opinion over the past several months had been diffuse, shifting, and often inconsistent.

The dominant public sentiment was, as public opinion polls registered again and again, sheer exhaustion with the war. A June 1968 poll found that only 18 percent of Americans believed the country was making progress in Vietnam; a quarter believed America was losing ground, and nearly half felt the U.S. was standing still. Another poll showed only one in ten people still believed allied victory was possible, while two-thirds thought the war would end in compromise. Rising frustration was also apparent in one of the long-standing gauges of public opinion on Vietnam: Gallup's "mistake ques-

tion." By early 1969 an unprecedented majority of Americans had come to believe that the U.S. "made a mistake in sending troops to fight in Vietnam." Weariness with the war was compounded by fears that the fighting would drag on indefinitely. As 1968 ended only a third of the country—35 percent—believed the war would end in the coming year. In short, frustrated and disillusioned, the public was rapidly losing patience with the American mission in Vietnam, and many Americans were looking for a quick end to the war.

A significant minority—32 percent—wanted one final all-out escalation. But the majority, as they had done since 1965, considered such a move dangerous and overly drastic. Instead, an increasing number of people simply wanted American involvement to end and the troops withdrawn. Throughout the campaign, polls showed that a majority of Americans was willing to back a candidate who would turn the fighting over to South Vietnam and withdraw American troops. Though few favored immediate withdrawal, more than half those surveyed in January 1969 approved a month-by-month troop reduction program.

The justifications Americans offered for withdrawal were mixed. Some, like a retired midwestern businessman, insisted that the U.S. had reached the limits of its responsibility in Southeast Asia: "We've done our part in Vietnam. I think the time has come now for the South Vietnamese to carry on. After all, they are going to have to run their own country sometime and decide what kind of relations they want to have with North Vietnam. That's none of our business." A New Jersey woman expressed more personal feelings: "Frankly, I don't care what happens in Vietnam anymore. I just want my son back."

Her sense of urgency was widely shared. According to the polls, between one-third and one-half of the country was willing to go ahead with withdrawal, even if it meant the collapse of South Vietnam. At the same time, however, Americans continued to insist on the importance of containing communism in Southeast Asia. A Harris poll taken in May 1969 found that 56 percent of Americans felt it was "very important" that the Communists not take over South Vietnam; only 9 percent were willing to accept a settlement that might allow an eventual Communist victory, and only 18 percent would accept a coalition settlement that left the Vietcong in a position to dominate Vietnam.

Americans' conflicting feelings about the war apparently were resolved by many through visions of a "neutralized" Southeast Asia: 83 percent told Harris pollsters they favored a solution that would allow the region to be neither pro-American nor pro-Communist. Ironically, that option, which had been politically unthinkable a few years earlier, was politically unattainable by 1969.

It would be up to the new administration to forge a policy that could pull together the contrary strands of public opinion. The problem was that, as one pollster noted, "On the one hand, the people urgently call for an early exit from Vietnam. Yet, on the other hand, the people are reluctant to see an outcome in Southeast Asia that is less than desirable." Americans wanted out but seemingly not at the cost of abandoning the country's long-standing political goals: They wanted to have their cake and eat it too. As candidate, Richard Nixon had promised that was possible; now, as president, he would have to find a way to make it come true.

The Politics of Disengagement

The year 1969 was one that Richard Nixon could later claim had laid the foundation for his greatest foreign policy successes. He had initiated the diplomatic signaling and maneuvering that would culminate in the highest points of his presidency: détente with the Soviet Union and rapprochement with China. But as far as his most pressing foreign policy challenge—the Vietnam War—was concerned, it must have been a year of bitter disappointment. All of his hopes for a quick settlement of the war were dashed, as the war in 1969 soon settled into a double stalemate in which the prospects for any dramatic breakthrough either on the battlefield or at the negotiating table vanished. The fact was that, though he had claimed one, Richard Nixon had no "secret plan" to end the war. Instead, his administration spent most of the year trying to develop a policy that might eventually lead to peace some years hence.

By midyear, the administration had settled, in

public at least, on a double-pronged approach: to pursue the negotiations at Paris while "Vietnamizing" the war itself so that the South Vietnamese would take over the fighting and American troops could begin to return home. But even this clearly stated public policy belied continued controversy among the highest placed actors in the administration. Severe differences emerged in answering basic questions: What was the objective of the continued American involvement in South Vietnam? How high a price was the administration—and the American public—willing to pay in pursuing those objectives? What military or diplomatic initiatives remained open? The inability of the administration to answer these questions in 1969 was not due to a lack of effort. On the contrary, Vietnam was uppermost in the minds of the new president and his national security adviser, literally from the moment that Richard Nixon took the oath of office.

The Kissinger way

Shortly after noon on January 20, 1969, almost as if on cue, messengers from the new White House picked up a thick sheaf of papers and distributed a copy to the Central Intelligence Agency, the Department of State, and the Department of Defense. State would forward an additional copy to the embassy in Saigon. DOD would make copies available to the Joint Chiefs of Staff and to MACV headquarters in Saigon. The document was not a statement of policy but a unique questionnaire consisting of twenty-eight major questions and fifty subsidiary ones covering virtually every aspect of the war in Vietnam. What were Hanoi's intentions? How strong was South Vietnam, militarily and politically? How were American tactics working? Could the war of attrition be won? Was the bombing effective? What were the prospects for pacification? These were the questions and Henry Kissinger wanted to know the answers.

Eschewing traditional bureaucratic procedures on this, his very first day as national security adviser, Kissinger asked that each agency's response be sent directly to his office. He forbade the general practice of bureaucracies to negotiate a common response that would represent no single agency's viewpoint but rather a lowest-common-denominator compromise. In the new administration, foreign policy would be made by the president and Henry Kissinger, not by bureaucratic accommodation.

Kissinger's approach, especially his requirement that each agency offer its own unedited answers, was not the result of personal pique. Rather, it came from a carefully thought-out approach to foreign policy that had shaped his academic career and that had been deeply influenced by his boyhood experiences.

Preceding page. Partners in policy. President Nixon and Henry Kissinger confer in the White House garden.

Heinz Alfred Kissinger was born in 1923 in the Bavarian town of Furth, a suburb of Nuremburg. Furth contained one of the few heavy concentrations of Jews in southern Germany, and Heinz's father, as a public preparatory schoolteacher, held a prestigious position. Like most Jews in the town, they led a comfortable existence.

In 1933, this comfortable world fell apart. The rise of Adolf Hitler to the German chancellorship deprived Heinz and his family of many basic civil rights. Kissinger faced repeated attacks from young Nazi thugs on the streets, expulsion from his school to assignment at a special "Jewish school," and finally the dismissal of his father from his teaching position. Despite these warning signs, the Kissinger family refused to leave. Finally, in 1938, at his mother's insistence, the family fled to England and then America. There they settled among fellow immigrants in New York City's Washington Heights neighborhood. Kissinger later insisted, perhaps too defensively, that "that part of my childhood is *not* a key to anything. . . . The political persecutions of my childhood are not what control my life."

While a diligent student in Germany, young Heinz had never distinguished himself academically. But in New York Henry, as he now called himself, became a straight-A student. With his solid record of achievement, he decided to enroll in an accounting program at City College of New York. But, before he was able to embark on his new career, Kissinger was drafted into the army at age twenty. Besides providing him with a short cut to American citizenship, his army experience radically altered Kissinger's future career. During his training as an infantryman, Kissinger met a fellow exile, a German Protestant named Fritz Kraemer, who traveled through American training camps briefing new recruits on the horrors of the Nazi enemy. Kraemer was immediately impressed with Kissinger's mind and effected a transfer for his new protégé to a position as German interpreter. With the war rapidly coming to a close, Kissinger was employed largely as an administrator to govern the areas now under American military occupation. Among his tasks was the identification of former Nazis for possible prosecution as war criminals.

In May 1946, Kissinger was discharged but spent an additional year as a civilian instructor in the army. He confided to Kraemer that he was thinking of returning to New York to enroll as a student at CCNY. Kraemer informed him that "a gentleman does not go to a local New York school" and encouraged his application to Harvard University. In 1947, at age twenty-four, Henry Kissinger became a Harvard freshman, determined to become an academic success. "He sat in that overstuffed chair . . . studying morning till night and biting his nails till there was blood," one of his roommates remembered. He was reserved with his classmates but found among the faculty a replacement for Kraemer as his mentor, the distinguished professor William Yandell Elliot. Under Elliot's tutelage, Kissinger devoured the Harvard curriculum, earning his bachelor's degree summa cum laude and immediately embarking on a graduate program resulting in his Ph.D. in government and a professorship.

As a tenured faculty member at Harvard, Kissinger became best known for the books he wrote on foreign policy and diplomacy in the nuclear age, largely under the auspices of the Council on Foreign Relations. His most creative and original work, however, was the one most often overlooked, his doctoral dissertation, later published as *A World Restored*. A detailed account of the diplomacy at the Congress of Vienna of 1815, which closed the Napoleonic period in European history, *A World Restored* was more than a path-breaking account of domestic political considerations at work at the congress. It also revealed, in embryonic form, the three major themes that were to guide Kissinger's actions when he finally was transformed by Nixon from diplomatic historian to diplomat.

Kissinger was preoccupied above all with the tension between creative diplomacy and career bureaucracies. Pointing out that the two leading figures at Vienna—Castlereagh of England and Metternich of Austria—both experienced greater problems with their cabinets at home than with enemy governments, Kissinger launched into an attack on foreign policy bureaucracies. They were "designed to execute, not conceive," he complained; their "quest for safety" blocked creative policy. Recalling that Castlereagh, who had done much to create the era of security, the *Pax Britannia*, was eventually repudiated by his countrymen and committed suicide, Kissinger argued that a statesman's first requirement was to overcome "the problem of legitimizing a policy *within* the governmental apparatus."

To overcome the inertia of bureaucracies, "whose primary concern is with safety and minimum risk," Kissinger saw the need for strong statesmen and diplomats. He rejected the trend in contemporary America that placed business executives and lawyers at the top of the foreign policy "establishment." "Our leaders have not lacked ability, but they have had to learn while doing," Kissinger complained. What was required was the emergence of new Metternichs or Castlereaghs, professional diplomats who served as plenipotentiaries for their governments.

The national security adviser skims the morning's news one day in August 1969.

But even such strong diplomats, Kissinger knew, still faced an important hurdle: public opinion. In *A World Restored* Kissinger remarked that statesmen "often share the fate of prophets, . . . without honor in their own country." The "acid test" of policy, he wrote, was "to obtain domestic support." A diplomat must understand that complete security is unattainable for any nation; one nation's security will inevitably create feelings of insecurity in the enemy camp. Rather, the statesman's task was "the reconciliation of different versions of legitimacy," recognizing the legitimate security needs of the enemy in order to assure a climate of peace. History, however, taught Kissinger that public opinion was seldom so enlightened. In matters of security, the public would demand nothing less than the whole loaf, while the successful diplomat knew that he had achieved his goal in assuring half.

This tension between diplomat and public opinion created a dilemma for which Kissinger had no sure answer. "A statesman who too far outruns the experience of his people will fail in achieving domestic consensus, however wise his policies. . . . A statesman who limits his policy to the experience of his people will doom himself to sterility," he wrote. The only hope was that "domestic disputes [remained] essentially technical and confined to achieving an agreed goal."

Kissinger's critique of existing foreign policy methods was trenchant, his vision less so. There existed a strong undercurrent of elitism in this vision, which called for a foreign policy "superstatesman" unencumbered with governmental disputes or domestic political strife. It was mildly disdainful as well, disdainful both of public opinion and of the foreign policy establishment that had taken Kissinger under its wing at the Council on Foreign Relations. The former may well have been the residue of boyhood experiences in Germany, where rabid nationalism and popular dreams of world power had shattered his adolescent years. Finally, the effort to achieve Kissinger's vision of foreign policy could be no better than the statesman who ran it. Unlike bureaucracies, which are designed to compensate for the weaknesses of individual members, Kissinger's foreign policy could only reflect the strengths and weaknesses of the "superstatesman" who controlled it.

Still, Kissinger's vision had a powerful attraction, especially in the year 1969 and especially for Richard Nixon. Lyndon Johnson's failures in foreign policy had resulted from his own insecurities in that field. He had demanded consensus and had in turn become a prisoner of the resulting bureaucratic compromises. If there was one area where Richard Nixon felt no hesitancy, it was in foreign policy. He would name a colorless corporate lawyer as nominal secretary of state and act as his own.

Unlike most professional politicians, and in sharp contrast to Lyndon Johnson, Richard Nixon had subordinated domestic politics to foreign affairs for most of his career. Ignoring the adage that a representative's first responsi-bility is to "take care" of his own district, Nixon had made his reputation in Congress on national security questions. His prominent role in the Alger Hiss affair and his defense of McCarthyism—"I think the majority of the American people favor it," he stated in 1952—were stepping stones to national office. As Eisenhower's vice president, he seemed to relish the often empty, ceremonial jaunts abroad. In many cases, he planned these trips on his own against the indifference, if not opposition, of Eisenhower and his chief advisers. He then exploited such personal "crises" as his angry reception in Venezuela and his "kitchen debate" with Nikita Khrushchev in Moscow to prove in the 1960 presidential campaign that his experience in foreign affairs was greater than John Kennedy's.

Nixon's interest in foreign affairs was unusual among presidential aspirants. Neither Lyndon Johnson nor Hubert Humphrey had used his years as vice president to achieve greater stature in that field. Perhaps this man, a loner by temperament, preferred the coolness and personal isolation of foreign affairs to the gregarious "glad-handing" that seemed so much a part of domestic politics. In any case, he was a willing listener as Henry Kissinger spelled out his concepts of diplomacy.

NSSM-1

The new approach was quickly put to a test. The answers to the questions posed by the NSC on inauguration day were completed by mid-February and formed the basis of Kissinger's first National Security Study Memorandum, NSSM-1. The questions focused more on the state of the war than on eliciting policy options from the various agencies. As such it forms a remarkable snapshot of where America stood in Vietnam at the end of 1968. More than that—and thanks to Kissinger's insistence on separate answers—it displays the deep divisions within the government over past performance and future prospects. Kissinger pointed out that the answers to the questions had a strong tendency to fall into two bureaucratic camps. "Group A usually includes MACV, CINCPAC, JCS, and Embassy Saigon, and takes a hopeful view of current and future prospects," Kissinger wrote to the president. A second group, "Group B, usually includes OSD [civilian Office of the Secretary of Defense], CIA and (to a lesser extent) State, and is decidedly more skeptical." And yet, on most answers, the optimism was only a matter of degree. Even "Group A" was markedly pessimistic on some of the more important questions. MACV recognized that a war of attrition was virtually unwinnable. Assuming that enemy casualties remained at the all-time record highs of 1968 (largely a result of the full-scale Tet attacks), "it would take thirteen years to exhaust the manpower pool." But MACV warned, "it is unlikely that the high enemy loss rates of January–June 1968 could be maintained." And as for the hope that ARVN could completely replace American servicemen, MACV predicted, "it could not now, or in the foreseeable future, handle both the VC and sizeable NVA forces without US combat support."

If nothing else, the results of NSSM-1 convinced Kissinger and Nixon that a solution to the Vietnam War would not come from the agencies but rather would have to be conceived in the White House itself. NSSM-1 seemed to indicate that a military victory was unattainable unless the American commitment of troops was doubled or tripled. The only solution seemed to be a negotiated settlement, a conclusion that obviously suited Kissinger's talents. But, NSSM-1 suggested as well that a negotiated settlement on American terms was beyond reach in 1969. Kissinger concluded from the agency answers that "Hanoi is in Paris for a variety of motives, but not primarily out of weakness." What was required—as had been the case in every review of the negotiating environment since 1965—was an improved allied military position in Vietnam. Despite his assurances to liberal friends that "we would be out in six months," Kissinger knew that 1969 was not a propitious time for negotiations.

Yet Kissinger was confident that the negotiations would ultimately succeed. In an article written shortly before he took office, Kissinger noted, "We are so powerful that Hanoi is simply unable to defeat us militarily. . . . Since it cannot force our withdrawal, it must negotiate about it. Unfortunately, our military strength has no political corollary; we have been unable so far to create a political structure that could survive military opposition from Hanoi after we withdraw." Moreover, Kissinger noted that Hanoi's long-term prospects were still strong: "As long as Hanoi can preserve some political assets in the South, it retains the prospect of an ultimately favorable political outcome."

Kissinger's analysis was not altogether different from those of the increasingly strident critics of the war. He seemed to be indicating that there was little chance that America could achieve its objectives. While the liberal critics used this analysis to press for a quick withdrawal of American forces in order to "cut losses," Kissinger had a different solution. He urged that America change its objectives.

Kissinger was openly critical of the decisions of the early 1960s that attached so much importance to saving South Vietnam from communism. That was irrelevant now. "The commitment of 500,000 Americans has settled the issue of the importance of Vietnam. For what is involved now is confidence in American promises." This became the guiding principle of Kissinger's thoughts on Vietnam. It was not Vietnam that was important but the American commitment. "However we got into Vietnam," he concluded, "whatever the judgement of our actions, ending the war honorably is essential for the peace of the world." And, he added, "The United States has no obligation to maintain a government in Saigon by force." Thus, for Kissinger, what was important was *how* America extricated itself and not what the final outcome proved to be.

Richard Nixon, of course, did not disagree with the importance of maintaining America's commitment—he supported it in countless speeches to the American public. But Nixon saw Vietnam as something more than a symbol of American promises. The long-term ability of South Vietnam to survive as a non-Communist sovereign state—of secondary concern to Kissinger—remained Nixon's primary objective. For four years, Kissinger and Nixon labored to achieve their objectives in Vietnam, and only at the very end, during the last few hectic days as Kissinger scrambled to sign a peace agreement with Le Duc Tho, did this difference emerge as a major issue in policymaking. The seeds of the final misunderstandings, halting steps, and frayed tempers of 1972 were planted in those early days of 1969.

Tet, 1969

The dilemma Kissinger outlined for President Nixon in NSSM-1 and from which he tried to escape by redefining American objectives was soon dramatized violently by the enemy on the battlefield in South Vietnam. On February 22, in what Henry Kissinger later called "an act of extraordinary cynicism," the North Vietnamese and Vietcong unleashed their 1969 post-Tet offensive. The attacks began one day before Nixon's scheduled departure on his first overseas trip to Europe. "Whether by accident or design," Kissinger wrote in his memoirs, it "humiliated the new President."

Tet '69 did bear some resemblance to the general offensive of 1968. As in 1968, Communist attacks were coordinated throughout the length of Vietnam. The enemy struck at precisely the same number of provincial capitals—twenty-nine out of forty-four—as they had a year earlier. And again, in 1969, Vietcong local and guerrilla forces carried the brunt of the enemy attack, while regular North Vietnamese divisions held back. But these similarities were only superficial.

Because of a substantial improvement in allied intelligence that tracked and screened the movement of enemy units deploying to attacking positions, the enemy was unable to repeat its performance of the previous year. American forces were able to screen populated areas from enemy concentrations and prevent the Communists from deploying sizable forces out of their base areas. The result was a pattern of Communist attacks far different from Tet 1968.

Most important, the Communists avoided large-scale ground battles, seldom using larger than company-size forces. Nor did they direct their attacks against civilian populations; only 1 percent of South Vietnam's hamlets experienced any Tet-related attacks during that year. Pacification chief William Colby said, "We expect our in-

Tet '69. South Vietnamese Rangers charge an enemy-held building in Bien Hoa on February 26. The Rangers captured three NVA soldiers.

dicators will wiggle a little, but so far, the effect of the new offensive has been slight." Nor did the enemy concentrate attacks against South Vietnamese forces as they had in 1968, when they hoped their offensive would leave ARVN in disarray. Rather, their primary focus seemed to be American military installations, a deliberate attempt to inflict as many casualties on U.S. troops as possible.

In this, the enemy achieved a signal success. In the first three weeks of the offensive, 1,140 Americans were killed in action, a total that almost equaled American losses in the same period of the 1968 offensive. Enemy losses, on the other hand, were only one-third of the previous year's high. The enemy tactics in 1969 may have been far different, but they were equally deadly.

Enemy attacks, generally suicidal assaults by small sapper units, were especially intense in III Corps near Saigon, although the capital itself remained generally undisturbed. At Dau Tieng, the VC attacked a brigade headquarters of the U.S. 25th Infantry Division, damaging six helicopters and shooting down two more that attempted to lift off. At the 25th's headquarters in Cu Chi, fifty sappers broke through the defensive perimeter—ten rings of wire—and destroyed ten helicopters with satchel charges. Cap-

tured sappers, as usual, were not carrying rifles. They had left their valuable weapons behind, they said, in the expectation that they would not survive the attack.

When the offensive had run its course the military balance of power on the ground had changed very little. There had been almost no redeployment of allied troops and no major defense had budged. The Communists had not even attempted to reverse the advances that the allies had made in pacification during the previous six months. But the offensive did serve one purpose of the enemy. If there were any doubters left in the Nixon administration, Tet '69 demonstrated that the war on the ground in South Vietnam was irrevocably stalemated.

The second stalemate

The stand-off in South Vietnam was matched by impasse in Paris. There were good reasons for this. Both sides emphasized what they had accomplished on the battlefield, while ignoring the "successes" of their opponents. The United States had proven that the Communists could not win a military victory while American troops remained in South Vietnam, nor could they force the exodus of those troops through military means. The enemy could claim, in response, that four years of fighting had shown that they could not be defeated by American military might. The result of these different readings of the past was negotiating positions that gave little room for compromise.

The U.S. stance in the early months of the Nixon administration remained, with only minor changes, the Johnson position. The primary purpose of the negotiations was to reach an agreement on the disengagement of "external" forces, both American and North Vietnamese. Henry Kissinger suggested that negotiations follow a "two-tiered" approach, with Washington and Hanoi concentrating on a mutually agreeable withdrawal, while the Saigon government and National Liberation Front negotiated a political settlement to the civil war within South Vietnam. Kissinger's avowed reason for this negotiating process was to permit South Vietnam to determine its own future, rather than have a solution imposed by the United States and North Vietnam. His approach, however, served another purpose: to separate the military and political questions. Under the two-tiered approach, America might very well be able to negotiate an honorable withdrawal of its own troops without regard to a final political settlement.

The American position, however, was acceptable neither to North Vietnam nor to South Vietnam. South Viet-

nam still adamantly refused any negotiations with the National Liberation Front, fearing that such talks would only serve to legitimize the insurgents. The two-month-long deadlock over the shape of the negotiating table had been precisely over this point. The compromise formula—two semicircular conference tables—permitted the South to join the talks while claiming that they were only negotiating with a single enemy represented by the North Vietnamese. In the minds of South Vietnam's leaders, there was really only one issue to negotiate: the withdrawal of North Vietnamese troops.

As criticism of South Vietnamese intransigence mounted, President Thieu was obliged to make some concession. On April 7, 1969, in a major speech before the National Assembly, Thieu spelled out the South Vietnamese negotiating stance. *After* North Vietnamese troops withdrew from South Vietnam, Laos, and Cambodia, Thieu promised the members of the National Liberation Front "national reconciliation," wherein its members—but not the organization—would be permitted "full political rights under the Constitution." But there was one provision; they must renounce their "communist ideology." It was an offer the Communists were guaranteed to refuse.

This provision by Thieu became the first of his notorious "Four No's," which he would later summarize succinctly

Vietnamese children flee from the battle in Bien Hoa during the enemy's Tet 1969 offensive.

on billboards throughout the country. "Everything is negotiable," said Thieu, "Everything except my four no's. One, coalition government. Not negotiable. Two, territorial integrity. Not negotiable. Three, the Communist party in the Republic of South Vietnam. Not negotiable. Four, neutralism. Not negotiable."

In part, Thieu's stance reflected his belief that his own personal power could be maintained only through the "four no's." Against the ultimate American threat, Thieu once told U.S. reporters, "If some day you say: 'President Thieu, if you do not accept coalition with the Communists, we abandon you,' then I will say, 'Thank you, we will continue the fight until victory.'"

In addition, Thieu realized that, even if he were more amenable to concessions to the NLF, his power base, the South Vietnamese army, would never support him in such a move. No less an authority on Saigon coups than Vice President Nguyen Cao Ky issued a warning: "If the new government tried to make a coalition with the Communists there would be a coup inside ten days." Ky continued, "Thieu cannot afford any more concessions. It is a matter of his survival."

Kissinger was understanding of Thieu's position. He termed it "comprehensible" that South Vietnam refused to talk with an organization claiming it, and not the government, was the rightful sovereign power in the country. But Kissinger had also written of his impatience. Speaking more to Saigon than to the American public, he pointed out, "A sovereign government is free to talk to any group that represents an important domestic power base without thereby conferring sovereignty on it; it happens all the time in union negotiations or even in police work." He concluded with a warning: "Clearly, there is a point beyond which Saigon cannot be given a veto over negotiations."

America's difficulties with its ally might have caused a major crisis had more progress been made in negotiating with the North Vietnamese. Yet, Hanoi was no more willing than Saigon to embrace Kissinger's two-tiered negotiating process. While Kissinger and the Americans believed that the separation of military and political issues could lead to a reduction of, if not an end to, violence and the withdrawal of U.S. troops, Hanoi's entire philosophy of warfare was based on the indivisibility of military and political issues. In 1954 at Geneva, Hanoi had been pressured into accepting a cease-fire and disengagement of Vietminh and French forces with the understanding that political issues would be settled later. They were understandably leery of heading down that path again.

The Communists countered Thieu's "four no's" with two of their own. There would be no withdrawal of North Vietnamese troops, which, in any event, Hanoi refused to acknowledge were present in the South. More important, there could be no political settlement so long as the "Thieu-Ky clique" remained in power. In Hanoi's view, such a solution would be the equivalent of surrender.

The president speaks

By early May, Richard Nixon realized that the traditional presidential "100-Day Honeymoon" was over, with neither a diplomatic nor a military breakthrough in sight. With his stalled Vietnam policy increasingly under attack, above all for its seeming drift, it was time to go to the public. In a major television address on May 14, 1969, the president attempted to break the deadlock in Paris with his own eight-point peace plan.

Nixon began by enunciating his "essential principles." "We have ruled out attempting to impose a purely military solution on the battlefield," he stated. "We have also ruled out either a one-sided withdrawal from Vietnam, or the acceptance in Paris of terms that would amount to a disguised defeat." The "essential principles" presented, in fact, the reality of the double deadlock on the battlefield and at the conference table.

Outwardly, the president seemed to join military and political issues into a single negotiating posture: "A settlement will require the withdrawal of all non-South Vietnamese forces . . . and procedures for political choice that give each significant group in South Vietnam a real opportunity to participate in the political life of the nation." While stating that "we do not dispute" the North Vietnamese position that military withdrawal could be discussed only in the context of a political settlement of the war, Nixon repeated Kissinger's two-tiered formula: "The political settlement is an internal matter which ought to be decided among the South Vietnamese themselves and not imposed by outside powers."

Nixon's eight-point plan reflected this belief. The first four points detailed a phased withdrawal of American and North Vietnamese troops. Three others also concerned military matters: an international body to supervise a cease-fire, release of prisoners of war, and agreement to abide by the Geneva accords of 1954 and 1962. Only one point, a vague promise of internationally supervised elections, suggested a political solution.

Hanoi's response to Nixon's talk was predictable. To the North, Nixon was merely repeating Kissinger's plan to separate military and political issues and to force the Communists to disarm themselves while the Saigon regime remained well-armed and in power.

President Thieu's response, however, shocked Washington. He had been given an advance copy of the speech and had voiced his approval, a fact pointed out to the press. But immediately after the speech, he objected to the "fine print," which he claimed to have misunderstood. A rereading of the speech convinced Thieu that Nixon had violated two of his "no's." The "opportunity to participate in the political life of the nation" accorded to "each significant group in South Vietnam," seemed to grant the Communists a role in South Vietnam's political future, which its constitution forbade. The phrase also seemed to indicate

On the Road to Watergate

At 10:35 A.M. on May 9, 1969, Henry Kissinger placed a call from the "Florida White House" at Key Biscayne, Florida, to J. Edgar Hoover at Federal Bureau of Investigation headquarters in Washington. That morning a front-page article in the *New York Times* by William Beecher had leaked the news of covert U.S. B-52 bombings of Communist sanctuaries in Cambodia. Kissinger requested that the FBI chief exert "a major effort to find out where [the leaks] came from." He later called back to remind Hoover to conduct the inquiry discreetly "so no stories will get out."

Hoover reported back to Kissinger at 5:05 P.M. that day with four suspects including three members of the National Security Council staff: Morton Halperin, whom Hoover considered the most likely source of the leak; Helmut Sonnenfeldt, a Soviet expert; and Daniel I. Davidson, an Averell Harriman protégé. The fourth was Colonel Robert Pursley who served as Melvin Laird's aide in the Defense Department. In a memo concerning their conversation, Hoover recorded that "Dr. Kissinger . . . hoped I would follow it up as far as we can take it, and they will destroy whoever did this if we can find him, no matter where he is."

That same day, FBI operatives placed a wiretap on Halperin's home telephone in Bethesda, Maryland. At 6:20 P.M., prior even to official approval for the wiretap from Attorney General John Mitchell, the first entry from Halperin's tap was made in the FBI logs. Three days later Davidson, Sonnenfeldt, and Pursley were also tapped. Mitchell later noted that it was "a dangerous game we were playing."

Kissinger had the most to gain from the wiretaps. Considered a member of the liberal eastern establishment in a conservative Republican administration, he needed to prove his loyalty and toughness. By agreeing to, if not specifically requesting, taps on colleagues such as Halperin and Sonnenfeldt, he solidified his position with Nixon and others within the administration, many of whom distrusted the new national security adviser.

Tapping Pursley was a different matter. By spying on Laird's aide, Kissinger hoped to keep tabs on the defense secretary, his chief rival for supremacy in foreign affairs. Although the tap on Pursley's office phone was lifted on May 27, it was renewed in 1970 and again in 1971, and an additional tap was placed on his home as relations between Laird and Kissinger deteriorated. Laird was never informed of the "suspicions" surrounding his aide and would not find out about the tap until 1974.

The FBI operation failed to reveal the source of the leaks; still, it continued for nearly seven months. During that time two more NSC staff members, Richard Moose and Richard L. Sneider, were placed under surveillance as well as several suspects outside the NSC. Reporters Hedrick Smith of the *New York Times* and Marvin Kalb of CBS, syndicated columnist Joseph Kraft, and Henry Brandon of the *London Sunday Times* all came under either physical or electronic surveillance. Finally, the tapping also spread to other areas of the administration as Nixon speech writer William Safire and John P. Sears, deputy counsel to the president in charge of Republican party patronage, joined the list of suspects.

In all, eleven wiretaps and four cases of physical surveillance were authorized by the White House in 1969. All but one, the tap on Morton Halperin (which remained in operation until 1971, many months after he left the government) were withdrawn by the end of the year. Round one was over.

The 1970 Cambodian invasion touched off a public outcry that stunned the White House. With anxiety and suspicion at a new high, another leak in the *New York Times* on May 2 regarding the renewed bombing of North Vietnam resulted in the renewal of wiretapping. While Kissinger unsuccessfully pleaded with *New York Times* Washington Bureau Chief Max Frankel to squelch the story, Haig forwarded a request to the FBI for more wiretaps. Round two was under way.

For Nixon and Kissinger, the May 2 leak broke the camel's back. With this second series of wiretaps they were, as journalist Seymour Hersh described it, "going for broke," trying once and for all to learn "who inside the administration was loyal and who was not." NSC members Tony Lake and Winston Lord were tapped. *New York Times* reporter William Beecher was tapped. Both Pursley and Sonnenfeldt were tapped for the second time. And, for the first time, the surveillance operation moved into the State Department, focusing on William Sullivan, the deputy assistant secretary of state for East Asia, and Richard Pederson, a close associate of Secretary of State William Rogers with whom he shared two private telephone lines. As one Kissinger aide recalled, it was a time of "general paranoia."

When these wiretaps were finally withdrawn in February of 1971 the source of the leaks still had not been uncovered. Perhaps realizing the growing risks of the operation, Kissinger and Haig curtailed their involvement in it (although Haig did continue to meet occasionally with one of J. Edgar Hoover's principal lieutenants at FBI headquarters to review some of the logs) and presidential adviser Robert Haldeman assumed control. Although the wiretaps were still a closely guarded secret, from there on, the game would get much rougher.

On June 13, 1971, the *New York Times* published the first installment of the Pentagon Papers leaked to them by Daniel Ellsberg. In July, the White House began the organization of the "Plumbers Unit" in an attempt to combat this, the most massive leak in White House history. Round three had begun. It would climax one year later on June 17, 1972, in a posh, Washington office building named the Watergate.

"Wolf Nixon in disguise...."

"Here is my generous offer."

"Listen to the 'impact' my eight–point plan might have."

"The reality of Nixon's eight–point proposal."

"Nixon's eight–point proposal."

A filmstrip of cartoons drawn from Hanoi newspapers of 1969 lampoons President Nixon and the eight–point peace plan.

an acceptance of a coalition government if the NLF won seats in the newly elected National Assembly. Long put off by Washington, Thieu now demanded a face–to–face meeting with Nixon. "The policies of the two nations cannot be solved very easily over 10,000 miles of water," Thieu informed reporters. Nixon reluctantly agreed to meet Thieu on Midway Island.

Before Nixon departed for Midway, he added another element to his emerging Vietnam policy. The May 14 television speech largely reflected the beliefs of Kissinger. But there was another view in the administration, that of the new secretary of defense, Melvin Laird.

Laird was not at all surprised at the early lack of progress in ending the war; nor did he believe that Nixon's new peace initiative would break the diplomatic deadlock. In his view, the United States was in need of a "trump card" to prevent either South Vietnam or North Vietnam from exercising a veto over America's extrication from the war. If Kissinger believed that the objective of American policy should be to preserve its credibility and prestige and Nixon believed that the U.S. could preserve the government of South Vietnam, Laird's views were more practical. He believed that so long as the administration was "bogged down" in Vietnam it would be unable to gain Congressional approval to fund defense

requirements that he felt were badly needed in other parts of the world. Moreover, the Nixon administration's domestic initiatives would become politically paralyzed and the reelection of the president would be endangered.

Laird was the first professional politician to serve as secretary of defense. Previously, presidents had hoped to keep that office bipartisan by appointing men with strong managerial backgrounds, all the better to cope with the Pentagon's sprawling organization and budget. It was a belief epitomized by John Kennedy's nomination of the Republican Robert McNamara. For all their difficulties with McNamara, the uniformed military had never confronted the politically oriented office run by Melvin Laird. William Westmoreland, by then army chief of staff, recalled that "Laird appeared to distrust the Joint Chiefs, seemingly unable to accept, as a consummate politician himself, that we were apolitical."

Laird was not only a "consummate politician" but a born one as well. His grandfather was a Wisconsin lieutenant governor, his father a state senator. After graduation from Carleton College and wartime service in the navy, Laird immediately embarked on his own political career. In 1946, he won a seat in the Wisconsin senate, at twenty–three, the youngest in the state's history. Six years later, he was elected to the U.S. Congress, quickly earning a seat on the Defense Appropriations Subcommittee. He developed a reputation as a "hawk" and committed himself early to Barry Goldwater's candidacy in 1964. Four years later, however, he turned to Republican moderates, backing first George Romney and later Nelson Rockefeller.

As secretary of defense, Laird persuaded Nixon to embrace Johnson's emphasis in 1968 on upgrading South Vietnam's forces and, in fact, to elevate that policy to strategy. It was Laird who coined the term Vietnamization. Speaking before the AFL–CIO Convention in October 1969, Laird explained the difference between his program and Johnson's plan:

The previous modernization program was designed to prepare the South Vietnamese to handle only the threat of Viet Cong insurgency that would remain *after* all North Vietnamese regular forces had returned home. It made sense, therefore, only in the context of success at Paris. It was a companion piece to the Paris talks, not a complement and alternative. Vietnamization, on the other hand, is directed toward preparing the South Vietnamese to handle both Viet Cong insurgency and regular North Vietnamese armed forces regardless of the outcome in Paris.

Thus when Nixon met Thieu at Midway Island on June 8, it was not negotiating procedures that he wanted to discuss. Already in Saigon, Ambassador Ellsworth Bunker had informed Thieu that the top item on Nixon's agenda was the reduction of American troop strength in Vietnam. Now Thieu told the American president, "We have claimed for years that we were getting stronger. If it is so, we have to be willing to see some Americans leave." After agreeing on a public statement, the two presidents went to meet the press. President Nixon began: "I have decided to order the immediate redeployment from Vietnam of the divisional equivalent of approximately 25,000 men. . . ." Vietnamization was policy; America was on its way out.

A midsummer's shadow dance

In the aftermath of the American initiatives, the eight–point peace plan, and the first announcement of a troop withdrawal, both sides took a series of steps, seemingly unconnected and deliberately ambiguous. Were they tentative steps toward accommodation? Tactical readjustments to prepare for future military operations? Politically motivated steps to appeal to world opinion? Each was conducted so as to disguise the real motive and therefore to obscure whether any progress was being made to end the war.

Immediately following the Midway meeting, the NLF announced that it had established a "provisional revolutionary government," which sought to give the insurgents equal status with the Saigon regime. The PRG was soon recognized as the legitimate government of South Vietnam by fifteen governments from among the Communist bloc

and their allies. The State Department dismissed the move as "the same old wine in a new bottle," but optimists suggested that it might be a hint that the NLF felt a political settlement was near. Under this assumption, the formation of the PRG would aid the Communists in their peaceful competition with Thieu's government.

More important was the news from the battlefield. By late July, it was clear that enemy activity had been dropping sharply for nearly two months. Enemy attacks diminished by nearly 50 percent from their rate in May, and U.S. combat deaths in mid–July reached their lowest level of the year. Of greater significance were the intelligence reports. For the first time in years, the American command was not predicting a new Communist offensive for the simple reason that captured documents indicated none in the offing. Pessimists argued that such lulls in the fighting were not unusual and simply reflected the normal tempo of the war, in which the enemy coordinated its attacks during the rainy season and refreshed itself during the dry summer. But others felt that this lull was different, a "gut feeling," according to one long–time correspondent. "Some of the highest American military commanders . . . will admit that something is now different."

Many of Nixon's critics thought they knew what that difference was. Pointing out that orders from Hanoi generally took about four weeks to be felt on the battlefield, they maintained that the lull, first registered in mid–June, was a response to Nixon's May 14 television address. Some, like Averell Harriman, former ambassador to the Paris negotiations, suggested that the war would be deescalated not through negotiations but through small unilateral steps recognized by the other side. They challenged the president to take the next step. Specifically, they urged Nixon to rescind President Johnson's standing orders to maintain "maximum pressure."

In mid–July, Nixon met the challenge. Secretly, he authorized Defense Secretary Laird to issue new guidelines to General Abrams in Saigon. The new instructions, effective August 15, ordered Abrams to give his top priority to providing "maximum assistance" to the South Vietnamese to strengthen their forces. Abrams was also ordered to "hold down" American battlefield casualties. Henry Kissinger later reported that at the last minute President Nixon changed his mind (probably fearing that he was making an undue civilian interference in the conduct of the war) and asked Laird not to send the orders, but it was too late. Laird had already sent them to Saigon. But Kissinger concluded that it made no difference. "Given our commitment to withdrawal, they reflected our capabilities, whatever our intentions."

In the end, the *pas de deux* of summer produced no results. Each side left the motivation for its decision deliberately vague. Each side felt that any announcement that it was deescalating the conflict would be perceived as a sign of weakness by the adversary. Kissinger himself followed this line of reasoning in his analysis of the enemy's "summer lull." "No one," he wrote, "asked the question whether the lull might reflect the fact that our strategy was succeeding." The ground was set, not for further deescalation, but for its opposite.

By early fall 1969, none of the major dilemmas faced by the administration as it took office had disappeared. The stalemates continued in Paris and South Vietnam. Thieu's government remained too weak for the U.S. to make any peace proposal that might prove acceptable to Hanoi. Vietnamization could produce no quick or dramatic solution; it was at best a long-term insurance plan.

Henry Kissinger now returned to a thought he had previously uttered only in private. In May, he had warned Soviet ambassador Anatoly Dobrynin that if there was no progress in Paris, the U.S. would "escalate the war." In early September, Kissinger called together a select group of NSC staff members to develop plans for what he called a "savage, punishing" blow aimed at North Vietnam. According to Roger Morris, a Kissinger aide at the time:

At a minimum, the attack plan would include the mining of the port of Haiphong and inland waterways, a naval blockade, and intensive bombing strikes at military targets and population centers. The group was also instructed to consider the options of bombing the Red River dikes to flood the vital farm land of North Vietnam and closing the rail supply lines at the Chinese border. The study was to be undertaken in total secrecy from the rest of the government.

Morris reports Kissinger as concluding, "I can't believe that a fourth-rate power like North Vietnam doesn't have a breaking point."

Fearing domestic and international reaction, Nixon shelved Kissinger's secret plan for a dramatic escalation of the war, for the time being at least. But it was more difficult to dismiss the thinking behind it. Earlier in his career, Kissinger had criticized America's defensive posture after negotiations began to end the Korean conflict. He believed that such timidity only prolonged the negotiations, concluding, "Our insistence on divorcing force from diplomacy caused our power to lack purpose and our negotiations to lack force." Understandably, Kissinger has been more circumspect in expressing his views on the relation of force and negotiations in the Vietnam conflict. But in his memoirs he does indicate that his own thinking had not changed much: "Analytically, it would have been better to offer the most generous proposal imaginable—and then, if rejected, to seek to impose it militarily."

There were, therefore, many unanswered questions within the administration in the early fall of 1969. Publicly, it appeared to have a well-established two-pronged policy: to pursue negotiations and, if they failed, to rely on Vietnamization as a means of extricating the United States. But this policy merely represented the areas of agreement within the administration. Still to be decided was how America's military might could be brought to bear, especially in light of the new battlefield orders issued by Laird.

Further complicating matters was a dramatic announcement from Hanoi on September 5, 1969. Ho Chi Minh had died. Now the Nixon administration faced a new line-up in the North Vietnamese Politburo. Would a firm display of force cause the enemy to buckle under the pressures of internal disagreements, or would a clear course of accommodation encourage the new leadership to reciprocate in order to get the war off their backs? If the president was not yet willing to make up his mind, it was at least clear that the shadow dance of summer was over. The "signals" from Hanoi stopped, while the message from the antiwar movement at home grew clearer.

Dissent

As the summer of 1969 drew to a close, the new administration began to sense a coming domestic challenge, and not without reason. Students would soon be returning to campuses across the nation. Over the summer, two separate groups representing the tactical poles of antiwar protest planned massive actions for the fall. At first operating separately and eyeing each other suspiciously and later coordinating their efforts, they would together lead the largest antiwar demonstrations in the nation's history.

The Vietnam Moratorium Committee was the first to weigh in with its plans. Led largely by moderate political veterans of the McCarthy and Kennedy presidential campaigns, the VMC announced an escalating program for a monthly "moratorium" on "business as usual" for the duration of the war. The moratorium would begin with one day in October and add one day each month. The first moratorium was scheduled for October 15.

Although focusing their organizing efforts on college campuses, VMC leaders hoped to reach far beyond the old antiwar movement. Sam Brown, chairman of the VMC, argued that "it's not just a small group of tired old peaceniks or a fringe percentage of radicals that are willing to protest the war. It's millions of Americans in every part of the country, even places like Mississippi—all they need is a little push and the right channel." The VMC kept its distance from the radical left and confrontational politics and, by early fall, began to collect the support of "establishment" figures, among them John Kenneth Galbraith, labor leader Walter Reuther, and even the chairman of Nixon's own Republican party, Rogers Morton. Forty members of Congress endorsed the moratorium, and a group of legislators attempted to keep the House in session the entire night of October 14 in recognition of Moratorium Day. The Nixon administration inadvertently lent a hand on September 27 when President Nixon, responding to a question on the protests, said, "Under no circumstances, will I be affected whatever by it." The administration's indifference only spurred antiwar activists to greater action.

On M-day, October 15, observances took place all over the country. The number of participants was estimated at 1 million, but in fact, it was uncounted and uncountable. As *Time* magazine pointed out, "the significance of M-day was less in the numbers of participants than in who the participants were and how they went about it." In North Newton, Kansas, an antique bell tolled 40,000 times, once for each American killed in the war; at Nixon's alma mater, Whittier College, a "flame of life" was lit as "a constant reminder of those who have died and are dying in Vietnam." Predictably, the largest demonstrations took place in such cities as San Francisco, Boston, and New York. But even in those cities, the participants were as likely to be in business suits as blue jeans. On Wall Street, observances began at Trinity Church with a reading of the names of the war dead. At noon, the Businessmen's Rally drew 20,000 from Manhattan's concrete jungle.

Nor were Moratorium Day activities confined to the U.S. Demonstrations by Americans took place in Copenhagen, London, Paris, Dublin, Tokyo, and Sydney, often with government employees participating. More poignant were the protests of American servicemen in South Vietnam. Fifteen members of a platoon of the Americal Division wore black armbands on patrol. Four of them were wounded later that day. At Tan Son Nhut air base, a half dozen airmen also wore the black armbands. It was a portent. Antiwar dissent was spreading even into the armed forces.

On October 20, the leaders of the Moratorium announced to the press their plans for a two-day Moratorium on November 13–14, to permit coordination with a march on Washington on November 15 directed by another antiwar group, the New Mobilization Committee To End the War. Unlike the VMC, the New Mobilization believed in confrontation and nonviolent resistance but excluded such violence-prone groups as the Weatherman faction of Students for a Democratic Society. Initially, the VMC had feared that the more radical direction of the New Mobe would frighten its moderate supporters, but assurances of nonviolence brought the two groups together.

While the New Mobe and the VMC were planning their November programs, the Nixon administration went on the offensive. First, the president unleashed Vice President Spiro Agnew. In a series of speeches, Agnew raised to new heights the level of rhetorical confrontation between the administration and its critics. After labeling the antiwar protesters as "an effete corps of impudent snobs who characterize themselves as intellectuals," he attacked the "liberal establishment press" for its coverage of the administration. Ironically, the most radical enemies of the administration cited Agnew's speech as confirmation of their own grievances against the press.

The highlight of the Nixon counteroffensive was a televised speech on November 3. Against the advice of his entire cabinet and Henry Kissinger, he made no concession to the protesters. Rather, he defended America's intervention in Vietnam and speaking to "the great silent majority of my fellow Americans," asked for "your support." Later, he informed the press that he would view a football game on the day of the great march.

The administration's rhetoric violated one of Kissinger's cardinal principles of the conduct of foreign affairs, to avoid the incitement of domestic passions, or what England's Lord Canning called "the fatal artillery of public excitation." In his memoirs, Kissinger wrote, "My attitude towards the protesters diverged from Nixon's. He saw in them an enemy that had to be vanquished; I considered them students and colleagues with whom I differed." In a private memorandum to the president he cautioned, "attacking this group head-on is counterproductive."

Kissinger's analysis proved correct. The demonstrations of November 13–15 surpassed the planners' expectations. The ceremonies began on November 13 with a dramatic "March against Death," in which a single file of 40,000 people walked in silent vigil from Arlington National Cemetery to the White House and Capitol. Each marcher carried a candle and a placard bearing the name of an American soldier killed or Vietnamese village destroyed in the war. Leading the march was Judith Droz, whose husband had been killed in Vietnam the previous spring. She came, she said, "to express my feelings and those of my late husband that the U.S. should get out of Vietnam immediately."

On Saturday, November 15, the warm drizzle of the previous two days gave way to clear blue skies and plummeting temperatures. In the freezing cold, 250,000 to 300,000 participants marched from the Capitol down Pennsylvania Avenue to the Washington Monument. Marchers bore placards reading "Silent Majority for Peace," and parade marshals carefully monitored the event. Its peacefulness defied all dire predictions. Only a splinter demonstration at the Justice Department disturbed the mood of the day.

In the end, the dissenters' "fall offensive" and the administration's response only introduced another stalemate into the administration's policy making. The government received notice that the antiwar movement was alive and growing, but the protesters gained little sense of having affected American policy. As Kissinger put it, "Neither could achieve what both yearned for: an early negotiated end to the war in Vietnam."

Hanoi mourns

The effects of the fall's antiwar activities were watched nowhere with greater interest than in North Vietnam. But Hanoi, in the fall of 1969, was a different place, subdued, in mourning, as it had been since September 5, 1969, when *Nhan Dan*, Hanoi's official newspaper, had tersely

Powers of the North

With the death of the charismatic Ho Chi Minh (right), leadership of North Vietnam fell to his comrades, among them the cool prime minister, Pham Van Dong (left above), and the fiery military leader, General Vo Nguyen Giap (left below), all three pictured here in November 1968, ten months before Ho's death.

reported "With deepest sorrow, the Central Executive Committee of the Vietnam Lao Dong Party . . . informs the whole party and the whole people of Vietnam that Comrade Ho Chi Minh, had passed away on September 3, 1969, at 9:47 A.M."

Even the Saigon-based *Vietnamese Guardian*, ignoring for a moment the division of Vietnam into two countries, admitted, "Vietnam loses its unique politician of truly international status. With President Ho's death, a legendary, almost mythological figure disappears from the international political scene."

Along with the mighty of the Communist world, thousands of Vietnamese filed in and out of Ba Dinh Congress Hall to catch a final glimpse of their beloved leader. Lying in a glass sarcophagus, his frail, thin body was clothed in his familiar, worn khaki outfit. At his feet, enclosed in a separate glass box, lay his sandals fashioned from old, used tires—a symbol of the president's privations and long marches during the French Indochina War.

At 7:30 A.M., on September 9, the funeral service began and all of Hanoi stopped to listen, nearly a million strong, at loud-speakers hastily erected across the city. Major Dinh Ngoc Lien led the People's Army Band in the national anthem, in the same place where twenty-four years earlier, almost to the day, he had opened the ceremony at which Ho proclaimed his country's independence.

Le Duan, the party's first secretary, delivered a short oration, his voice quavering with emotion. On the podium several of North Vietnam's leaders, including Pham Van Dong, burst into tears, as Le Duan concluded, "President Ho Chi Minh, the great leader, the loved and revered master of our party and people, lives forever."

American policy makers were naturally less interested in Ho's place in history than in trying to fathom what his death would mean for the conduct of the war. Douglas Pike, perhaps America's foremost authority on the Vietnamese Communists, predicted interparty strife: "I have no faith in collective leadership. They will all claim the mantle of Ho Chi Minh and they will start to get grabby." An official National Intelligence Estimate agreed: "It would be surprising if Ho's death has not introduced some uncertainties within the top leadership. Although, his disciples have been working together for common goals for nearly four decades, they almost certainly have held differing views on key issues over the years and it would be most unusual if they were devoid of personal ambitions."

Later events proved both Pike and the NIE poor prophets. Perhaps their expectations were a consequence of America's selective experience with Communist leaderships. Having little contact with such countries as China and Cuba, American policy makers were most familiar with the second generation leadership of the Soviet Union and its satellites. For most of these rulers, the revolutionary experiences of their predecessors had become ossified,

the philosophy of Marxism a rhetorical device to mask self-interested pursuit of power. But Ho and his surviving comrades—Le Duan, Pham Van Dong, Truong Chinh, and Vo Nguyen Giap—were not Kosygin or Brezhnev. These men were revolutionaries.

Ho's legacy—Hanoi's strategy

For Ho and his followers, Marxism was the driving force of their lives, a philosophy that had attracted each of them forty years earlier because it answered Lenin's question, *What is to be Done?* Each had come to Marxism first as a Vietnamese nationalist, but they had adapted Marxism to their own national conditions. Marxism provided a blueprint for ending the colonial occupation of the French and achieving independence for their country. Above all, however, it gave them a certainty of their ultimate success. Central to Marxist thought is the idea that the historical process cannot be stopped. Neither weapons nor strategies nor personal courage—though all three were needed—could insure success. The great vindicator was not power but time.

Not only did Marxism tell them that this was so, but their own lives seemed to prove the Marxist vision correct. All of Ho's closest comrades, like Ho himself, had spent most of their lives not in the comfort of national power but in the privations of resistance. Each had spent time in jail or in exile. Each had experienced the battle for physical existence in the jungles and mountains of Vietnam, when not lack of weapons but lack of food and shelter wasted their physical condition. And yet, they had triumphed. They had defeated France, one of the world's recognized great powers; they had marched victoriously into Hanoi; they had fought the world's greatest power to a stalemate for over four years.

While Nixon and Kissinger agonized over the stalemate in Vietnam, the new North Vietnamese leadership embraced it. It was confirmation anew that their strategy was working. Perhaps the only matter that both sides could agree upon was that time was on the side of the Communists, the one side from the devout belief in the correctness of their Marxist theory, the other from their recognition of political reality.

That America would tire of the war was not, in the view of Ho's successors, a matter entirely of their own doing. In their theory of revolutionary warfare, successfully applied against the French, their enemies would be ground down not so much by direct military action as by demoralization. The death of Ho Chi Minh after fifty years of labor for their cause served to remind them that patience was their most greatly needed virtue and time their ally. They would wait.

Moratoriums

Above. A shop owner closes his doors in observance of the moratorium in Washington.

Right. A participant listens to the speaker during one of Boston's October 15 Moratorium rallies.

Far right. Antiwar protesters in Berkeley are undeterred by rain during the October Moratorium rally at the University of California's Sproul Plaza, a landmark of protest.

Preceding page. Demonstrators fill Washington's 15th Street on the final leg of the march on Washington, November 15, 1969.

Left. Antiwar actors perform street theater in front of New York's Plaza Hotel as part of the October Moratorium.

Far left. Demonstrators at an "antiwar lie-down" in Manhattan's Central Park during the November Moratorium.

Below. Businessmen join a rally at noon on Wall Street, October 15.

Above. Protesters begin the long "March Against Death" from Washington's Arlington Cemetery to the Capitol building on November 13.

Left. New York City's October Moratorium concludes with an evening rally in front of St. Patrick's Cathedral.

Right. On patrol near Chu Lui, a soldier of the 198th Infantry Brigade and more than half his platoon wear black armbands to show support for the Moratorium.

One War: A New Strategy

Of all the controversies surrounding the Vietnam War, few seem so difficult to unravel as an assessment of the Communist Tet offensive of 1968. One point, however, on which every observer seems to agree is that the offensive resulted in a psychological setback for the American and South Vietnamese cause. This psychological defeat has largely been perceived as affecting the civilian political leadership and public opinion in America. But the psychological effects of Tet were also visible within the ranks of the army itself, as veteran officers began, for the first time, to question publicly the prevailing military strategy.

One such officer, Lieutenant Colonel Richard A. McMahon, had served in intelligence units both in Vietnam and at CINCPAC headquarters in Honolulu. Writing in the journal *Army* in early 1969, McMahon argued, "When a fighting machine as good as this one is unable to achieve its purpose, the reasons probably lie not with the forces in the field but with the strategy governing

their employment." He termed the prevailing strategy a "direct approach . . . the heritage of Clausewitz," in which the "primary objective [is] the destruction of the enemy's armed forces by . . . bringing them to battle." McMahon concluded, "It has failed."

McMahon suggested that the United States reject the Clausewitzian paradigm in favor of another classical theory of warfare, "the indirect approach," as enunciated by Britain's famous military theorist, Sir Basil Liddell Hart. McMahon described this indirect approach as seeking "to dislocate the enemy rather than destroy him. . . . It relies heavily on surprise and psychological means to lower the enemy's morale, and upon maneuver to disrupt his dispositions, interdict his lines of supply and cut off his routes of escape." McMahon concluded that this approach would have many advantages. "It would avoid search-and-destroy operations in favor of clear-and-hold actions designed to drive the insurgent permanently and completely away from his population base. . . . It would rely on intensive patrolling by small units and highly effective intelligence agencies to find insurgent bases and caches, and to round up insurgent leaders, agents, and sympathizers."

McMahon found company in an increasing number of junior officers. Captain Brian Jenkins offered his views to the Rand Corporation in early 1969. He suggested that "in Vietnam, the Army simply performed its repertoire even though it was frequently irrelevant to the situation." Jenkins, like McMahon, argued that American commanders took a traditional view of the war in which "the losing side will be determined primarily by personnel losses. Essentially it is a strategy of attrition. . . . Other notions, such as 'winning hearts and minds,' have been added, but these other notions are considered incidental. Our army remains enemy-oriented and casualty-oriented. War, then, is assumed to be a battlefield where tactics rather than strategy are important." Continuing this theme of the primacy of tactics over strategy, Jenkins concluded that the criteria to measure success in the war were "operational criteria," and hence, *the operations are the strategy.*"

LORAPL

Jenkins had a unique perspective on the subject. In October 1968 he had joined a special task force created in July 1968 by the new COMUSMACV, General Creighton Abrams, to study America's strategy over the previous four years and to recommend any needed changes. Called the Long Range Planning Task Group, or LORAPL, the group concluded its work in March 1970.

To head the task force Abrams chose an army lieutenant colonel, Dr. Donald S. Marshall. Abrams's first contact with Marshall had come in 1966, when Marshall, then a member of the army's PROVN ("Program for the Pacification and Long-Term Development of South Vietnam") study team had briefed Abrams on its work.* This study had urged the army to adopt a pacification-oriented strategy in Vietnam rather than emphasize the "main-force" operations then being conducted. Abrams was, at the time, deputy chief of staff of the army.

Thus when Abrams chose Marshall he had a good understanding of the type of man he was getting. In fact, he asked Marshall "to bring your papers with you," in other words, to use PROVN as the basis for the reconsideration of American strategy. Within a month after assuming command Abrams had, according to Marshall, a "clear understanding that Westmoreland's strategy was not adequate to do the job that had to be done." In particular, Abrams felt that insufficient attention had been given to the "political and human aspects of the war."

What Marshall and his group set out to do was to create a new strategy for the United States in Vietnam. In fact, Marshall believes that "this was the development of a national strategy for Vietnam . . . where none had existed before. . . . Attrition is a component of a strategy, but it is inadequate."

On November 26, 1968, LORAPL gave a special briefing to General Abrams and his senior aides to announce its preliminary conclusions. This report evolved, with very few changes, into the official, secret MACV Objectives Plan, adopted by Abrams in March 1969. Addressing the current military situation, the group concluded,

All of our U.S. combat accomplishments have made no significant—positive—difference to the rural Vietnamese—for there still is no real security in the countryside! Our large scale operations have attempted to enable the development of a protective shield, by driving the NVA and Vietcong main force units out of South Vietnam. . . . In pressing this objective, however, we have tended to lose sight of *why* we were driving the enemy back and destroying his combat capability. Destruction of NVA and VC units and individuals . . . has become an end in itself—an end that at times has been self-defeating.

In addressing this situation LORAPL realized that it was essential first to define those American objectives in Vietnam toward which a strategy could be directed. They immediately faced a problem. While the development of such objectives was clearly the responsibility of figures with more authority in Washington, American political leaders had been loathe to articulate clear and explicit goals. Instead LORAPL found a bewildering array of statements from State, Defense, and the White House, of-

---

* For more information on the PROVN study, see page 59 of *A Contagion of War,* another volume in "The Vietnam Experience."

A Popular Force soldier, armed with his new M16 rifle, stands guard in the village of Dai Phuoc, near Da Nang, in 1970.

Area Security Concept

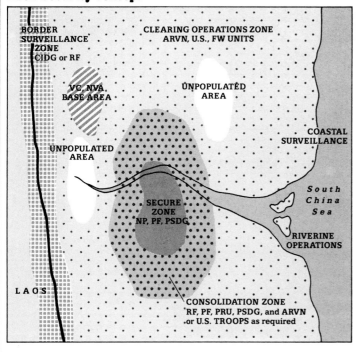

ten contradictory in nature. LORAPL's first task was to shape these statements into a "single, internally consistent, coherent statement of objectives," according to Marshall. The result was the first set of precisely defined American objectives in the war. LORAPL described the "ultimate objective" as

A free, independent and viable nation of South Vietnam that is not hostile to the United States, functioning in a secure environment both internally and regionally.

Since the achievement of this objective depended to a great extent on the abilities of the government of South Vietnam rather than on American military performance, LORAPL was unable to summon much optimism: "In view of socio–cultural and economic factors that preclude successful rapid planned change, most social scientists would estimate that at least two decades would be required to achieve the ultimate U.S. objective in Vietnam." Abrams's planners were well aware that the American public would never accept another twenty years of American combat in Vietnam. "Lack of time," they concluded, "is the greatest threat to achievement of the present U.S. objectives in Vietnam."

To remedy this depressing conclusion, LORAPL recommended the adoption of "immediate" and "intermediate" U.S. objectives that could be accomplished in a reasonable period of time. They further urged that achievement of these objectives be labeled "a win," which would increase public confidence in America's role in Vietnam and perhaps buy sufficient time to reach the "ultimate" objective. LORAPL suggested two immediate objectives:

- An environment of reasonable security within key areas of South Vietnam.

- A realistic basis for the government of Vietnam and its people to proceed with building a free and independent nation.

If these objectives could be met, then the U.S. effort could proceed toward the two "intermediate" objectives:

- Expanded areas of secure environment within which the GVN carries out national development programs.

- Solidified basis for the GVN and its people to continue developing meaningful institutions and an environment for beneficial economic growth and social change.

In his Commander's Summary of the final MACV Objectives Plan, Abrams accepted these objectives. He also secured Ambassador Ellsworth Bunker's approval of them. In fact, according to Marshall, Abrams had "kept the ambassador totally informed" of LORAPL's work and the two men "were working hand in glove." Abrams and Bunker then sent the objectives to Washington for approval but never received a reply. Still, Marshall concluded, "We continued to work under that set of objectives. . . . We had to have these objectives from both the planning and operational standpoints."

The unwillingness of America's political leaders to endorse these objectives was probably a result of their wish to maintain freedom of action in pursuing a Vietnam policy, especially in the negotiations. It left open the very real possibility that while Abrams was pursuing a particular set of objectives in Vietnam, Kissinger might be trying to achieve entirely different ones in the negotiations in Paris.

In accepting the LORAPL objectives, Abrams elaborated on the thinking behind them. A foremost concern was American public opinion; the electoral process would serve as his milestones. "A failure to achieve measurable success by July 1970 may be expected to result in widespread disillusionment with the Congress. By the time Congressional campaigns reached their peak in the summer of 1970, we may expect to see a change of support on the part of Congressional incumbents as they attempt to retain control of the electorate." July 1970 was thus adopted as the deadline for achievement of these immediate objectives. Similarly, Abrams reported, "The intermediate objective must be achieved by 30 June 1972, prior to the Congressional and Presidential campaigns. . . . Additional 'time' for achieving a 'win' beyond that point cannot be reasonably expected."

In a major departure from earlier planning, MACV decided to use pacification gains and not enemy reversals as the major index of progress. Abrams established the specific goal "to increase the relatively secure areas to include 90 percent of the population by June 1972" as an indication that the intermediate objectives had been met.

"One war"

Establishing new objectives was only a first step. Still to be answered was, how do we get there? Looking at America's earlier strategy, Abrams saw three "interrelated thrusts": "Destroying enemy main force units," establishing a "militarily secure climate," and "improving national development." However, Abrams concluded, "Although all three thrusts were conducted simultaneously well into 1968, high priority was given to the first. The other two were given a relatively low weight of effort." Now MACV adopted the "one war concept" earlier proclaimed by Ambassador Bunker. Abrams described this as "a strategy focused upon protecting the population so that the civil government can establish its authority as opposed to an earlier conception of the purpose of war—destruction of the enemy's forces."

Under the one war concept Abrams approved a strategy based upon developing "area security." This divided Vietnamese territory into three types of zones and provided for a division of responsibility between American and South Vietnamese forces in conducting the war in those areas. Under the concept of area security the three area classifications were "clearing operations zones," "consolidation zones," and "secure zones." "Clearing zones" would fall under the responsibility of ARVN commanders and under the protection of all "Free World" Forces. As a clearing zone became free of enemy troops it would become part of the "consolidation zone," responsible to the province chief and protected by South Vietnamese auxiliary troops and American battalions when required. Finally, "secure zones" would be created in which only South Vietnamese Regional and Popular Forces would be required to provide security (see illustration, page 52).

Abrams cautioned that the security concept was not designed to provide security for an area. Rather,

the requirement is to provide security for the *populace* in the areas. Security must be continuous. A hamlet which belongs to the enemy at night or even one night a month cannot be considered a secure hamlet.

Once Abrams approved the new MACV Objectives Plan in March 1969, he faced the much more serious task of gaining its adoption by his superiors in Washington, his senior colleagues in the South Vietnamese armed forces, and his subordinate American commanders in the field. He adopted a different strategy with each group.

Abrams decided not to send the plan to Washington for Defense Department approval. Abrams told Marshall that he feared that it would be "nit-picked to death like flies buzzing around an elephant." Instead he dealt with his superiors informally, gradually explaining the most controversial concepts to them and gaining their piecemeal approval.

With the South Vietnamese, Abrams and Ambassador Bunker used gentle persuasion. Keeping President Thieu informed and gaining his full approval of the plan, Abrams then succeeded in making the MACV Objectives Plan the basis for the Combined Strategic Objectives Plan of the allied armed forces. Abrams and South Vietnamese chief of staff General Cao Van Vien signed the plan in March 1970, making it the official strategy of the war. The Combined Strategic Objectives Plan may well have been the most important document to come out of LORAPL's work, since it committed the South Vietnamese armed forces to carrying out Abrams's strategy. With American forces already rapidly withdrawing from the war, the South Vietnamese were going to have to make it work.

The most difficult group to deal with proved to be the American field force and divisional commanders, all highly qualified generals. While issuing no direct orders to them, Abrams did use his weekly commanders' conference to urge consistently that they operate in accordance with the guidelines expressed in the objectives plan. Abrams often felt frustrated. On one occasion he told Marshall, "I have one hundred-odd generals, and only two of them understand this war!" Still, Colonel Marshall believed that the generals' willingness to carry out the new strategy "varied considerably between commanders, in space and over time." Some, like Prov Corps commander army Lieutenant General Richard Stilwell, gave Abrams their full support. Stilwell, of course, was backed up by the marine generals in I Corps. As for more recalcitrant gen-

"Fighting Abe." General Creighton Abrams at his MACV headquarters in early 1969.

erals, Abrams would personally send Marshall to their headquarters to brief their entire staffs. Marshall described one such encounter with the II Field Force commander, Lieutenant General Julian J. Ewell, in III Corps:

Ewell sat there during the briefing. He chewed up and spat out an entire yellow pencil in the course of listening. When it was over he stood up, turned around to his staff, and said, "I've made my entire career and reputation by going 180 degrees counter to such orders as this," and walked out.

In the end Marshall concluded that the acceptance of the plan by American commanders was for the most part "moot" because American units were, in any case, withdrawing from the war. Rather, he pointed out, "We believed that it was the important thing for the ARVN to adopt it and in many senses ARVN had adopted it before the Americans had."

The war's new face

Although he did not approve the final MACV Objectives Plan until March 1969, Abrams did not wait that long to begin implementing the new strategy. Journalists were able to detect a new thrust in American military policy earlier that year. The approval Abrams gave to marine General Raymond Davis to free most of the troops manning the "strong points" along the DMZ was only one signal.

For operations in the clearing zones Abrams began to adopt the tactics of the enemy, capitalizing on the great mobility of American troops to break down or build up his units with even greater speed than the VC. Abrams told reporters, "We work in small patrols because that's how the enemy moves—in groups of four and five. When he fights in squad size, we now fight in squad size. When he cuts to half squad, so do we." American operations of battalion size or larger slowly began to decline, beginning in mid-1968 when Abrams took command. In the second half of 1968 there were only 384 such operations, compared with nearly 600 in the first half of the year. The decline continued into 1969 and 1970 when the number of large operations dropped to 620 for the entire year. *Time* magazine reported, "Few of these actions produce any spectacular battles. But they are calculated to cripple the Communist fight[ing] man's whole style." And the magazine concluded by contrasting "the vast, multi-division-sized 'search-and-destroy' missions of General William Westmoreland and the sting-ray 'spoiler' raids that Abrams has specialized in."

In emphasizing this small-unit war, American troops quickly realized that the war among the population had not changed much since 1965 or 1966, nor was it any less deadly than the main-force war. An army medical study reported the grim facts of American casualties, finding that those wounded "from fragments (including mines and booby traps) rose from 49.6 percent in 1966 to 80 percent in 1970. The incidence of these wounds was more than triple the level incurred in World War II and Korea." The army study concluded, "These injuries, often multiple, always devastating, pose the most formidable threat to life and the greatest challenge to the surgeon."

One division upon which General Abrams's new tactical thrust had little impact was the 1st Marine Division, now commanded by Major General Edwin B. Wheeler from his headquarters near Da Nang. The 1st Marine Division had considered population security its major objective ever since the original deployment in early 1966. By 1970 the division had committed over 2,000 men and officers to the Combined Action Platoons to increase efficiency and performance in that task. In addition, squads from the division conducted thousands of patrols in the environs of villages to keep the Vietcong from coming back. The task was not merely to provide security but to make it permanent.

The marine division experienced the frustration of confronting an enemy "satisfied with just being able to exist." There were few glorious battles for the 1st Marine Division, but examples of individual valor were still numerous, such as the actions of Lance Corporal Emilio A. De la Garza, Jr.

De la Garza had enlisted in the marines in 1969 and was assigned to Marine Corps exchange duty in Da Nang, a relatively safe rear-echelon position. In December 1969 De la Garza volunteered for transfer into the 2d Battalion, 1st Marines, 1st Marine Division. As a member of Company E, he was engaged in a routine nighttime patrol on April 11, 1970, when his squad spotted two enemy soldiers armed with an RPG rocket launcher. The marines fired, killing one, but the other guerrilla dove into a nearby flooded paddy. The marines flushed him out by throwing grenades into the water. As De la Garza and his platoon commander began to drag the enemy soldier from the water, the corporal noticed the struggling guerrilla reach for a grenade. De la Garza pushed his platoon leader aside and smothered the grenade. De la Garza's death represented the only marine casualty; he was posthumously awarded a Medal of Honor for his "prompt and decisive action, and his great personal valor in the face of almost certain death."

Abrams's strategy spread the experiences of the 1st Marine Division to countless other units, such as the 1st Battalion, 50th Infantry, and the 4th and 25th infantry divisions, as the American military effort shifted from the war of battalions to the search for guerrilla fishes. With his concentration of troops near population centers and with his new orders to hold down American casualties, Abrams was still confronted with the problem of the "clearing zones." How could he prevent enemy build-ups in these largely unpopulated areas and push outward the frontiers of consolidation and secure zones in the face of declining

Soldiers of the 25th Infantry Division march an enemy prisoner into camp near Cu Chi in III Corps in mid-1969. The 25th was among the units redeployed to protect the population.

American force strength? His answer was the B-52 Strato-fortress and overall American air power. If the American arsenal was deliberately sheathed in the delicate war among the population, it was unleashed as never before in the clearing zones and in Laos and Cambodia.

The sledgehammer

Because of his cigar-chomping manner, his gruff exterior, and his reputation as a protégé of General George S. Patton, General Abrams's keen intellect and devotion to classical music went unnoticed by many. Often he would describe his tactical approach in musical terms. "Sometimes you need to play the *1812 Overture* and now and then you have to let the violins play," is the metaphor he used for his "sting-ray" tactics in populated areas. But if Abrams brought a new pianissimo to the American tactical repertoire, he also realized that there was still a place to play it fortissimo.

In the clearing zones Abrams believed that saturation bombing was the most efficient means to keep the enemy off balance and to prevent his massing for attack. He could thus use his combat troops for "mop-up operations" rather than initiate contact through large troop sweeps.

Electronic surveillance of the jungles and mountains—with portable radar units, various devices that could detect body heat and heat from engines, and even "people sniffers," which picked up the scent of human urine—enabled U.S. and South Vietnamese forces to spot the enemy more accurately and without deploying large numbers of troops. MACV even used IBM 1430 computers to analyze patterns of enemy operations to predict likely times and places of attacks, thus helping to pinpoint the enemy.

In clearing zones nearer to populated areas, Abrams used a technique known as "cordon and pile on" or simply "pile on." This technique differed in crucial respects from earlier cordon operations as well as from search and destroy missions. Previously, the cordon had been used largely to conduct police operations. Allied soldiers would cordon off a village in an attempt to snare unwary guerrillas. More often such cordons provided an opportunity to search a village for possible VC weapons caches and to conduct small "civic action" programs such as MEDCAPs. In such cases, in the middle of villages, little use was made of artillery or air fire support.

By late 1968 the cordon technique was more commonly used in less populated areas, augmenting if not replacing search and destroy operations. In such situations the "cordon and pile on" technique made use of improved technologies. Not only could electronic surveillance devices make "discovery" of the enemy easier, but the increased availability of helicopters made it possible for fewer soldiers to be "thrashing about in the jungle," as one general put it. If the enemy was found, reinforcements could be

ferried in more quickly and in larger numbers to cordon off the area. After the cordon was complete, the area would be pounded by artillery and bombers. These tactics made increasing use of B-52 aircraft.

Although B-52s had first been deployed in Vietnam in 1965, their use had not been widespread until 1968. Substantial use of B-52s during the siege of Khe Sanh had given American commanders new confidence in the Stratofortresses as they hit enemy positions within less than a mile of friendly troops. By the end of 1968 and throughout 1969 the B-52s were heavily relied upon as both tactical and strategic bombers.

Once a clearing zone had been saturated with fire, ground troops could sweep through the area. It was considered the most efficient way to engage the enemy in the countryside, preventing him from nearing the population

While many American troops were redeployed to populated areas, the men of the 101st Airborne Division, including these members of the 2d Battalion, 506th Infantry, transfer ammunition in the sparsely inhabited region along the DMZ.

centers. "Everyone is employing cordon and pile-on now," said Major General Keith L. Ware of the 1st Infantry Division in September 1968.

Much of South Vietnam's territory was wholly unpopulated, and Abrams did not want to tie down his troops in those areas. Here, more than ever, the B–52s did the work, continually pounding enemy rear base areas and keeping him off balance. In both 1968 and 1969 the number of B–52 sorties flown in Southeast Asia surpassed the previous total for the entire war, before beginning to decline in 1970 as the U.S. Air Force withdrew slowly from the war. From 1968 until the end of the U.S. commitment in 1972, B–52 bomb tonnage represented more than 50 percent of the total bomb tonnage dropped on South Vietnam.

For the most part these sorties were not flown in support of combat troops. Only 10 percent of the air strikes were flown to support allied forces in immediate contact with the enemy. Another quarter of the sorties fulfilled a request for an immediate strike on a target of opportunity spotted from the ground. The other two-thirds of the strikes were simply flown over suspected enemy targets derived from all intelligence sources. If there were increasingly fewer American soldiers patrolling the unpopulated regions of South Vietnam, Abrams was not going to let the enemy forget that the Americans were still around.

The B–52 became one of the many controversial weapons employed in Vietnam. Some reporters likened it to killing a fly with a sledgehammer. But many field commanders were impressed with its accomplishments. General Westmoreland stated, "Enemy troops fear B–52s, tactical air, artillery, and armor, in that order." Psychological operations officers reported that they were most successful in encouraging enemy defections in units recently hit by a B–52. While some field officers gained great faith in the bombers, others were less impressed. Colonel Joseph B. Conmy, Jr., who as commander of the 3d Brigade of the 101st Airborne Division directed the attack on Hamburger Hill, was reluctant to use B–52s in that situation. While acknowledging that the enemy placed a high priority on retrieving their dead, Conmy claimed that he never saw a dead enemy soldier in the aftermath of a B–52 raid. He, like many others, became convinced that the enemy received prior warning from such strikes.

Air force Lieutenant General John Vogt, a deputy COMUSMACV and former commander of the 7th Air Force, reasoned that Soviet trawlers in the South Pacific radioed Hanoi whenever B–52s took off from Anderson Air Force Base on Guam. He believed that enemy radar picked up the Stratofortresses 240 kilometers from the coast. A captured NVA platoon leader seemed to confirm Vogt's suspicions: "I know that on the B–52 strikes we normally had advance warning as to where and when they would occur. The warning usually came by a message from division to the regiment and it normally arrived two hours prior to the strike." Like most of the arsenal deployed in Vietnam, this "most feared weapon" could make a major contribution, but it was far from a panacea.

The use of the B–52 was not limited to its tactical deployment within South Vietnam. As Abrams's consolidation zones and secure zones spread outward, the enemy was steadily pushed outward to South Vietnam's western borders and into his sanctuaries in Laos and Cambodia. B–52s were sent to strike the Ho Chi Minh Trail in Laos for the first time in 1969 with both total tonnage and sorties increasing in subsequent years, even as the total of B–52 strikes declined. Here, even more than in South Vietnam, a virtual armada of electronic sensors, bearing such colorful names as Spikebuoy, Acoubuoy, Adsid, and Acousid, attempted to keep tabs on enemy movements.

The most important technological advance, however, was in the development of precision guided munition, the so-called "smart weapons." These weapons, which homed in on their targets, greatly increased the efficiency of the weapons employed and lowered the costs of the air war, both in money and human life.

An important dimension of the air war over the Ho Chi Minh Trail was the interdiction of enemy supply trucks. New technological developments in airborne radar systems, such as low-light-level television and forward-

A B–52 lifts off from Guam on its way to a mission over South Vietnam. Under General Abrams, B–52s increasingly replaced the soldier in fighting the enemy in unpopulated areas.

looking infrared radar, greatly enhanced interdiction capability at night and during poor weather conditions. The development of the AC-130 gunship, considered the best truck-killing weapon in the war, added even more to the enemy's cost of supplying his troops.

The net effect of this increased activity over the Laotian panhandle was mixed. The B-52 undoubtedly had the effect of keeping the enemy from massing for attack, a substantial contribution as the American military effort concentrated on providing population security. But the results of the interdiction campaign were uncertain at best. As a postwar Department of Defense study concluded, the interdiction sorties "did hamper the flow of supplies down the Ho Chi Minh Trail, and the enemy had to increase his efforts to maintain the net flow of material he received in [South Vietnam], but interdiction did not choke off VC/NVA activity in the South, and all of the estimates of supply flows along the trail were uncertain."

The new Communist strategy

On August 23, 1968, North Vietnamese Politburo member Truong Chinh, who had been a leading opponent of the Tet offensive strategy of 1968, took to the airwaves of North Vietnam for a major speech outlining his proposals both for future development of North Vietnam as well as for the war effort. "We must," he urged, "grasp the motto of 'long-drawn out fight and relying mainly on one's self.' At times, under certain circumstances, we must shift to the defensive to gain time, dishearten the enemy, and build up our forces to prepare for a new offensive." Truong Chinh's speech, according to Radio Hanoi, was followed by "several sessions of heated debate" within the ruling Politburo. It was clear to all members of that group that with the beginnings of negotiations in Paris, North Vietnam would embark on its "talk-fight" strategy, first employed during the French Indochina War. But the question remained open as to how the Communists would conduct the "fight" portion of the equation. After the discussions within the Politburo were over it became clear that Truong Chinh's words had been heeded.

Much of the pressure for a reexamination of tactics undoubtedly came from the Communist southerners themselves, who had borne the brunt of the Tet '68 attacks. One year later in April 1969, COSVN announced in Directive 53: "Never again and under no circumstances are we going to risk our entire military force for just an offensive. On the contrary, we should endeavor to preserve our military potential for future campaigns." While the directive probably reflected the thinking of Communist cadres in the South, the subsequent release of Resolutions 9 and 14 (a resolution is a COSVN decision that is more fundamental than a directive) explicitly confirmed agreement by the North Vietnamese Politburo.

Resolution 9, issued in July 1969, was a frank appraisal of shortcomings and mistakes made during the Tet offensive and included a call for more economical means of continuing the fight. The new tactical emphasis was discussed in detail in Resolution 14, entitled "On Guerrilla Warfare." This resolution called for the cadres to break up main- and local-force units into companies and to transform the companies into sapper units where possible.

The term sapper originally referred to combat engineers. Within the NVA and VC, however, the name, while retaining the idea of technological expertise, became associated more with commando-raider units. By October 1969, the enemy had made rapid strides in the changeover. One sapper regiment, forty-seven sapper battalions, and thirty-one sapper companies had been accepted into MACV's enemy order of battle. This total did not include the many smaller sapper units organic to local-force battalions. MACV also estimated that one regiment, ten battalions, and two companies were in the process of being converted from infantry to sapper units. Many of them were manned entirely by NVA soldiers.

An enemy document captured in June 1969 had already made clear the reasons behind the changeover:

We have created a method of conducting our attacks, successfully using small forces against larger ones. We always develop the traditions of such particularly Vietnamese [fighting outfits] such as the special action units, the commandos and direct fire artillery units.

The document concluded, "We secure victory not through a one-blow offensive, not through a phase of attack, not even through a series of attacks culminating in a final kill. . . . Victory will come to us, not suddenly, but in a complicated and tortuous way."

The new enemy tactics were immediately reflected in MACV's statistical compilations. During the second half of 1969 the level of guerrilla activities—harassment, terrorism, and sabotage—remained at the same level as in the previous six months. However, conventional actions dropped significantly. Battalion-size attacks dropped from 29 to 5 and smaller conventional attacks from 2,185 to 1,602. In the years 1970 and 1971 combined, only 15 battalion-size attacks by VC or NVA forces were recorded. As one South Vietnamese general put it, "From this time on, sapper actions were to become the mainstay of enemy activities."

As if to punctuate the change in tactics, the Communists staged a daring sapper attack on the huge U.S. base at Cam Ranh Bay on August 7, 1969. Just after midnight a squad of sappers, obviously aided by a thorough knowledge of the base, slipped through the northern perimeter and made their way through the R & R area to the army hospital. Hurling satchel charges through the open doors and windows, they followed with several bursts from their automatic rifles. The sappers quickly quit the area, blowing up several buildings as they left the base along a pre-

Overhead grenade. *A grenade, with its pin pulled, attached to a trip wire, is placed inside a can hanging from a tree. When a soldier passes underneath, he trips the wire, causing the grenade to fall and explode on or near him.*

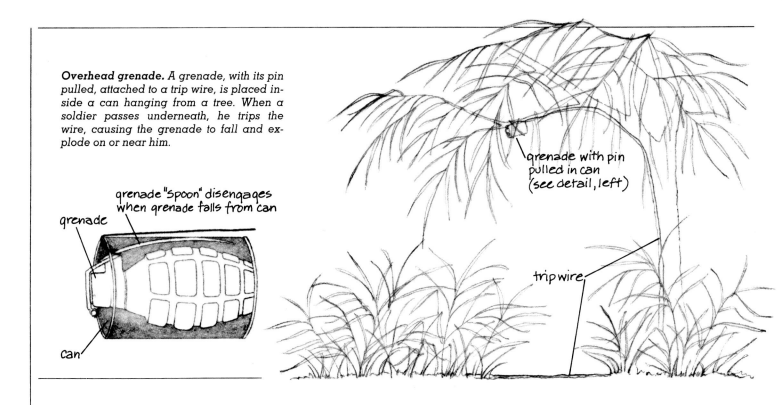

grenade with pin pulled in can (see detail, left)

trip wire

grenade "spoon" disengages when grenade falls from can

grenade

can

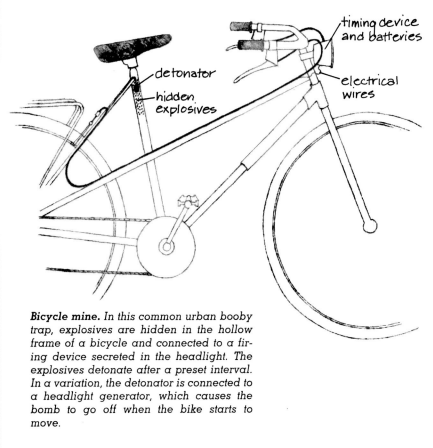

timing device and batteries

detonator

hidden explosives

electrical wires

Bicycle mine. *In this common urban booby trap, explosives are hidden in the hollow frame of a bicycle and connected to a firing device secreted in the headlight. The explosives detonate after a preset interval. In a variation, the detonator is connected to a headlight generator, which causes the bomb to go off when the bike starts to move.*

Coconut mine. *A hollowed-out coconut shell filled with black powder and buried beneath the ground, this mine is detonated when a passer-by snags the trip wire, which triggers the explosive.*

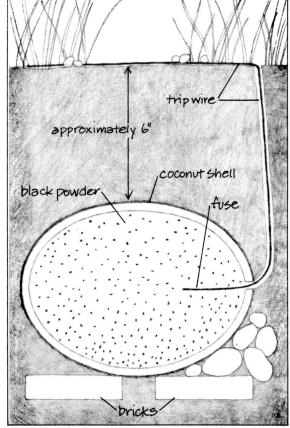

trip wire

approximately 6"

coconut shell

black powder

fuse

bricks

Booby Traps

Vietcong booby traps were rudimentary in their make-up but often brilliant in their design and lethal in their effects. Most were commonly constructed by old men, women, and children, often from American dud rounds. Thousands of American casualties were caused by these unseen weapons. U.S. Marine officers in 1967 estimated that booby traps caused about 16 percent of their casualties; the men in the field estimated that figure at closer to 50 percent. Even if the traps didn't wound or kill a soldier, they made him hesitate over every step he took. Men on patrol took care to follow precisely in the footsteps of their predecessor, carefully watching the point man whose value often lay in his "sixth sense" in discovering trip wires. Said one booby trap victim from his Saigon hospital bed in 1967, "I'd rather be over on the Cambodian border fighting North Vietnamese regulars than taking my chances with VC booby traps." The traps depicted here were among those most commonly encountered by Americans in Vietnam.

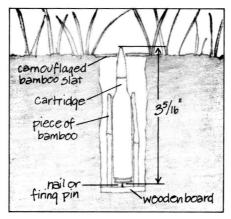

Cartridge trap. One of the most widely encountered booby traps in Vietnam, the trap is activated by a soldier stepping on the bamboo slat. This causes the cartridge to press down on the firing pin, setting off the bullet into the soldier's foot. The bullet shown is an AK47 round, but other bullets were also used.

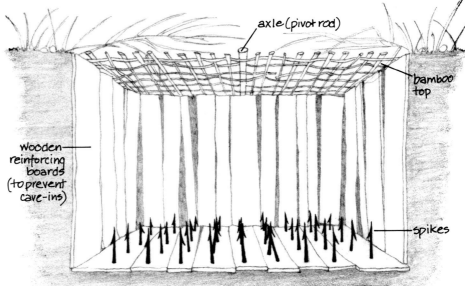

Spike pits. Two larger versions of the punji trap. The above trap is activated by stepping onto the bamboo top, causing the lid to turn on the axle, dropping the man onto the spikes, and close again. Below, a wooden bridge is first weakened by the partial sawing of the boards at the middle of the span. Anyone crossing would cause the bridge to give way and drop him onto the spikes below.

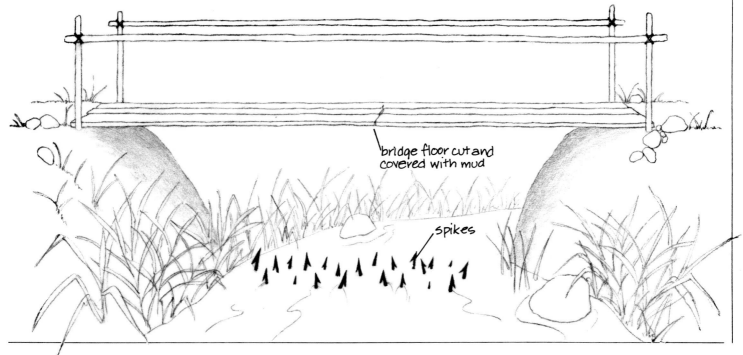

Boonierat Song

I landed in this country,
One year of life to give,
My only friend a weapon,
My only prayer, to live.

I walked away from freedom
And the life that I had known,
I passed the weary faces
Of the others going home.

Boonie Rats, Boonie Rats,
Scared but not alone,
300 days more or less
Then I'm going home.

The first few days were hectic
As they psyched my mind for war,
I often got the feeling
They're trying to tie the score.

The first day with my unit
We climbed a two klick hill,
To find an enemy soldier,
To capture, wound, or kill.

Boonie Rats, Boonie Rats,
Scared but not alone,
200 days more or less
Then I'm going home.

The air was hot and humid,
The ground was hard and dry.
Ten times I cursed my rucksack
And wished that I could die.

I learned to look for danger
In the trees and on the ground,
I learned to shake with terror
When I hear an A-K round.

Boonie Rats, Boonie Rats,
Scared but not alone,
100 days more or less
Then I'm going home.

'SKYHAWKS' is our motto,
'AIRBORNE' is our cry,
Freedom is our mission,
For this we do or die.

Boonie Rats a legend
For now and times to come,
Wherever there are soldiers
They'll talk of what we've done.

Boonie Rats, Boonie Rats,
Scared but not alone,
50 days more or less
Then I'm going home.

They say there'll always be a war,
I hope they're very wrong,
To the Boonie Rats of Vietnam
I dedicate this song.

Boonie Rats, Boonie Rats,
Scared but not alone,
Today I see my Freedom Bird,
Today, I'm going home.

arranged escape route. The results of the attack: two U.S. dead and ninety-eight wounded, nineteen buildings damaged—and no Communist casualties.

Despite such apparent successes, Resolution 14 was, according to interrogation reports, not popular among the rank-and-file of the Vietcong. The massing of main-force units in 1964 had seemed to be an indication to the enemy "grunt" that victory was near. Now the return to more pure guerrilla tactics and the breakdown of large units seemed to put their ultimate triumph beyond the horizon. Many wondered whether a deal with the United States was in the offing and whether the North Vietnamese would sacrifice their southern counterparts as part of such a deal. The Communist leadership went to great lengths to offer reassurance to the fighters but with only limited success. In 1969, over 28,000 enemy soldiers rallied to the South Vietnamese government side, more than double the number of 1968.

Although the new Communist strategy was not a response to the unveiling of Abrams's new tactics—the two appeared simultaneously—it did at least partially neutralize much of the new American approach, especially in III and IV Corps where NVA troops were unable to operate in the quasiconventional manner they used in I Corps. First, the scattering of combat forces into smaller sapper units made them much less vulnerable to American firepower, especially B-52 bombings. In addition, the breakdown of main-force units was preceded by a dispersion of supplies as well. Large caches of weapons and food were no longer necessary for the support of regiment-size units. Rather, more numerous and smaller stockpiles were used. This put greater stress on the complicated enemy logistics system, since planning had to be extended from the regiment all the way down to the company level. Still, such stockpiles were much less vulnerable to discovery and individual destruction of caches would be much less harmful. In a pinch, sapper units could even live off the land. Finally, the conversion to sapper units permitted the enemy, after suffering such large personnel losses during 1968, to concentrate its best and most experienced troops into elite smaller units.

That the new enemy tactics served so well to counter the Abrams strategy was not altogether a coincidence. While Abrams's approach was designed to buy as much time for the American effort as possible, the new enemy tactics were designed to stretch out their most valuable resource: time. Sapper tactics permitted the enemy to continue to fight on his own terms, at the time and place of his own choosing. They could regain control of the level of their own casualties while the high drama of sapper attacks was sure to grab headlines and remind the American public that American soldiers were still dying. In the final analysis, the enemy merely wanted to survive until the day the Americans went home.

"The dollars and blood sharing plan"

By early 1969 American political and military leaders

were well aware of what the enemy was up to. If the Communists were simply waiting for U.S. troops to withdraw, then the Americans would leave behind a surprise for the enemy: an improved and modernized South Vietnamese armed forces (RVNAF) capable of outlasting the Vietcong and NVA. The question would no longer be whether the Americans could remain in Vietnam longer than the Vietnamese but whether the South Vietnamese could outlast the Communists.

The origins of the Vietnamization program—a term coined by Secretary of Defense Laird—stretched back into the final months of the Johnson administration. Under Secretary of Defense Clark Clifford's direction, Johnson approved a plan that called for large-scale expansion and equipment modernization of the RVNAF and improvement in command and control, administration, and logistical support operations. The plan established two phases, with Phase I based on the assumption that "for the indefinite future, the U.S. would continue to participate in the war at then approved levels." Phase II, on the other hand, envisioned a mutual withdrawal of U.S. and NVA troops and was designed to prepare the RVNAF to fight the remaining "VC units receiving external support in the form of replacements and supplies." Neither phase was designed to prepare the RVNAF to face both the VC and NVA.

Following Laird's lead, the new Nixon administration expanded upon Clifford's plan to enable the RVNAF to handle the threat of continued insurgency within South Vietnam as well as that posed by NVA regulars. When Nixon and Thieu met on Midway Island on June 8, 1969, to announce the withdrawal of the first 25,000 American troops, the two presidents also agreed upon an acceleration of Clifford's Phase II plan. Called the "Midway package," the new plan was designed to raise the total strength of the RVNAF to nearly 1 million men by 1971.

Nixon's Vietnamization program was to be implemented in three stages: 1) ground combat responsibility was to be turned over to the RVNAF, with the U.S. continuing to provide air, naval, and logistical support; 2) the RVNAF would develop its own combat support capabilities in order to achieve self-reliance with the help of U.S. military aid and training; and 3) the American role would be reduced to a strictly advisory nature.

Through 1969 Vietnamization began to show some steady progress in modernizing RVNAF units. By April 1969 all ARVN units were equipped with M16 rifles, replacing the older, heavier M1s. ARVN units also received supplies of M79 grenade launchers and M60 machine guns. The Vietnamese air force grew to 400 aircraft, including one squadron of F-5s, as well as 100 helicopters, with 300 more on the way. All told, the U.S. had supplied the South Vietnamese with over 700,000 M16s, 12,000 M60s, 1,200 armored vehicles, 500,000 wheeled vehicles, and 900 artillery pieces among thousands of items rapidly filling South Vietnamese warehouses.

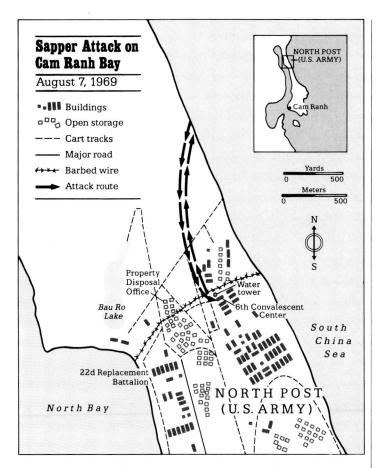

Sapper Attack on Cam Ranh Bay

August 7, 1969

In some ways these statistics represented an epitaph to the sorry neglect of the RVNAF over the previous four years. Almost all the equipment supplied to the South Vietnamese had been standard for American units since 1966. For example, the 1st Air Cavalry Division possessed more than 400 helicopters of its own in 1965. Now, in 1969, the Vietnamization program was slated to provide the entire RVNAF with fewer helicopters than this single American division. It was no wonder that the Americans had borne the brunt of the fighting.

Still, Secretary of Defense Laird was not convinced that the relative paucity of technological equipment was a total disadvantage to the South Vietnamese. Laird, like other critics of America's military policy in Vietnam, feared that the U.S. armed forces had become too dependent on weapons like the helicopter. Laird later explained, "I think it was proven that the helicopter was very, very expensive. We used helicopters effectively on many occasions, but certainly on interdiction a helicopter isn't very good. The interdiction has to be done on the ground." At least to this limited extent Laird was trying to avoid duplicating in ARVN some of the problems he perceived in the American military.

Perhaps of greater importance for the future of Vietnamization were the efforts to improve and develop RVNAF combat support capabilities. Members of their air force required specialized instruction in the United States; by August 1969, 1,700 of them were undergoing training at bases in America. For most, it was necessary to learn

English, and by January 1969 an English language center at Tan Son Nhut had 1,086 enrollees.

Outside of the classroom, MACV instituted on-the-job training programs and mobile training teams to reach more RVNAF personnel. On-the-job training was especially favored by logistics and technical personnel. Operation Buddy, initiated by the U.S. 1st Logistical Command, matched a South Vietnamese unit with a U.S. logistical unit. After a period in which the Vietnamese first watched and then performed the duties of the unit, they returned to their former outfit to perform the logistical functions. Under Operation Switchback the South Vietnamese returned to their own unit along with the American equipment with which they had been trained.

Despite the careful planning by MACV, the Vietnamization program was attacked by numerous critics and skeptics. The Vietnamese dubbed it the "U.S. dollar and Vietnamese blood sharing plan." Some Americans questioned the technical skills of the South Vietnamese in maintaining highly sophisticated equipment. "They will have to divert thousands of men from combat units to keep it in repair, which they won't be able to do in the long run anyhow," one said. Others called attention to the weaknesses of the South Vietnamese in coordinating supporting firepower with actual combat operations, a fact of concern to South Vietnamese commanders dependent upon U.S. air and artillery support. "We live with the military assistance of the U.S." said one ARVN general. "Without that aid, our army would die." Lieutenant General James Gavin, one of the developers of the airmobile concept, was particularly concerned about the fate of U.S. helicopters. "I don't see leaving sophisticated helicopters and continuing to replace them. Oh, no," he prophesized, "that would be like dropping them into the Pacific Ocean."

Many Americans were sympathetic to ARVN's handicaps. A typical South Vietnamese infantry unit could expect only one-third the number of machine guns, fewer radios, and a very small number of the sophisticated weapons employed by American units. Whereas a U.S. battalion had eighty-two starlight night observation scopes, especially effective in aiding nighttime ground reconnaissance, an ARVN battalion was slated to receive only three. And an American pilot summed up his counterparts' language difficulties: "I couldn't imagine myself going over to learn Vietnamese and fly."

MACV, itself, understood these problems and, indeed, was aware of even more severe ones than those posed by technology or language. Structural problems within the RVNAF itself were the gravest threat and were particularly immune to American solutions. ARVN soldiers were drafted at age eighteen and served until they reached forty, if they lived that long. Although entitled to fifteen days of leave per year, it was nearly impossible for a soldier to secure even one day. As a result, many soldiers simply deserted: 125,000 in 1969 and 150,000 in 1970, al-

though 25,000 of the 1970 deserters subsequently returned. Low pay was an even greater problem. An ARVN captain with three children received a salary worth $40 per month in 1970; by comparison, a civilian janitor employed at an American facility made $60.

Social problems also deeply divided the RVNAF. Most officers came from the upper and middle classes and were inclined to treat their socially inferior subordinates with contempt. Other social divisions—officers tended to be Catholic and urban, enlisted men Buddhist and rural—exacerbated the situation. Even within the officer corps social distinctions and connections severely hampered the army's efficiency. In its report to Kissinger for NSSM-1, MACV spotted a cleavage between actual "combat officers" and "political officers" who served at division headquarters and in provincial capitals. "Promotions," MACV reported, "are still made through negotiation and compromise at promotion boards between general officers." Since the "political officers" were more likely to have the "right connections," "combat officers" were often passed over in promotion. "Morale, thereby, is low among these Vietnamese field officers who had held the same rank for eight or ten years while witness[ing] his colleagues at Saigon or Corps rapid advance due to favoritism," MACV concluded. Since nearly every military expert believed that the quality of officers was the single most important determinant of ARVN's combat effectiveness, MACV pessimistically predicted "the increase in RVNAF effectiveness may well be limited."

Despite these problems, Laird remained confident that Vietnamization could succeed. Still, he admitted later that there was one variable beyond America's control: "There was one thing we could never ensure with the Vietnamization program, and that was the will and desire of the South Vietnamese." In fact, Laird's statement was an ingenous acknowledgement of the structural and social problems within the RVNAF. The "will and desire" of the Vietnamese was not something that could merely be summoned forth by an act of courage but rather required an organization that inspired such motivation. Its intractable problems prevented the RVNAF from becoming such an organization.

An early test

By mid-1969 the RVNAF modernization program was nearly one year old, facilitating Abrams's redeployment of American troops to populated areas. The slack was being taken up by ARVN in the clearing zones, as the number of battalion-size operations conducted by the South Vietnamese almost doubled between 1968 and 1969. Increasingly, ARVN units rather than American ones received the call when the enemy attacked.

Such was the situation in May 1969 when the CIDG camp at Ben Het came under siege. Ben Het was an iso-

The siege of Ben Het, June 1969. American Special Forces soldiers and South Vietnamese Rangers defend the besieged CIDG camp.

lated fortification near Cambodia similar to such strong points as Khe Sanh and Con Thien in the north. Until April 1969 it relied on a security umbrella provided by the 4th Infantry Division. But when the 4th was redeployed that task fell to the South Vietnamese 24th Special Tactical Zone commanded by marine Colonel Nguyen Ba Lien. Five hundred American artillerymen remained behind to provide fire support for the Vietnamese marines.

When the NVA attacked Ben Het in early May, Lien sent his men to the rescue. For the first month of the siege they fought well, but in a performance reminiscent of the mid–1960s, they soon wearied and retired to their secure bases, leaving the initiative to the enemy. The American artillery forces—stationed at nearby Dak To—had been counting on Lien's men to provide base security. Now they were forced to perform double duty, guarding their own perimeter as well as working overtime to support the besieged camp at Ben Het.

More serious were the conditions confronted by American engineers trying to keep the road between Ben Het and Dak To open. In early June, when the NVA opened fire the South Vietnamese guard detail simply vanished, leaving the Americans to drag their dead and wounded to shelter. In two months the engineers suffered 19 men killed and 120 wounded.

As the noose around Ben Het tightened, Lien simply made himself scarce. Attempting to direct the counterattack from his vantage point in Kontum, fifty kilometers away, he was unable to make maximum use of the available American airpower and artillery.

And then suddenly, after a two–month siege, the NVA simply disappeared. Hanoi announced that Ben Het displayed "a humiliating failure for the U.S. in its plot to de–Americanize the war and use Vietnamese to kill Vietnamese." For once, at least, the enemy's propaganda seemed not to have far surpassed its deeds.

The CIDG camp at Ben Het could be resupplied by helicopter only with the aid of a giant smoke screen to hinder the fire of the North Vietnamese.

Ben Het was hardly a conclusive test of Vietnamization. Many years would pass before the "final test." But it again displayed many of the intractable problems of building an effective South Vietnamese fighting force, particularly the devastating effect of poor command leadership.

In many ways the Vietnamization program showed the American military at its best and worst. In constructing detailed training programs down to company level, in providing massive amounts of hardware and supplies, in constructing the physical infrastructure to fight a modern war, the American military had again shown its genius for logistical management. But in confronting the endemic problems of the RVNAF the Americans were much less successful. The failure was not that the Americans were unable to solve these problems; they could hardly be expected to do so. Deeply embedded in the very social system the United States was committed to saving, these problems were simply not amenable to an American solution and perhaps could be solved by nothing short of a revolution in South Vietnam itself.

That the American military was aware of these problems cannot be disputed. General Abrams's response to Kissinger's NSSM-1 questionnaire made that clear. They chose to ignore these warnings partly out of political pressure from Washington and partly because Vietnamization simply had to work. Otherwise, the attainment of America's ultimate objective was an illusion. But somewhere in the bowels of the Pentagon, in the swarm of memoranda and progress reports, the lesson of Ben Het echoed over and over again: It won't work.

A wounded South Vietnamese soldier retreats and another is carried into the camp at Ben Het after they tried to break through the NVA siege on June 25, 1969.

Back to Basic

New recruits expand the ranks of ARVN in July 1969 as Vietnamization becomes U.S. policy.

The newest members of the 5th ARVN Division crawl through an infiltration course in 1969. The recruits are carrying older M1 rifles, since M16s were considered too valuable to be used by trainees.

Teaching the ancient art of map reading was as important to Vietnamization as courses in modern weaponry. Here new ARVN recruits learn their lessons in infantry school in Thu Duc in September 1969.

To the average American, Vietnamization seemed to mean an endless stream of equipment and supplies contributed to the South Vietnamese, courtesy of the American taxpayer. But to the South Vietnamese army and their American advisers, Vietnamization meant a lot of hard work. For the new equipment to do its job, the Vietnamese had to be trained to use it. Throughout 1969 ARVN showed undoubted improvement, but the results were nonetheless spotty.

Good performances by such units as the 51st ARVN Infantry Battalion were offset by the continued poor showing of others, such as the 22d ARVN Division. Employing what was derisively described as "search and avoid" tactics, the 22d set 1,800 ambushes during the three summer months of 1969 and netted only six enemy KIAs while suffering ten deaths themselves.

The difference between improved and lackluster units often lay in the quality of Vietnamese NCOs and commissioned officers. The American advisory effort gave a high priority to the training of these officers, but there was only so much that could be done. Much of the advanced equipment given to the South Vietnamese proved to be technologically baffling to them. Said one American pilot of his American mechanics, "My boys have been tinkering with cars since they were fourteen. They feel comfortable working with helicopters. The Vietnamese don't."

For all the imponderables in the Vietnamization program, it wasn't going to fail because of lack of effort.

At NCO combat school in Nha Trang, Vietnamese youths practice firing their M16 rifles.

UH-1C helicopters recently delivered to the ARVN line up to carry South Vietnamese soldiers into the field.

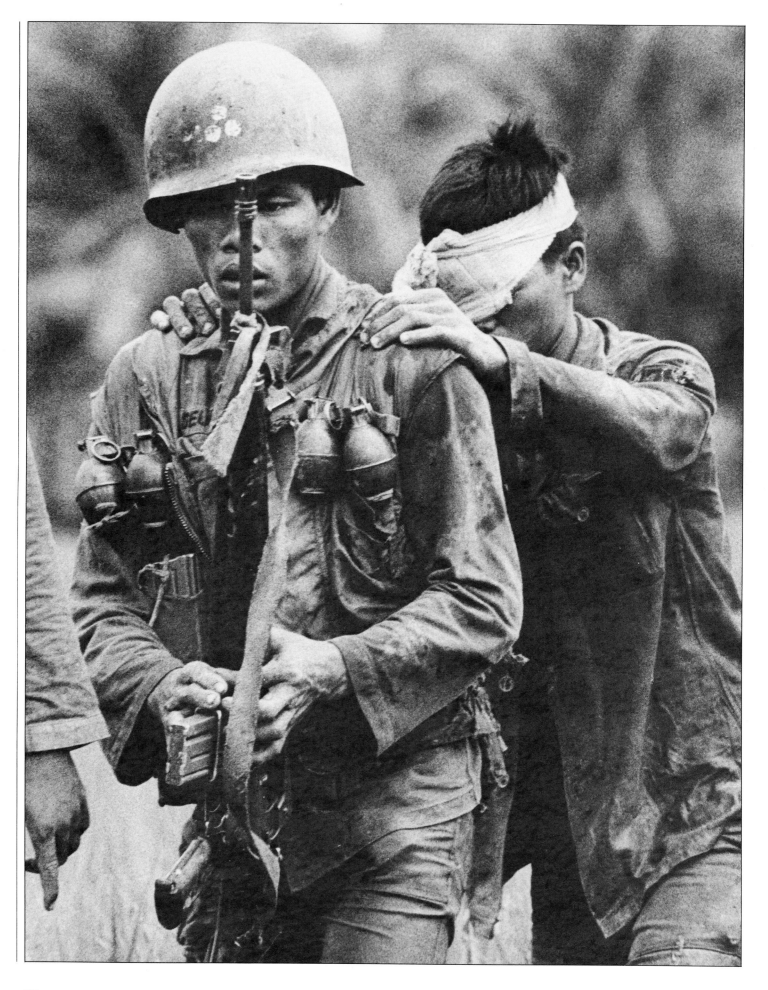

ARVN marines of the 4th Battalion, Marine Division, are transported by truck during the Parrot's Beak operation in Cambodia in May-June 1970. American advisers judged ARVN's performance during the operation, one of the first real tests of Vietnamization, as "better than expected."

Left. Vietnamization meant more South Vietnamese casualties as well. Here a soldier from the 7th ARVN Division leads a buddy back to camp after he was blinded during a firefight with the VC in the Mekong Delta, January 12, 1970.

A soldier of the 1st Battalion, 15th Regiment, 9th ARVN Division, hustles across a rice field during a sweep near Can Tho in the Mekong Delta in September 1969.

The War in the Village

It may well have been the greatest success of America's two-decade-long involvement in Vietnam, but it was a story that seldom made the front pages, or even the back pages, of American newspapers. One newsman complained, "There is nothing very dramatic going on to write about." But William Colby, director of CORDS—Civilian Operations and Rural Development Support—since late 1968, had an answer for him:

Surely he must see that the life of the Vietnamese woman in the village . . . was "dramatically" different from what it had been a year before, when she had huddled in a refugee camp, fearing that mortar attacks would drive her and her family back to her village to provide food, concealment, and recruits for the enemy. Now she had "returned to the village" under the refugee program, was protected by a Territorial Force unit with her son in a self-defense group, had voted for the village council, had participated in a village discussion that had led to the decision to spend its development funds on a bridge across the canal to give her easier access to the local market, and her husband had received title to the land they

worked and had made a start in planting the new miracle rice.

Pacification in Vietnam, long the Achilles' heel of the American effort, had finally come of age. By the end of 1970 COMUSMACV, General Creighton Abrams, had met not only his immediate goals as outlined in the MACV Objectives Plan but also the intermediate goals (all approved by President Thieu), whose target date was July 1972. Over 90 percent of the Vietnamese population lived in secure or relatively secure villages.

The groundwork for the American side in this success had been laid in 1967 with the development of CORDS by Robert Komer. Colby was free in his praise of what his predecessor had accomplished: "Komer was the man who saw the necessity of putting the military and civilians together into a common strategy and then to solve the problem of the military's concern about unity of command by putting Westmoreland in as the commander. . . . That solved all the problems of having a unified strategy under military command, but essentially a political strategy rather than a military." Abrams took the next step by making pacification "the number one strategy for the war," according to Colby.

As Abrams's deputy for CORDS, Colby developed a three-pronged program from his experiences in the early 1960s when he had worked closely with the Diem government as a CIA official: "self-defense, self-government, and self-development."

It isn't a matter of building a school for them. It's a matter of getting *them* to help build the school. It isn't a matter of defending it, it's a matter of getting *them* to help defend themselves with your support.

Pacification had never been short on pretty phrases or philosophies. The important thing was to translate the program into accomplishments, and here the American effort had always foundered where South Vietnamese responsibilities began. But not after 1968. The shock of the Tet offensive finally spurred President Thieu and his government to action. "The basic factor," according to Colby, "was that we had finally discovered that the main element of the war was the war at the village, rather than the war between battalions."

In late 1968 Thieu organized the Central Pacification and Development Council, an umbrella organization which coordinated the work of the various GVN agencies involved in pacification. He put his personal prestige behind the council by acting as its presiding officer, in fact as well as name. He established the goals and shaped the annual pacification plans. He made it a habit to visit regu-

larly the training camps organized for local officials. More than that, he fought for and secured passage of important legislation and governmental directives that revitalized the villages as no previous government had. He was rewarded for his efforts. By the early 1970s some observers believed that the local, southern-based insurgency "had been defeated." Even the more cautious agreed that it had been made "manageable."

Self-defense

The provision of constant security for villages had always been the first prerequisite of a successful pacification program. Without it, the benefits of development programs could either be shattered by enemy attack or their fruits fall into the hands of the insurgents. Recognizing this fact, one of the first steps Robert Komer took when CORDS was organized was to separate the American advisory program to the Vietnamese Territorial Forces—Regional Forces and Popular Forces (RFs and PFs)—from the American military chain-of-command and place it directly under CORDS' management. This step, coupled with the new resources provided by the Vietnamization program, began to bear fruit. By early 1970, 95 percent of all RFs and PFs were equipped with M16s, a vast improvement over their old carbines. Units also received a supply of M79 grenade launchers and M60 machine guns. In addition, RF-PF troops were given the same fourteen weeks of basic training as regular ARVN soldiers. Territorial Force strength increased sharply, climbing from 360,000 in 1968 to over 550,000 in 1971.

Beginning in 1970 RF-PF units were permitted to recruit from among the draft-age classes (ages eighteen to thirty), normally restricted to the regular armed forces. The RFs and PFs proved a popular choice among young men. Although paid as full-time soldiers, they were able to remain near their villages and families. South Vietnamese officials, while preferring that such men join ARVN, realized that they would otherwise be good candidates for desertion or for a local Vietcong unit.

In addition, the GVN established eight new training centers for territorial forces—two in each Corps zone. RF-PF units were also required to undertake periodic refresher courses. Such efforts, however, often proved ineffective, as they had since 1961, because province chiefs were reluctant to give up their troops for the training period or pay the required transportation costs.

In part to remedy this situation, the American military instead came to the Territorial Forces. The marines had initiated such a program in 1965, the Combined Action Platoons. Now these were expanded into Combined Action Groups. Where CAPs had been limited to a marine rifle squad operating with an RF company, the CAG assigned an entire marine company to an RF battalion. Company headquarters worked with battalion headquar-

Preceding page. The chief of a village near Da Nang, carrying a submachine gun, poses with his family at the time of a propaganda photo session in 1970.

76

MACV personnel attend a briefing on pacification at MACV headquarters, Tan Son Nhut air base, 1970.

ters; a marine platoon was assigned to each RF company; each squad to an RF platoon, and so on down the line. Like the CAPs, the CAGs produced mixed results, but they did make the advisory effort more comprehensive.

The army, as well, came up with an innovation—the Mobile Advisory Teams, first developed in late 1967. Operating under the supervision of the local province and district advisory teams, each MAT consisted of two U.S. Army officers, three enlisted men, and an interpreter. They offered advice on such matters as field fortifications, barrier systems, small-unit operations, and ambushes and also gave instruction in medical treatment and the care of weapons.

These different efforts greatly enhanced the effectiveness of the RFs and PFs in providing rural security. Throughout 1969 the number of small-unit and nighttime operations showed a steady increase. RF operations increased from 150,000 to over 200,000 per month during that year, while PF operations increased some 40 percent. These operations were a crucial part of providing security, since they prevented entry by the VC into a village during the night. The common experience of the years prior to 1967, when Territorial Forces retired to the safety of their

bunkers at darkness, thus giving the insurgents free access to the villagers, had become a thing of the past. By March 1970 MACV determined that nearly 90 percent of all RF–PF units possessed firepower equal or superior to that possessed by the enemy.

Of less significance militarily, but of far greater importance psychologically, was the organization of the civilian population into the People's Self-Defense Force. The idea was not new. Rather, it had been consistently rejected by South Vietnamese leaders who feared that the weapons given to villagers would either fall into VC hands, or worse, be used by the villagers themselves against the government. Colby offered persuasive counterarguments. The VC, he argued, had a sufficient supply of modern AK47s and had little use for the ancient carbines he proposed to parcel out. The second argument he turned on its head: "The concept was the political one of indicating confidence in the villager, of giving him a gun that he could use to shoot you."

With the cautious cooperation of the Saigon government, the PSDF began slowly under Komer in 1968 and grew rapidly, but not haphazardly, after Colby took over in November 1968. Using an "oil-spot concept," Colby be-

Men of the 5th Battalion, 10th Regional Forces, completing a search and clear mission in an enemy-held forest in 1970, run to a UH-1D helicopter that will carry them from the field.

gan in the most secure and trustworthy areas and gradually extended outward. PSDF members were all volunteers, worked without pay, and were required to perform a certain number of patrols per month. By the end of 1970 over 3.5 million villagers, young and old, male and female—there were no restrictions—had joined. Weapons were in short supply, so the half million RF-PF carbines replaced by M16s, were shared by the new force. At the beginning of the program Colby expected to lose up to one-quarter of the weapons, but the actual loss rate was less than 2 percent.

"They weren't fighters," Colby admitted. "They weren't good at it, but they were there. The difference is, if you live in a small isolated village and five men walk in with guns in their hands, they dominate the village. Whereas, if there are ten people there with guns in their hands, the five don't get in free. That's the whole difference."

The improvement in Territorial Forces, augmented by the PSDF, had a decisive effect on the security of Vietnamese villages. At the end of 1968, CORDS reported that 47 percent of the population was considered to live in secure areas. By the end of 1970 that figure had risen to 75 percent, with another 20 percent living in "relatively secure"

villages. While the absolute figures were subject to controversy, the overall trend was clear.

There was another winner in the bargain—the American taxpayer. A leading Pentagon systems analyst, a frequent critic of the military's conduct of the war, concluded his discussion of the Territorial Forces with uncommon words of praise:

It seems clear that the RF-PF, by their combat performance and their permanent presence in the countryside, had a profound and perhaps decisive effect on improving the security of the rural population. Yet they consumed less than 5 percent of the costs of the war. There can be little question that the Regional and Popular Forces were the most cost-effective military forces employed on the allied side. However, until the big pacification effort began in 1967-68, they were consistently neglected by both the GVN and United States.

Phoenix

The development of local defense forces was only one phase in the battle to bring security to the Vietnamese villages. To win the war in the countryside, not only would the enemy military forces have to be neutralized but its political apparatus, the Vietcong infrastructure, would also have to be destroyed. Until late 1967 no concerted or organized effort had targeted the VCI. In that year Robert Komer developed, with substantial assistance from the CIA, what was destined to become one of the most controversial programs of the war: Phoenix.

Although formally initiated by President Thieu in mid-1968, Phoenix did not really get off the ground until 1969 when the GVN finally provided an organizational basis for the program to exist. Phoenix was *not* a military program: It commanded no troops and conducted no operations of its own. It was instead an intelligence-gathering, sharing, and coordinating effort designed to identify individual members of the VCI so that armed Vietnamese forces—regular troops, RFs and PFs, National Police, and Provincial Reconnaissance Units—could take action against them. Members of the VCI could be "neutralized" through arrest, voluntary rallying to the GVN under the Chieu Hoi program, or death.

The purpose of Phoenix was to obtain the cooperation of Vietnamese jurisdictions, which had often squabbled with each other. The American advisory effort was organized

to resolve these problems and facilitate cooperation through local Intelligence Operations Coordinating Committees, which consisted of representatives of the responsible Vietnamese agencies and local village and hamlet officials.

In theory, once a VCI suspect had been identified—three independent sources were required—the Coordinating Committee would develop a plan of action to capture him or induce his surrender. This might involve the use of any available Vietnamese armed unit, depending upon the known circumstance of the targeted cadre.

The program immediately ran into serious problems. VCI quickly learned that they could enjoy a "sanctuary" along the border between any two districts. It was common practice for each district to leave a one-hundred-meter "buffer zone" along its border to prevent its forces from stumbling into the operational area of the adjacent district, resulting in accidental casualties. Only by careful joint planning—always a difficulty among the South Vietnamese—could this problem be corrected.

Perhaps a more serious problem was the system of quotas announced by Saigon in August 1969. Under this

Peoples Self-Defense Force members attend a class in hamlet defense.

plan each district was required to neutralize an assigned number of VCI cadres each month, which quickly resulted in an all too common pattern of abuses. VC guerrillas killed in combat were often arbitrarily labeled members of the infrastructure. As one adviser put it, "It would give many of our peers a chance to 'clear up' a lot of dossiers that were still active."

More troublesome was the incentive that the quotas gave to local officials to concentrate on the more easily captured VCI "small fry," at the cost of neglecting the time-consuming task of identifying the important cadres. Under the quota system both the "small fry" and the truly important members each counted as "one."

Available statistics on the program substantiate the problem. Through mid-1971 only 40 percent of the VCI captured were even members of the Communist party, and only 3 percent of all cadres neutralized were party members at the regional, provincial, or national level. (Nationally, over 50 percent of the NLF were Communist party members.) Without making inroads into this "hard core," Phoenix could not stop the VCI from regenerating.

Other statistics also suggest that the Phoenix Program was considerably less effective than desired. Over half of the VCI members reported neutralized were killed or captured by regular military forces in the course of normal operations. Another 30 percent voluntarily rallied to the GVN. Only 20 percent were neutralized as part of Phoenix operations, and of those only half had been specifically targeted by the Coordinating Committees. As a Pentagon study concluded, "Only ten percent of the job was being done in an organized way by the forces chiefly tasked to do it."

Despite its relative lack of success, the Phoenix Program was immediately confronted with a series of sensational charges. To this day it is still routinely described as a program of organized assassination. Colby vehemently denied such charges: "To call it a program of murder is nonsense. . . . They were of more value to us alive than dead, and therefore, the object was to try to get them alive." His instructions to field officers leave no doubt as to his intentions:

Our training emphasizes the desirability of obtaining these target individuals alive and of using intelligent and lawful methods of interrogation to obtain the truth of what they know about other aspects of the VCI . . . [U.S. personnel] are specifically not authorized to engage in assassinations or other violations of the rules of land warfare.

It was one thing, however, to issue such instructions and another to make sure that they were carefully carried out in the field. Lieutenant John Cook, an army adviser in Di An District, recalls that he always reminded his Vietnamese counterparts of the desirability of capturing a suspect alive. Yet he knew that many GVN troops would exert little effort to do so. Still, even the opportunities for assassi-

nation were very rare. Of those 10 percent of the VCI neutralized by actual Phoenix operations, only one-fifth were killed. Thus, of all the VC cadres captured, rallied, or killed, at most 2 percent were even potentially victims of planned assassination.

To be sure, there were some notorious incidents. When informed that a VCI suspect had been captured, one district chief arrived in his Jeep, pulled out a gun, and shot her. When the incident was reported to Colby, as he required American advisers to do, he prevailed upon the prime minister to fire the district chief. It turned out that the dead cadre had assassinated a member of the chief's family. Commented Colby, "That's the kind of hatred you get in a civil war. You see it in Lebanon, you see it everywhere."

But such events were clearly unusual. Robert Kaiser, then a respected reporter for the *Wall Street Journal*, went to Vietnam to investigate the charges against the Phoenix Program and reported to Colby that he could find no evidence to substantiate them. The more defensible charge against Phoenix was that it was inept and ineffective. Even Colby admitted that such charges "have a certain validity." And Robert Komer, the father of the program, writing in 1970, concluded, "To date Phoenix had been a small, poorly managed, and largely ineffective effort."

Though Phoenix could be credited with only a small part of it, the VCI was severely hurt during 1969 and 1970. Ongoing military operations and the general increase in rural security made their work ever more difficult and dangerous. In many cases cadres were pushed back into isolated regions of a province and in some cases provincial-level leaders were running their territory from beyond South Vietnam's borders. Where the enemy infrastructure chose to remain in a pacified area its efforts were often limited to occasional leaflet distribution. Still, the VCI proved impossible to eradicate completely. As late as December 1972, just prior to the cease-fire, over 90 percent of the villages were labeled "secure," but only 29 percent of the Vietnamese population lived in villages fully freed of all VCI influence.

The rural renaissance

As important as the new measure of security was, it remained only the first step in creating a true national community within South Vietnam. The next step was to revitalize the most important institution in Vietnamese society—the village. In this, too, President Thieu enjoyed considerable, if sometimes uneven, success.

The first order of business was to implement the promises of 1967 to permit the free election of village officials. Under the election laws, the voters directly elected the council, whose members in turn elected a village chief. A few village elections were held in 1968 and more in March, June, and September of 1969. By the end of that

Village Chief Tran Huu Quyen of Chon Than District in Binh Long Province stands in front of an RD cadre in mid-1969. Life for elected village officials remained dangerous, despite the increased security in 1969: Tran had just received a threatening letter from the VC.

year 95 percent of the villages under government control had functioning village councils.

On April 1, 1969, Thieu took another important step, placing purely local security forces under the control of the elected village governments. Included in this group were the Popular Forces, the People's Self-Defense Forces, and the National Police. A deputy village chief, also selected by the full council, managed these forces. For the first time in the history of the GVN, the village itself would become responsible for its own defense.

After sanctioning the election of village councils, the GVN also had to provide the villages with something to govern. In the past almost all decisions affecting the villagers had been made by officials representing the Saigon regime. Now, in April 1969, Thieu made available to each village, after it had elected a council and village chief, a lump sum of 1 million piasters (approximately $10,000) annually to be used at its own discretion.

The response to this decree revealed the problems Thieu faced in his decentralization program and in providing villages with real power. William Colby recalls the

reaction of village officials when informed of their new rights: "They were awed at the revolutionary idea that they would actually make decisions about anything as important as money." But he also saw the opposite side of the coin, the reaction of regional and provincial officials—mostly military personnel appointed from Saigon—who had previously controlled the village purse strings. These officials denounced the idea, arguing that the money would be misspent. But Thieu's government made its position clear: The villagers had a right to make their own mistakes; provincial officials should report any cases of outright abuse but permit the villagers to learn from their errors. Colby concluded, "Some money was certainly wasted, and some was undoubtedly stolen, but the real purpose of the program—stimulating local leadership and responsibility—was equally certainly achieved."

Thieu's efforts to revitalize the villages were creating the foundation for a possible second power base, a position which was, up to then, the exclusive preserve of ARVN. Much of Thieu's future would depend upon how he positioned himself between these two competing bases.

"Land-to-the-Tiller"

Perhaps Thieu's most impressive and important reform was the long-sought redistribution of land. President Diem had attempted a program of land reform as early as 1955, but it had ended in failure. Diem's program had required the peasants to pay for the land over a period of ten years. The Vietcong quickly pointed out to the peasants that this was a trick—requiring them to pay for land the VC had in many cases already given to them for free.

President Thieu learned from Diem's mistake. Under his "Land-to-the-Tiller" program, enacted in 1970, the peasants received their land for free. The old owners would be repaid by the Saigon government, 20 percent in cash and the remainder in government bonds redeemable over eight years. For its part, the American treasury provided 10 percent of the total funds needed by the GVN. In addition, Thieu recognized all grants of land made by the Vietcong since 1954. Many landowners were delighted, since they received compensation for land that had long since been confiscated by the enemy. Others bowed to the inevitable once President Thieu's determination became apparent, and the program passed through the National Assembly with ease.

The execution of the program equaled the quality of its conception. Relying on local officials who knew which farmers actually farmed what land to undertake the massive land survey necessary for implementation of the program, and making use of a central computer bank in Saigon, the government was able to parcel out the land with great speed. The statistics on landownership quickly reflected the success of the program. When the program began in 1970 only 40 percent of South Vietnam's farmers could claim to be landowners, but within two years that figure had almost doubled to 77 percent.

One U.S. government report concluded that the effects of the land reform program went well beyond the economic advantages for the peasant. The program, it reported, "had hurt the VC/NVA politically, reduced peasant neutrality, helped unify the village as a local government and community, created an appetite for land among the landless, and received credit for more changes than it probably should have." The *New York Times* may well have been right: It probably was "the most ambitious and progressive land reform of the Twentieth Century."

Pacification: the unsolved problem

The successes of CORDS and the GVN's Central Pacification Council in 1969 and 1970 displayed the pacification effort at its constructive best. But ever since the beginning of the insurgency, pacification had shown a destructive side as well: the generation of refugees. The refugees were a constant reminder of the delicate relationship be-

Old style pacification: In a 1967 operation, villagers are relocated by the U.S. Army Task Force Oregon, as the 4th Battalion, 31st Infantry, 196th Infantry Brigade, sweeps through and destroys their village.

By 1969, pacification planners aimed at keeping villagers in their homes: Here villagers display a South Vietnamese flag in their paddy so soldiers sweeping through their village will know whose side they are on.

tween the military and political sides of the war. If the refugee problem was largely created by the military war, it could be solved only through the various programs that made up the pacification effort.

And yet, ironically, until late 1968 increasing numbers of refugees were considered the greatest success of pacification. A State Department memorandum written in 1966 explained:

This helps deny recruits, food producers, porters, etc., to VC, and clears the battlefield of innocent civilians. Indeed in some cases we might suggest military operations specifically designed to generate refugees—very temporary or longer term depending on local weighing of our interests and capacity to handle them well. Measures to encourage refugee flow might be targeted where they will hurt the VC most and embitter people toward US/GVN forces least.

William Colby admitted as much when he described the pre-1968 pacification policy as designed to "bring the people to security." In other words, the population would be moved to secured areas, rather than bring security to the villages. In some cases, such as Ben Suc in Binh Duong Province, entire villages were evacuated in order to prevent the population from aiding the enemy. MACV estimated that in 1967 alone at least 100,000 refugees were generated in "relocation sweeps." The claim that nearly 1 million Vietnamese had been freed of VC control from 1965 to 1967 was largely the result of this process, rather

than any success in making the people's home villages more secure.

Under Abrams, this concept was reversed. The new policy, one advanced first by Komer and then by Colby, was to bring security to the population. Severe restrictions were placed on pressuring villagers to leave their villages. All relocations required advance approval from GVN authorities and warning to the population. The tactics of "cordon and search" rather than "search and destroy" further served to lessen the number of refugees generated.

Of course, this policy was possible only in the context of the rapidly improving pacification programs. The provision of village security as well as the success of the village revitalization program made it possible not only for more people to stay in their homes after military operations but also for many former refugees to return to their villages or to new ones not far away.

The available statistics on the refugees seemed to indicate a great success in the new strategy. The number of refugees generated in 1969 was slightly more than 100,000, compared to 340,000 in the previous year. Similarly the population of South Vietnam's refugee camps dropped from 735,000 to 216,000, while the number of "out-of-camp" refugees dropped from 500,000 to 50,000.

Many critics of the refugee program, however, were unimpressed with the statistical progress. A U.S. Senate

Refugees from the Mekong Delta village of Phu Huu receive their cash allowance as part of their resettlement benefits. Typically a family of four received $35 a month.

Vinh Dien, a thirty-year-old mechanic, conducts a thriving business in his motorcycle repair shop in Hue. Vinh is playing hooky: He should be carrying out his assignment as an RD cadre at provincial headquarters.

investigation of the refugee problem argued that the main achievement had been to implement a new bookkeeping system designed "to show progress, but not failure." The report concluded, that the refugee problem had been "'solved' . . . by classifying refugees out of existence."

One way this was done was to create a new category called "war victims," whose homes had not been completely destroyed. And indeed, the 1969 statistics show an additional 300,000 Vietnamese listed as "war victims." One adviser in I Corps told the *Washington Post*, "We've been instructed not to report any new refugees. Sure we're generating new ones, but they're going on the rolls as war victims, not refugees." The situation worsened in 1970 when President Thieu decreed that there be no new refugees. Now many civilians were caught in a "Catch-22" situation: After being forced from their homes by allied

military actions, they were denied refugee status by officials who cited Thieu's decree.

Finally, the GVN's accounting of "refugees resettled" was highly misleading. In reality, the figures referred to the number who received "resettlement benefits," which consisted of six months' food allowance, a small cash payment, and ten sheets of tin roofing to build a new home. Such recipients were classified as "resettled" whether or not they were actually able to leave a refugee camp and, if so, to return to their home village. In 1970 Colby ended the statistical manipulation by labeling the "refugees resettled" category more descriptively as "resettlement benefits received." Still, the category was misleading for those unfamiliar with the process.

If refugees were not returning to the land in the numbers suggested by the GVN's glowing progress reports, then where were they? Some lived unofficially and uncounted on the periphery of official refugee camps, others eked out an existence without government support in their old villages, while still others banded together in unofficial camps. But by far the most succumbed to the age-old siren of the cities.

In 1955 only 15 percent of the South Vietnamese lived in cities; by 1970, 60 percent were classified as urban dwellers. The population of Saigon swelled from 300,000 to nearly 3 million. Qui Nhon grew from about 40,000 to 140,000, while Da Nang's population rose by about 300 percent from 1967 to 1973 alone to a total of one-half million. The flight to the cities was not acknowledged as part of the refugee flow; urban migrants were never officially counted as refugees. But, *de facto*, many were pressured into the more secure urban areas by military operations.

Not all who moved to the cities were forced to do so. Some were drawn by the prospect of a booming wartime economy and the hundreds of jobs created by the American presence. By 1970 nearly one-half million Vietnamese worked for the Americans; counting their families, perhaps 2 million out of Vietnam's 17 million people were dependent upon Americans for their livelihood.

Inevitably, as security in the countryside increased, many returned to the land. But for most, urban life was addictive and few people believed that a majority of the South Vietnamese would ever again lead a rural existence. Even the most squalid Saigon slum offered comforts and conveniences that were rare in the villages: running water, electricity, and television.

Nguyen Huu Khoa had lived in Saigon for eight years, after the war forced him from his ancestral home in Long Thoi in 1962. His life was hardly luxurious. He worked in a car wash and lived with his wife and children in a tiny three-room house in one of Saigon's shantytowns. Khoa was uncertain if he or his wife would return home after the end of the war. But his daughter had already made up her mind: "I could never go back now, and neither could my brothers. We'd be lost as peasants in a village, working in the rice fields and sowing crops. We're city people now."

A decade of warfare had made Vietnamese society very different from the one that Diem had led in the 1950s. Urbanization had created the seeds of a new political force, city dwellers who, like urbanites throughout the world, depended upon the government rather than a sense of community cooperation to insure their well-being. Thieu's imaginative initiatives in the countryside had created a rural population at once both more autonomous and more deeply entwined with the fate of the central government. These developments presented Thieu with a unique opportunity to carve out a new political foundation for his country, one that might bring substance to South Vietnam's claims to democracy. But these same developments also posed a grave danger to the stability Thieu had fashioned over the four previous years and, in particular, to the armed forces upon whose strength his regime had rested and depended.

Unfinished business

Despite Thieu's undeniable success in the countryside in 1969 and 1970, there were still important gaps—perhaps intentional—in a foundation for a true national community. Of greatest importance, the trend toward grassroots democracy ended abruptly at the village gate. Almost without exception, district and province chiefs and lesser officials were chosen from the ranks of ARVN officers, appointed by Saigon, and dependent upon Thieu for their privileges. Since most of these officers came from comfortable urban backgrounds, the gap between the rural peasant and the urbanized district and provincial officials was perpetuated.

These officials naturally saw the revitalization of the villages as a potential threat to their own power and, armed with the authority to control all political movements, they prohibited any drive toward intervillage political mobilization. The dialogue between the peasants and the Saigon

Caught in the flood of migrants to the unprepared cities, several families create homes in sewer pipes near Saigon's central market in 1969.

President Thieu and Vice President Ky are joined by U.S. Ambassador Ellsworth Bunker in reviewing South Vietnamese airmen during a ceremonial transfer of American attack bombers to the Vietnamese air force in 1969.

regime remained one-sided, with Thieu parceling out reforms as he thought prudent, without permitting the rural population to use these reforms as a means of influencing the central government. As one student of Thieu's policies concluded, "In the end, the peasant was left to his own resources with no organization to speak for him above the village level."

By 1969 President Thieu found himself facing a difficult dilemma. His political power base had long been the ARVN, but to create a truly popular government he needed an alternate civilian base for his rule. To shift from one base to another would require delicate timing. Ambassador Colby, who recognized Thieu's dilemma and sincerely believed that he was trying to effect the switch, used the analogy of a "man standing on an ice floe building a wooden boat." Colby continued:

The ice floe is melting. If he builds it fast enough and steps in it, fine. If he steps in it before he's ready, he sinks. If he waits too long, the ice floe melts and he goes under.

Colby concluded, "He was not able to build the new

[power base] because he depended so much on the continued cohesion of the military."

Whether Thieu was sincere in the desire to create an active civilian power base or whether his maneuverings were designed largely to impress the American embassy is open to question. But what seems clear in retrospect is that most of these steps did more to enhance Thieu's position than to create any truly democratic movement.

Thieu had begun the consolidation of his rule by isolating Vice President Nguyen Cao Ky during the crisis provoked by the Communist Tet offensive of 1968. He continued these maneuverings in his anticorruption campaign of late 1968 and his sponsorship of the National Social-Democratic Front in the spring of 1969. The real target of Thieu's anticorruption campaign was not corruption but, once again, Vice President Ky. Half of the country's forty-four province chiefs, most of them loyal to Ky, were replaced by Thieu's men. His majors became colonels and Ky's colonels became majors. As one American observer pointed out, "Each man owed his new insignia to Thieu and could be expected to act accordingly."

Student Protest, South Vietnamese Style

Doan Van Toai

The shock of the Tet offensive intensified opposition to the war in Vietnam not only in America, but among the South Vietnamese as well. Of greatest importance, the urban population, which had not been directly affected by the war until 1968, got a bitter taste of the fighting and they were frightened by it. While President Thieu insisted on fighting to the last man, fewer and fewer people were willing to support him in his efforts.

As the opposition grew, Thieu renewed his insistence that with increased American aid he would defeat the Communists. Peace activists were a frustration to him and he fought back with repression. His police arrested people and charged them with being Communist agents.

This happened to two men with whom I worked very closely. One, Nguyen Long, was a lawyer and president of the Self-Determination Movement. I was editor of the movement's magazine Tu Quyet (Self-Determination). The other was Huynh Tam Mam, president of the Saigon Students Union. I was his vice president. Both men were arrested several times, but the government was unable to prove that they were Communists. Ultimately they were exchanged for prisoners held by the Vietcong, and the Communists used the opportunity for their own propaganda purposes by granting the men "political asylum" from the Thieu regime.

My relationship with Long was a well-kept secret, but I knew that my open association with Mam would eventually lead to my own arrest. That moment came after the Tet offensive when Thieu ordered the mobilization of the students, placing Vice President Ky in charge of the program. All students were to be trained part-time in a military school in order to protect the cities while the regular army was on the battlefield. As one of the Student Union leaders, I organized demonstrations at Saigon University. We boycotted classes, conducted hunger strikes, participated in sit-ins, and pressed our case among the people in public places, such as markets. These peaceful demonstrations soon spread to other universities. Finally the government gave in, in part because Thieu feared that Ky might turn the students into a power base for his own political struggle against the president.

As the student movement grew and joined the larger peace movement, Thieu ordered the arrest of many student leaders, including myself, and charged us with being "Communist agents" or "manipulated by the Communists." Some of us were imprisoned; others were sent into the army. The Thieu regime often considered its army a place to punish "stubborn elements."

I myself was sent to prison rather than into the army because I had the necessary papers to prove that I was exempt from the draft. But Thieu's prisons were brutal, as Amnesty International confirmed in the 1970s. When I was in jail I knew that the police forced Communist prisoners to drink soapy water and then ran 220-volt electrical shocks through their bodies. I personally witnessed the torture and death of some of my fellow prisoners but was spared this treatment, probably because I was not considered very dangerous. Other prisoners were spared torture because they were well known and the government feared adverse public reaction.

Thieu's attitude and behavior toward the people in the peace movement was a terrible, costly blunder. He believed that the Communists directly manipulated the peace movement or that, at the very least, those who called for peace were cowardly defeatists. In fact, some of the leaders did have contact with the Vietcong, and after Tet a number of prominent opposition leaders decided to join the Vietcong. Many students also joined at this time. But it was Thieu's own insensitivity to the needs of his people and the unwise manner in which he dealt with them that often turned patriotic peace activists into professional Communists.

The goals of the opposition groups were to increase democracy, improve human rights, and work out a negotiated peace with the Vietcong. Their guiding philosophy was "national concord without reprisal," which was in accordance with the platform of the NLF. I believed then, and still believe, that this was the most practical solution and the best expression of the aspirations of the Vietnamese people. The immediate aim of the group was to have better, more capable leadership with which to fight the Communists.

For the most part, the opposition groups wanted to carry on their struggle legally by becoming part of the official opposition. Their ambition was to speak with a third voice, to demonstrate to the people that they lived in the South but were neither on the side of Thieu nor on the side of the Communists. Thieu dealt with them unwisely. Being short-sighted, he refused to have any dealings with them. The Vietcong were much smarter. They accepted the presence of this third force (later recognized by the peace agreements of 1973) and encouraged its anti-Thieu activities.

In July 1971 I wrote a seven-part article entitled "Anti-American or Anti-Communist?" It was published in an opposition paper called Dien Tin (The Telegraph) on seven consecutive days, and each day the government confiscated the paper. In my article I argued that there was no place for patriotic people in South Vietnam. One had to choose between protesting what Thieu was doing to the country and risk being arrested and thrown into jail or else join the Vietcong. Many people chose the latter. The Communists were certainly skillful in the art of propaganda. But their own efforts were less effective in winning over the people to their cause than were the errors of the Thieu government.

Today in Vietnam, under the Communists, the situation is worse than it was under Thieu. But if I had to live through the 1960s again I am sure I would do the same things I did then, without regret, because I could not support a regime such as Thieu's and the stupid policy of the United States, which has a habit of relying on bad elements.

Doan Van Toai, author of The Vietnamese Gulag, was a leader of the Vietnamese student movement in the 1960s and early 1970s. He is now a senior fellow at the Institute for Southeast Asian Policy Analysis in Fresno, California.

Similarly, among the civilian bureaucrats, Thieu promoted his own men and demoted Ky's. Corruption was a perfect charge since a dossier could be compiled against virtually any official, documenting major or minor acts of misconduct. As one Vietnamese journalist wrote, "The charges can always be used and it's hard to argue against it and look good."

There was another victim of Thieu's campaign: Prime Minister Tran Van Huong. Huong made the fatal mistake of taking Thieu's anticorruption campaign seriously. In speeches he made throughout the nation, Huong voiced impatience with Thieu's policy of prosecuting small fry rather than the major sources of corruption.

Thieu, however, chose not to deal with Huong directly. He was a favorite of the American embassy. As a civilian, a native southerner, and a Buddhist, he had brought some balance to the regime. But by 1969, with Thieu's position secure, he could now afford to jettison Huong. Thieu called his leading supporters together and gave the green light for a public criticism campaign against Huong, including the submission of a petition asking for his ouster. Huong, however, refused to heed the signal and would not resign. Thieu escalated the pressure as legislators blamed Huong for everything from rising prices to, ironically, rampant corruption. Newspapers joined in the attack. Finally, in late August, Huong and Thieu reached an accommodation. Rather than resign or be fired, the premier paid the price of his independent acts by making the face-saving move of "stepping aside."

Huong's ouster capped a four-month campaign by Thieu that resulted in a reshuffling of his cabinet and in even greater control by Thieu of the governmental apparatus. The cabinet reshuffling had begun in April 1969, when Thieu invited major party leaders to the presidential palace and asked them to join his new National Social-Democratic Front. Thieu answered their skepticism by "promising a redistribution of power after the alliance is formed," according to one reporter who was present. Privately, Thieu promised a special place in his new cabinet for each leader. Whether the party leaders accepted his bait, or whether they simply feared being left on the outside, six of them—representing 48 percent of the vote for the National Assembly—joined the front. Within a year the front had been forgotten, and most of the party leaders had to settle for Thieu's offers of minor cabinet posts at best. Most rejected these offers as insulting.

This left Thieu with a free hand in reconstituting the cabinet. As prime minister he chose his old military academy classmate General Tran Thien Khiem. Khiem's new cabinet spread power more thinly than ever, with thirty-one ministers replacing Huong's twenty-one. More important, not one of them was a popular figure in his own right, one who could threaten Thieu's power. The new cabinet was also packed with military men. Contrary to the wishes of the American embassy, the key posts—the pre-miership and the ministries of interior, defense, and rural development—all went to soldiers. Thieu was not only more firmly in power than ever, but he had also more closely intertwined his fate with the ARVN. Vice President Ky was left powerless, with plenty of free time to mull over his fate at his villa in Nha Trang. Thieu had well earned his French nickname, "Le Grand Louvoyeur," which roughly translated means "the Great Tacker," one who maneuvers well when the winds blow against him. By such tactics Thieu did much to undercut his own village reform program and to deprive himself of the potential rewards of his efforts.

Ironically, the Americans who had long hoped that Thieu might develop a strong civilian constituency may have contributed to his caution. The Vietnamization policy in effect gave Thieu a mere four or five years to create the well-functioning political community Abrams and his LORAPL staff had concluded would require a generation or more to build. In addition, Vietnamization actually encouraged Thieu to solidify his support within ARVN since it was clear that the day would come when the Americans would depart and leave him to live with the policies they were trying to force upon him.

Thieu was clearly in a no-win situation. If he chose to build his civilian base, which could only be accomplished at the expense of ARVN's control of the political system, he risked a coup attempt. At the very least ARVN would wind up divided and demoralized and in no position to fight a successful war against the Communists, especially as Americans pulled out. But a failure to create this civilian constituency would deprive the nation of the cohesion and sense of mission required to carry out the long struggle.

Again it was the peasants who were the losers and the Vietcong the winners. Writing before he took office, Henry Kissinger remarked, "Our military strength has no political structure that could survive military opposition from Hanoi after we withdraw." More than a year later, after many of the gains from the invigorated pacification program had already become apparent, Kissinger was unable to conclude differently in a secret memorandum to President Nixon: "Most reports of progress have concerned security gains by U.S. forces—not a lasting erosion of enemy political strength."

In the critical year of 1969, President Thieu succeeded in squandering the fruits of the greatest allied success of the war. By failing to take advantage of the opportunity to mobilize civilian opinion in support of his government, he insured that his future would be determined by ARVN and ARVN alone. And by the early months of 1970 it was apparent to all—to Thieu, to Washington, and above all, to the American soldiers—that time was running out.

General Thieu vs. Colonel Chau

The history of General Nguyen Van Thieu's rule in Vietnam is replete with examples of the repression of patriotic, anti-Communist South Vietnamese whose only crime was to oppose the president. Of all these cases none so dramatically shows the acquiescence of the American government in that repression than that of Colonel Tran Ngoc Chau.

A former Buddhist monk and a highly decorated army colonel, Chau had earned a reputation as one of Vietnam's most creative and dedicated public servants, above all for his work as a pacification leader in the delta with the American adviser, John Paul Vann. Chau used his popularity as a springboard to election to the National Assembly. In October 1969 he circulated a document that accurately detailed the illegal activities of Nguyen Cao Thang, a close Thieu associate, known as the "King of War Profiteering." Thieu immediately branded Chau a Communist and urged the assembly to try him for treason.

The colonel had long been a thorn in Thieu's side, especially because of his advocacy of negotiations with the Communists. While rejecting a coalition government, Chau urged that the NLF be given full freedom to compete peacefully in South Vietnam's political arena. Chau's reasoning was that if the Communists became an open political party, the non-Communist parties would be forced to form an alliance to compete successfully.

Chau's goal was precisely what upset Thieu. "In the new political struggle," Chau argued, "the army will no longer play the main role, but the political parties, religions, and the people will have to directly and totally resist the Communists."

Thieu pursued him with a vengeance. Chau was protected by parliamentary immunity from prosecution, but Thieu sought to strip him of this safeguard by gaining the signatures of three-quarters of the assembly on a petition that would require Chau to stand trial. Despite the use of bribery, blackmail, and forgery, Thieu was unable to gain the required signatures.

Next, Thieu adopted a less oblique approach. He sent armed police into the legislative chamber with orders to instigate a riot. Reporters and assemblymen were beaten and pistol-whipped. The police assaulted Chau, tore his war medals from his shirt, and, according to observers, "beat him to the floor, handcuffed him, dragged him down a flight of stairs by his feet . . . and tossed him into a waiting Jeep."

Jailed in the notorious Chi Hoa prison and barred from a thirty-five minute military tribunal hearing the charges against him, Chau was sentenced to ten years' hard labor.

After the melee in the chamber, Thieu emerged with the signatures of the required three-quarters majority on the petition, although many representatives later claimed that their signatures had been forged. One last wrinkle in the case indicated the lengths to which Thieu was willing to go to lock up Chau. The Supreme Court, in an almost unprecedented display of independence from Thieu, ruled the conviction illegal and later annulled the sentence. But the military prosecutor simply placed ARVN above the law, announcing that the Supreme Court ruling "would have no bearing whatsoever on the verdict already handed down by the military court."

Chau's case would not have been unusual were it not for the fact that the charges against him of conspiring with the Communists were based on work that Chau had done for the American embassy. Chau had met several times with his Communist brother, a captain in the intelligence service of the NVA. Chau passed on information received from his brother to John Paul Vann, who reported it directly to Ambassador Lodge and later Ambassador Bunker. Some American intelligence officials believe that Chau provided the critical information on plans for the 1968 Communist Tet offensive that resulted in the reinforcement of Saigon on the eve of the attacks. Ambassador Bunker himself attended a three-hour meeting with Chau in late 1967. In addition, Chau had undertaken negotiations on behalf of the U.S. Embassy for the release of American POWs.

When the embassy realized that Thieu was launching a major campaign against Chau the American role changed. According to closed-door testimony given by Vann before a U.S. Senate committee, Bunker warned all senior American officials in Saigon not to intervene on Chau's behalf. When a group of Chau's American friends attempted to arrange for him to "visit" the U.S., Bunker ordered that he be denied a visa.

Rumors of Chau's connection to the Americans began to surface as he went to trial. Bunker suggested to Washington that the embassy deny having had any meeting with Chau, but the State Department rejected the idea since Vann's Senate testimony clearly contradicted such a statement. When questioned about Bunker's handling of the Chau affair, President Nixon's press secretary, Ronald Ziegler, commented: "There is no displeasure on the part of the president whatsoever in relation to Ambassador Bunker's handling of his post in Saigon."

According to Cao Van Tuong, liaison minister with the National Assembly, if the embassy had publicly confirmed Chau's assertion that he had worked with the CIA, the assembly "might have adjusted or taken action accordingly. But so long as we had not heard anything from the American authorities or the American embassy here, we could not start any action to go to his defense." Prosecuted by the government he had served so well, and abandoned by the government he had secretly aided, Chau met the fate of so many of Nguyen Van Thieu's opponents: he went to jail.

Colonel Chau remained in jail until 1975. In 1981 he left Vietnam by boat and eventually settled in California.

America's Disengagement Army

The ceremony bore all the trappings of a victory celebration. The 814 men of the 9th Infantry Division's 3d Battalion, 60th Infantry, were the first contingent of the 538,500 American troops in South Vietnam to withdraw. They stepped smartly to the tune of the "Colonel Bogey March." The soldiers—all spit-and-polish for the occasion with GI haircuts and neatly trimmed mustaches and sideburns—snapped to attention on the steamy tarmac at Saigon's Tan Son Nhut airport. On all sides banners and flags waved. A bevy of South Vietnamese girls held up neatly lettered signs reading "Farewell to the Old Reliables," the division's proud nickname. South Vietnamese president Nguyen Van Thieu inspected the ranks, shaking hands with the soldiers and presenting them with cigarette lighters engraved with his signature and seal of office. The highlight of the elaborate three-hour affair was a speech by General Creighton Abrams. Abrams praised his troops "who fought well un-

der some of the most arduous and unusual combat conditions ever experienced by American combat soldiers.''

Despite the military pomp, the troops were not leaving as victors. While their war was over in that July of 1969, the war they had come to South Vietnam to fight was not. If the abandonment of U.S. hopes for military victory and the somber reality of the ongoing war did not dampen the upbeat mood of Thieu, Abrams, and the other dignitaries gathered at Tan Son Nhut, it left many of the departing soldiers uneasy and frustrated. For some soldiers the ''heroes' sendoff'' was sullied by the fact that they were leaving a war unfinished. Said one GI, ''If it were the end of the war, a big reception would be natural.'' Others expressed disillusionment. Specialist 4 Gary Doss commented, ''I can truthfully say that I can't see any good reason for 36,000 Americans to have died here.''

Any sense of triumph the men felt as they boarded C–141 Starlifter transports for the flight home to McChord Air Force Base in Seattle, Washington, had to do with

their own survival. As he embarked on one of the waiting Starlifters, Staff Sergeant Cleveland Brown breathed a sigh of relief: ''I only had a month to go. But I'm glad to be getting out alive. It's been a long, hard eleven months.'' A Bravo Company platoon sergeant found his chance to go home almost too good to be true. ''I don't think anybody is going to believe it until they get back. You ain't never lucky until you leave this place,'' he said.

To the 500,000 Americans still looking forward to withdrawal from South Vietnam, the onset of disengagement signaled the winding down of America's war. All that was lacking was the termination date. That all–important date, President Nixon had stated, ''will depend upon the extent of the training of the South Vietnamese, as well as developments in Paris.'' Such uncertainty had an unsettling effect upon the morale and effectiveness of American troops in South Vietnam, and a phenomenon called short–timer's fever broke out among the ranks.

''Short–timer's fever'' was an affliction that began with the first American sent to serve in Vietnam, and almost every soldier was exposed to it under the twelve–month rotation system (thirteen months for marines), as he approached his last month or so in–country. The most virulent cases flared up among combat troops. The symptoms

Preceding page. Members of Company D, 2d Battalion, 12th Cavalry, 1st Air Cavalry Division, hang loose at the Rock Island East cache site in Cambodia during the Fishhook incursion, May 15, 1970.

His tour nearly over, Sgt. John D. Cameron of the 3d Brigade, 1st Cavalry Division, says good–bye to fellow troopers heading off on patrol from Firebase Joy on June 11, 1969. His long bout with ''short–timer's fever'' was about ended.

Tossing a smoke grenade in a familiar farewell gesture, Cameron leaves Firebase Joy on June 19 for Bien Hoa, where on June 23 he will board the "freedom bird" for home.

were easily recognizable. With only five or six weeks left of his year's tour, a soldier's efficiency in combat would begin to wane, causing reluctance to engage in combat and sullen, irritable, or even hostile behavior toward others in his unit. He was haunted by fear of being wounded or killed just before he was to be rotated home.

One veteran of short–timer's fever described himself as obsessed with seeing that final entry on what he called his "Figmo chart," standing for "Fuck it, got my orders," (to return to the U.S.). Frequently, commanders tried informally to reduce demands on short–timers. Paul Lapointe, a lieutenant in Company D, 1st Battalion, 52d Regiment, 198th Light Infantry Brigade, Americal (23d Infantry) Division, recalls, "Certainly in my company, if I had somebody who was getting down to fourteen days or a month we'd try to get him back to the rear and have him drive a truck for a month or so. At the very least, I'd try to make sure that he wasn't walking the point."

As the United States began pulling out of Vietnam in 1969, short–timer's fever became widely contagious. "If Nixon is going to withdraw," remarked one 1st Infantry Division soldier, "then let's all go home now. I don't want to get killed buying time for the gooks." This apprehension soon became ingrained in the outlook of many soldiers to-

ward the war and their role in it—whether they had eleven, five, or only one month to go in their tours.

Reinforcing this attitude were reports from home about huge peace demonstrations in Washington and other cities and the growing legion of students and other protesters opposed to the war. Antiwar protesters—especially students exempt from the draft—were not exactly popular figures to American soldiers, and in 1969, as the withdrawal began, the antiwar movement worked a particularly depressing effect upon military morale, sometimes evoking resentment and rage against those involved. As one nineteen–year–old infantryman vented his fury: "I think someone ought to kill those long–haired, queer bastards back in the world. Anyone who demonstrates against the war ought to be lined up and killed, just like any gook here."

Many soldiers interpreted antiwar talk as criticism of them personally, not of the war in general. A GI angrily asked, "Do they think I voted myself to come here? Why pick on the poor grunt? You'd think I wanted this war." Stories that made the rounds in 1969 about protesters jeering at men in uniform as "baby-killers" further infuriated the fighting men. Above all, the troops' antipathy toward the antiwar movement reflected their general perception in 1969 that America, weary of the war and wanting to forget it, was simply turning its back on its fighting men. "The feeling of the men," as an officer conveyed it, "is that if there must be a war, it should be a total war supported by everybody—or no war at all."

Ironically, as soldiers lost faith in the purpose of their being in Vietnam, some of them became as ardent about getting themselves out of the war as were the antiwar activists in their protests. There were some soldiers who also expressed contempt for prowar groups. "They ought to send over some of those people who are for the war," snarled Specialist 4 Steven Almond. "Send some of those brave politicians and hard hats and let them see if they like it so much. I'll change places with any of them." Strangely enough, as signs of their alienation from America's Vietnam policy and their yearning to end the war, more and more soldiers donned the symbols of the hated antiwar protesters—peace symbols worn on their helmets and peace medallions and love beads hanging from their necks. The two-finger peace sign became a widespread enlisted man's salute. Short-timer's fever was rapidly eroding the men's commitment.

Crisis in command

Neither MACV nor Washington could ignore the sagging troop morale of 1969. The morale "emergency" and its prompt treatment were uppermost in the minds of officials at the Defense Department. "The spirit of our military men is beginning to be tested and strained," said Assistant Secretary of Defense for Manpower and Reserve Affairs Roger Kelley. "We darn well better do something about it," he warned, "if we want him [sic] to stand up to the difficult job we are asking him to do." The job of maintaining morale, imparting a sense of purpose and mission to the soldiers, and preserving unit cohesion fell to the officer corps in South Vietnam—in particular to junior officers, captains, and lieutenants—and to the noncommissioned officers. In the troubled days of 1969 and 1970, it turned out to be an exasperating mission. For one thing, many members of the officer corps were experiencing their own crises of confidence. America's disengagement policy and the associated taint of retreat disgusted these officers, causing them to feel betrayed. "We won the war," complained a major, "that's what kills us. We fought the North Vietnamese to a standstill and bolstered the South Vietnamese Army and Government. But we can't persuade anybody of that."

The general decline of morale among American troops during the withdrawal also disheartened officers. In the spring of 1970, for example, forty combat officers sent President Nixon a letter expressing their serious concern about "the extent of disaffection among the American troops."

A number of such discouraged officers went so far as to

Sgt. Willum T. McCoy of the Reconnaissance Intelligence Technical Squadron at Tan Son Nhut air base sports a pair of heart-shaped sunglasses.

resign. Pentagon statistics on West Point graduates reveal that the class of 1965 had entered almost as many resignations in five years as the class of 1961 did in nine. Many of those who did not resign adopted the attitude, as one officer put it, "if that's the way they want to play then all I'm going to do is to come over here [to Vietnam], enhance my career, and get the hell out." According to a Defense Department study, a disturbing number of officers in Vietnam shared this negative outlook: "the confusion of political, social, and military goals and requirements which dominated U.S. involvement in Vietnam created an extremely frustrating environment for many senior officers, some of whom might therefore respond with suspicion [and] distrust."

While resignations depleted the number of officers available for command slots in South Vietnam, the pool of men from which junior officers were drawn was also shrinking. Enrollment in Reserve Officers' Training Corps (ROTC), a traditionally valuable source of college-educated officers, dropped from a total for all services in 1960 of 230,000 to 123,000 by 1969. This marked fall-off in ROTC enrollment was caused primarily by a general antimilitary climate on college campuses. Dwindling ROTC enrollment forced the Pentagon to meet the spiraling demand for junior officers by relying more heavily on Officers' Candidate Schools (OCS), which sought would-be officers from the enlisted ranks.

By 1967 half of the newly commissioned officers were soldiers who went through OCS. Even there the unpopularity of the war was taking its toll. Because of draft deferments for college students and a drop off in enlistments, the overall caliber of junior officers in Vietnam declined. Even the quality of noncoms suffered as a result of the pressing need for junior officers. By granting temporary company-grade commissions to thousands of its experienced noncoms, the military had to fill the gap by promoting generally younger and inexperienced enlisted men to the noncommissioned ranks. Soldiers sarcastically referred to them as "instant NCOs" or "shake-n-bake sergeants."

An army in search of a mission

The toughest challenge for officers in South Vietnam was to remotivate combat troops beset by short-timer's fever. Motivation had not been a great problem in the days of fighting before the Tet offensive. Then the troops' confidence that their actions made a difference, that they were winning the war, was all the incentive they required. But the beginning of withdrawal changed that. The soldiers heard no more talk of victory, of big, coordinated search and destroy offensives, of aggressive tactics of attrition. The army's mission had become mainly defensive, or as a senior U.S. officer summed it up, "to hold the fort until the Indians make peace."

Tactics were revised accordingly, as small American patrols fanned out across the countryside to seek out enemy bases and caches. One American general described them as "windshield wiper tactics." "We just kept going, going," he said, "going back and forth to keep the countryside clear."

American commanders considered the shift to defensively oriented "windshield wiper tactics" essential to the U.S. withdrawal strategy that emphasized pacification and security in the villages. Although these tactics were enthusiastically implemented by MACV, they tended to exacerbate discontent among combat troops. Risking their lives for victory was one thing. But exposing themselves to danger for other than that seemed pointless. Specialist 5 Charles Thornton, a medic with the 1st Air Cavalry Division, articulated the distinction: "The first time I was here, in 1968, we were more aggressive. Then people felt that if we really went at it, we could finish the war. Now we know that it will go on after we leave, so why get killed?" Captain Richard Gayle, a battalion surgeon, attributed the troops' flagging motivation to their lack of understanding of the purpose and value of their efforts. "To the enlisted ranks," he said, "the men don't always understand why the war is being fought. They would like to know why they have to risk their lives in a particular mis-

sion. To them," Gayle continued, "it looks like an endless war."

The prevalent "search and clear" tactics, forcing the troops day in and day out to hump the same hills or wade the same rice fields, strengthened the men's impression that their mission mattered little to the war's outcome. "The men see very small returns for their accomplishments," remarked Lieutenant Sonny Tuel. "The very nature of the war makes them patrol the same patch of ground over and over again. They kill a few Vietcong, but more will be there next time. They know the army will be leaving and that the job is not going to be finished. Six months or a year from now Vietnam won't be much different from today. That's how they see the war."

The slackening enemy activity through much of South Vietnam in 1969 and 1970 should have offered some relief to grunts stricken with short-timer's fever. It did not. If anything, scant contact with the enemy tended to confirm their cynicism about the usefulness of their patrolling. Furthermore, the enemy could still wreak casualties on Americans with mines and booby traps, two of the big, if not the biggest, sources of U.S. casualties. They could disable anyone or anything moving anywhere on the ground. In August 1970, Specialist 4 Charles Staples of Chicago, helping load his wounded buddies aboard a helicopter, set off a booby trap. He was lucky enough to survive his second booby trap wound in ten months. "It blew shell fragments into my calves and knees," he recalled. "I guess I triggered it just as I was passing the men in." That same day, on a routine visit to Firebase Bronco, south of Chu Lai, First Lieutenant Franklin Nelson, a company commander in the 11th Infantry Brigade, and eighteen of his men joined the list of mine victims. As they drove along a supposedly secure road, a powerful explosion, detonated by a mine alongside the road, killed Franklin and wounded everyone else.

This daily round of random death and incapacitation from mines and booby traps, combined with short-timer's fever and skepticism about the worth of "search and clear," steadily lowered American morale. One GI muttered, "A lot of our buddies got killed here but they died for nothing. Our morale, man, it's so low you can't see it." An American officer rendered this diagnosis: "A man cannot release any adrenalin against a mine or booby trap. We train him to be a skilled, aggressive infantryman, and then his skills never get to be used. But he still bears the fears and stresses of combat. It can be very debilitating."

Search and evade

American officers soon discovered how debilitating the combat environment could be to unit effectiveness and discipline. Trying to bolster combat unit morale, officers encountered conditions they were not prepared to deal with. "Back in 1967," said Colonel Joseph Ulatowski, "officers gave orders and didn't have to worry about the sensitivities of the men and find new ways of doing the job. Otherwise you can send the men on a search mission, but they won't search." "Not searching" was what American officers had been chastising South Vietnamese units about for years. But in 1969 it was becoming part of the tactical repertoire of some American combat units, particularly at the squad and platoon level. The procedure was simple. Instead of searching areas possibly "hot" with enemy activity, American patrols searched somewhere else.

There were other evasion techniques. When ordered out on patrol some soldiers just halted a few yards outside their base perimeter, stalled as long as their patrol might be expected to take, and then returned to base with a bogus report. Sometimes troops on "evasion maneuvers" had to concoct a complicated charade to cover themselves. Marine lieutenant William Broyles, Jr., who served in Vietnam from 1969 to 1970, recalls a situation when his infantry unit deliberately "faked" a patrol. His unit, whose patrol sector included an area thought to be infested with NVA regulars, was told by the commander to "go get some." Concluding that "it would have been suicide," as Broyles tells it, the unit "faked the patrol on our radios, talking to each other from a few feet away as if we were crossing rivers, climbing hills, taking up new positions. We weren't about to risk our lives."

Pressure from their troops to "search and evade" put some junior officers and noncoms, who led small patrols, in an untenable ethical position. On the one hand, their sworn duty as officers bound them to obey their superiors' orders and to accomplish their missions to the best of their ability. On the other hand, their responsibility for the welfare of their troops, enhanced by close contact at the small unit level, made them feel their first priority during the withdrawal was to avoid unnecessary dangers and, above all, to keep their men alive until redeployment. Despite the motivational problems they encountered, the majority of officers tried to accomplish their missions to the best of their ability. Some adopted a look-the-other-way policy. Rather than risking a confrontation with their men that might cast a blemish on their command record, these officers and noncoms simply let things slide.

A small but growing number of officers, however, chose concern for their men as their chief priority and deliberately cooperated with "evasive measures" to hold combat risk to a minimum. "The most important part of my job now," one army lieutenant colonel felt, "is to get as many men as possible back to the U.S. alive." For these officers, leading their men through the motions of searching for the enemy was a conscious command decision. "Whenever we can get away with it," one young lieutenant admitted, "we radio the old man [the commander] that we are moving our platoon forward . . . to search for the enemy. But if there is any risk of getting shot at, we stay where we are until the choppers come to pick us up."

Not all occasions for contact with the enemy were avoided by such officers and noncoms. But they usually would not lead their men into combat without first evaluating the pros and cons of their mission. "If I think a mission will be too costly," declared Sergeant Ralph Mitchell, "I weigh the value of it, and my men come first." Specialist 4 Douglas H. Michels, leading his squad on patrol near Camp Eagle just southeast of Hue, headquarters of the U.S. Army 101st Airborne Division, opted first for the safety of his men and it cost him his rank. Ordered to ascend a hill he knew to be recently mined and booby trapped by the Communists, Michels decided otherwise: "It just wasn't necessary. Some of my men might have been killed." After scaling another hill, Specialist 4 Michels and his squad returned to base. There Michels's superior busted him to private. Michels still has no regrets: "You know, one general told me that it was a disgrace for me to refuse an order in combat. And another told me that I did the right thing."

For most officers, however, duty did not mean yielding to their troops' short-timer's fever or to "democracy in the foxholes," or to the disobeying of orders. Because of their insistence on following orders such soldiers, many of them career officers and noncoms, were characterized by enlisted men as "Regular Army" or by the more disparaging term, "lifer."

The fact that combat units consisted largely of draftees, who often openly denigrated the military establishment, or the "Green Machine" as they scornfully called it, aggravated relations between officers and their men. Some soldiers defiantly printed "Fuck the Green Machine" on their jackets and helmets. Others wore peace medallions and other antiwar symbols to irritate their "lifer" officers.

Troops in combat units especially resented the fact that army and marine officers served only six months of their one-year tour in combat while enlisted men served a full year. MACV had instituted the six-month limit for officers in combat units in 1965 to "blood" as many officers as possible and to build a large reserve of experienced combat leaders. Enlisted men in combat units sometimes referred to their rotating officers as "ticket punchers" whose only interest lay in acquiring a reputation for aggressiveness and combat results—measured in statistics such as the body count—to earn a promotion and a step up the career ladder. A Defense Department study found that "rather than feeling that they were led by an officer corps which was worthy of respect and which was sharing the burden of sacrifice, the feeling became widespread [among the soldiers] that they were expendable pawns being used to further the development of an experienced corps of officers. Soldiers frequently had more combat exposure than their officers." The soldiers often called their officers "REMFs" (standing for "Rear Echelon Mother Fuckers"), a derogatory term for men who spent half or all their tours in the rear.

The officer rotation system had been a source of antagonism between officers and enlisted men in combat units from 1965 onward. But, during the withdrawal, when the aggressiveness and combat results demanded of career-minded officers became anathema to many troops, that antagonism, at its most extreme degree, could turn to outright hatred. *Newsweek* reported a bizarre incident in late 1970 in which an American entertainer heard "grunts cheer enthusiastically when they learned that two of their own officers had just been killed by a Vietcong ambush." Such hatred severed the bond of trust between officers and men, pitting one side against the other. In a small but still alarming number of cases the result was willful insubordination.

"Sir, my men refuse to fight"

August 1969, Song Chang Valley, I Corps. For five days, Alpha Company, 3d Battalion, 196th Light Infantry Brigade, Americal Division, had been assaulting the labyrinth of NVA bunkers on the rocky, jungle slope of Nui Lon Mountain. Each time Alpha Company had been re-pulsed by a concealed enemy who let the men come close and then cut them down with deadly crossfire. American casualties ran high. Only forty-nine men of Alpha Company were left. Then, on August 24, Lieutenant Colonel Robert Bacon, commander of the 3d Battalion, ordered Alpha Company to attack the bunkers a sixth time. Alpha Company did not move.

Bacon, impatient at the delay, repeated his order. Still nothing. Finally, the nervous voice of Lieutenant Eugene Schurtz, Alpha Company's commander, crackled over the radio at Bacon's headquarters. Two newsmen, Peter Arnett and Horst Faas, were with Bacon when the call came in. "I am sorry, sir," Schurtz informed Bacon, "but my men have refused to go. . . . We cannot move out." Bacon shot back, "Repeat that please. Have you told them what it means to disobey orders under fire?"

"I think they understand," Schurtz replied, "but some of them simply had enough. They are broken. There are boys here who have only ninety days left in Vietnam. They want to go home in one piece." Bacon sent Major Richard Waite, his executive officer, and Sergeant Okey Blanken-

At Fire Support Base Betty near the Cambodian border, Capt. Brian Utermahlen (second from left) of Company A, 1st Battalion, 8th Cavalry, 1st Air Cavalry Division, has a beer with his men. "I can put myself in the PFC's shoes without any bother," Uter-mahlen said. "I went to school with guys like these. I know them."

ship to give the insubordinate troops a "pep talk and a kick in the butt."

Waite and Blankenship found the men exhausted. Schurtz was sobbing. After talking with the men, Blankenship realized a pep talk was fruitless. So he "lied," telling the men that "another company was down to fifteen men and still on the move." An Alpha soldier asked why, and Blankenship replied, "Maybe they got something more than you've got." The soldier, with clenched fists, charged Blankenship, shouting, "Don't call us cowards, we are not cowards." Blankenship's ploy roused the men a little. But they would not budge until assured the NVA had already abandoned the bunkers. The NVA had, and Alpha Company moved out.

The Alpha Company incident—the bureaucratic term for an incident of this sort is "combat refusal"—was headlined in newspapers across America. Despite the attention it attracted, the army downplayed the incident. Major General Lloyd Ramsey, commander of the Americal Division, called it "a slight ripple on the water. It was settled in a few moments. The whole thing was blown out of proportion." Ramsey even pronounced the morale of his men "great, amazing." An Alpha Company soldier contradicted him, snapping, "Those patriots [the officers] are trying to get us all killed."

The glossing over of Alpha Company's combat refusal was shortsighted. Although the number of soldiers of the 100,000 American combat troops involved in combat refusals was few, the increasing frequency of such incidents reflected the severely deteriorating morale of U.S. forces. According to a report issued by the Senate Armed Services Committee in 1971, there were at least thirty-five individual combat refusals during 1970 in the 1st Air Cavalry Division alone. That same year the Department of the Army released documents showing a steady increase in court-martial cases involving "acts of insubordination, mutiny, and willful disobedience" to a total of almost 382 in 1970. Unit-sized refusals were also on the rise. In November 1969, at Cu Chi near the Cambodian border, twenty-one men of the 1st Platoon, Company B, 2d Battalion, 27th Infantry, 25th Infantry Division, refused to advance into combat. Most of them were combat veterans and short-timers. When Captain Frank Smith ordered them directly to move, the soldiers defied his command.

If Americans held any doubts about the authenticity of combat refusal reports, they got the chance in April 1970 to see one live on television, courtesy of CBS News. The scene was a dirt road in War Zone C. The cast consisted of Captain Al Rice and the men of Charlie Company, 2d Battalion, 7th Cavalry, 1st Air Cavalry Division, as well as CBS newsman John Laurence and his cameraman. The drama began when Captain Rice ordered his unit down a jungle path presumably surrounded by the enemy, toward a landing zone. The men balked. Before the sound cameras, Rice told Laurence, "We're going to move on the

road, period." Charlie Company remained obdurate. One soldier spoke up: "I'm not going to walk there. Nothing doing. My whole squad ain't walking down that trail . . . [it's] a suicide walk. . . . We've had too many companies, too many battalions want to walk the road. They get blown away." While the camera filmed the incident, Charlie Company took an alternative path to its landing zone.

Military authorities had difficulty coping with the unprecedented rise of combat refusals. The traditional method for dealing with such an act of insubordination was the general court-martial. But the military justice system in Vietnam proved an inadequate means of bringing offenders to trial, prosecuting, and sentencing them in a way that deterred others from risking similar punishment. Military courts and legal staffs were already overburdened with cases involving corruption in the ranks, AWOL offenders, and deserters. With the rotation policy, the rapid turnover of personnel affected the legal staff, the potential defendants, and witnesses. Furthermore, since the cumbersome court-martial procedure was impractical in the field, senior commanders frequently imposed lesser administrative penalties at their discretion, such as loss of pay, demotion, or punishment duty. Combat officers sometimes felt that sending a man to the rear to stand trial constituted a "reward" because it freed him from combat duty. So military justice for combat refusals was often inconsistent, leaving punishment to be set according to the individual standards followed by the field commanders. The men of Alpha Company, for example, did not even receive a reprimand for their insubordination. Nor did the troops of Charlie Company for their combat refusal, which one of the unit's senior commanders, a colonel, said was not "even a near rebellion." A member of Company C, 2d Battalion, 501st Infantry, who refused to move with his combat unit to another position, was removed from his unit, prosecuted, and found guilty of disobeying a direct order. He received a suspended sentence.

An army at war with itself

For junior officers and noncoms combat refusals were unnerving, disorienting traumas. When word got around that a television audience of millions of Americans saw and heard Captain Rice "bargaining" with his company, the effect was depressing to many officers. One platoon leader confessed, "I've got to run a sort of carrot-and-stick operation. The idea I got in training was that I give an order and everyone would obey. But when I got out here, I realized things weren't that simple." To their dismay, officers of many units discerned among their troops the "us against them" mentality. The volatile division in the ranks almost inevitably ignited violence.

Those officers who spurned the carrot-and-stick for a hard-line, traditional approach to command and discipline exposed themselves to danger. The cost to aggressive leaders could be severe. "Fragging" is a seemingly innocuous word with a dark meaning. It derives from the fragmentation grenade, which leaves no fingerprints, and came to be the term for soldiers' efforts to murder their officers without leaving incriminating evidence. Fragging also became a general term for all attacks on fellow servicemen with grenades, rifles, or knives. The killing of officers and noncoms by U.S. troops was not unknown during earlier wars. In World War I, involving over 4.7 million U.S. personnel, fewer than 370 of what are now called fragging incidents came to court-martial. The ratio of fraggings to personnel was about the same during World War II and the Korean War. In Vietnam fraggings increased conspicuously. After a young West Pointer from Senator Mike Mansfield's Montana was fragged and killed in his sleep, Mansfield asked for an inquiry into the practice. The Pentagon reluctantly disclosed that fraggings in Vietnam during 1970 totaled 209, more than double those of 1969. Forty-five Americans, mostly officers and noncoms, lost their lives. A Defense Department study concluded that in 1969 and 1970 fraggings "reached disturbingly high" levels in South Vietnam.

In previous wars, fraggings normally took place in the field, usually in combat situations. Incompetent or overzealous officers, reckoned by the men to be "dangerous" to them, were the targets. During a battle or skirmish, one or more soldiers would shoot the intended victim, and he would be reported as killed in action. Vietnam had its share of these executions. Stories circulated of despised lieutenants or NCOs who were killed in the field by their men. There were cases when hatred for "overaggressive" officers ran so high that soldiers dared to place fragging bounties on their heads. Sometimes money for bounties of $50 to $1,000 was raised among disgruntled troops. The most notorious was a $10,000 bounty offered in the underground newspaper *GI Says* for the fragging of Lieutenant Colonel Weldon Honeycutt, who ordered and led the costly assault on Hamburger Hill in mid-1969. There were, in fact, several attempts on his life, but Honeycutt managed to survive his tour and return stateside. Other officers tagged for murder were not so fortunate.

A striking aspect of the pattern of fraggings in South Vietnam was that an inordinate number occurred in rear areas, away from the perils of combat. The likely victims in these cases would be a REMF, or a "strictly by-the-book" officer, or an NCO representing to the enlisted men the regimented values of the "Green Machine." Captain William Paris of the 11th Armored Cavalry Regiment remembers a fragging threat to one such "lifer" sergeant. "He was, you know, an old soldier. To him the army was the army and didn't have any problems . . . which was totally the wrong attitude." Captain Paris advised the sergeant not to try to enforce strict military discipline among the troops and told him "to cool it." The sergeant ignored

his warnings and continued to insist upon strict adherence to military regulations by his men. Finally, his resentful troops decided to "frighten" the sergeant. "They set up a claymore mine by the sergeant's bed," Paris recalls, "with a trip wire that wasn't set up to detonate. That scared the sergeant so we had him reassigned."

Fraggings sometimes involved a macabre ritual. A smoke grenade might be rolled into an officer's sleeping quarters as a first warning. If that failed to change the officer's behavior, a second warning, in the form of a tear gas grenade, would follow. If that failed, the fragger would employ the real thing, a fragmentation grenade. Usually the second warning was sufficient. Bill Karabaic, who served with the 101st Airborne Division, remembers a rookie lieutenant who, because of his niggling enforcement of petty regulations, ran the risk of getting the full treatment. "The first day he was smoked," said Karabaic. "The second gassed. The third day he was building a frag-proof hootch." Fortunately for that young lieutenant, his men—for reasons of their own—made no further attempts to frag him.

"You've got to stop . . ."

The military authorities acknowledged the rash of fraggings and related acts of violence in South Vietnam. In testimony before the Senate Armed Services Committee, Robert Froehlke, a nominee for secretary of the army, declared that "fraggings by any other name are murder, clear and simple murder, and we must deal with them as we deal with any other murder." To this end the marines organized Operation Freeze in mid-1970, a coordinated command and judicial program "to make escape more difficult for fraggers and conviction more certain." The operation was organized by Lieutenant General William Jones. "I went out there," he recalls, "and had a big session with all the division commanders [and] said 'you've got to stop this!' " The army undertook similar programs to identify and prosecute fraggers.

But the perpetrators could not be so easily singled out and prosecuted. Although only one man might toss the grenade or pull the trigger, he usually acted with the tacit if not express approval of his comrades. The silent bond of "us against them" made identifying the culprit or obtaining witnesses extraordinarily difficult. In part because of this, only about 10 percent of fraggings came to trial.

If responsibility for fragging was collective, the victim was not just the individual officer injured or killed. His colleagues also suffered the intimidation and fear that the fraggings were designed to convey. Captain Barry Steinberg of the Army Judge Advocate General Corps called it "the troops' way of controlling officers," adding that it was "deadly effective." The psychological terrorism of fragging not only made officers think twice before issuing an order, it bred a debilitating paranoia among them. Said a colo-

At Camp Tien Sha in Da Nang navy lieutenant Owen Heggs teaches one of the first black history courses in Vietnam in 1969.

nel in Vietnam who received a box of cigars from his unit as a Christmas gift, "You know, my first thought was that maybe a frag was hidden inside."

Since 1948, when President Harry Truman had ordered the military to desegregate, the armed forces had made significant strides in eliminating racially discriminatory practices. But in the 1960s pockets of discrimination remained. Blacks, for instance, were more likely than whites to be assigned to low-skilled specialties, including infantry duty. By 1971, although blacks comprised less than 12 percent of the population, they made up 16.3 percent of the infantry and 19.6 percent of service and supply positions. In contrast, fewer than 4.9 percent of electronic specialists were black. Project 100,000, a manpower recruitment program instituted by the military at the prodding of President Johnson and Secretary of Defense Robert McNamara, was partly responsible. It lowered the educational standards required for acceptance into the military. Thus the military had to take men, many of whom were black, whose poor educations led to their being assigned to low-skill support and combat specialties.

The burgeoning civil rights movement of the 1960s heightened black soldiers' awareness of these disparities, and mounting resentment often found expression in violent protests and racial strife. Starting in 1968 racial violence disrupted American military bases around the world. After touring marine bases in 1969 to assess the racial climate, Lieutenant General Leonard Chapman concluded, "There is no question about it, we've got a problem."

It was not surprising that South Vietnam, especially during withdrawal, became the military's racial pressure cooker. Blacks there in 1969 and 1970 angrily denounced obvious discrimination. Although they represented only one-ninth of U.S. forces in Vietnam, blacks constituted one-fifth of combat troops. Some infantry units were nearly 50 percent black. And blacks accounted for 14 percent of all battle casualties. Racial violence, however, rarely broke out in combat units while they were in the field. "When you drink out of the same canteen and eat off the same spoon," said one black paratrooper of the 173d Airborne Brigade, "you get real tight together." Captain William Paris, a white officer, agrees: "In a tactical unit, you didn't have racism, 'cause that guy wasn't a 'nigger,' he was your best friend. And if you didn't believe it, the first time the rounds flew you found nothing but [GIs] in those foxholes that didn't have a racist bone in their body."

It was in rear areas where racial enmities that might have been suppressed in combat were likely to burst into violence. A 1972 army inspector general's report on racial incidents in Vietnam in 1969 and 1970 observed that "192 or 81 percent of the serious incident reports addressing blacks and whites are concentrated in built-up military areas." A black army lieutenant colonel commented: "What happens to us in Vietnam is no different than what happens in the United States—except for combat. The threat of death changes many things, but comradeship doesn't last long after you get to the village." At Tien Sha, near Da Nang, a civil rights protest rally ignited an all-out brawl between black and white onlookers. Ronald Washington, a twenty-year-old soldier from California, gave this account: "As our sessions ended two white guys stopped and asked what we were doing. We told them to leave but they yelled 'black mother fuckers' and threw rocks. So twelve blacks caught them and did a job." After more whites joined the fray, the base commander arrived to restore order. At first a black militant armed with a rifle threatened the commander. But Washington persuaded the soldier to surrender his weapon. In 1970, at Camp Evans near the DMZ, groups of white and black soldiers, after hurling racial epithets at each other, rushed for their weapons and faced off. A racial firefight was barely averted when the commander "cooled things down."

American officers did not possess, nor could they have been expected to possess, the training to solve long-standing racial inequities. And traditional military discipline gave them inadequate means to punish racism. In just ten months of 1969 the Marine 1st Division reported seventy-nine racial assaults and three racially motivated fraggings. One grenade attack at an enlisted men's club killed one marine and injured sixty-two others. The military did institute several measures to reduce racial friction. It eliminated restrictions against modified Afro haircuts and no longer prohibited black soldiers from performing the "dap," an elaborate handshake greeting consisting of a series of hand, wrist, and arm slappings and finger snappings. Discrimination against black soldiers practicing the Black Muslim religion was also forbidden. The most important measure required commanders to establish formal grievance sessions and integrated civil rights committees to hear and discuss racial complaints. These sessions provided the opportunity for blacks and whites to discuss openly their differences. Still, many black soldiers doubted that anything beneficial would come of them. A 1971 Defense Department study of air force units in Southeast Asia "found minority group frustration so high that [at grievance sessions] many men found it difficult to articulate their complaints." Ronald Washington, after his first such session, said: "I wish now that I had let that brother blow the base commander's head off."

Dropping out

Several thousand soldiers of America's disengagement army, instead of ticking off the days until the magic date of redeployment, chose a different course. They deserted. (Being absent without leave for more than thirty days amounts to desertion.) Soldiers rarely deserted while in combat. Out in "the boonies"—the hills, jungles, and rice fields—there was no place to go. "What are you going to do," quipped a GI, "walk through Cambodia?" As for deserting to the enemy, the few Americans who tried it discovered it was no easy matter. The Vietcong were not interested in giving sanctuary to deserters. A VC spokesman cautioned, "If GIs desert and go over and live with our forces, they will have a difficult life to lead."

Throughout the war, only 5,000 servicemen were discharged for deserting during a combat tour in South Vietnam. Tens of thousands of other soldiers seeking to escape the war opted for a different form of withdrawal, a psychological one through drugs. Marijuana was the most popular choice. A MACV survey of marijuana availability in Saigon found that it could be purchased in almost every shop in the city. Marijuana cigarettes that cost a dollar in Da Nang cost only ten cents in Saigon. Between 1965 and 1967 only a small percentage of U.S. troops were known to be indulging in marijuana. According to Defense Department studies, the percentage of troops smoking marijuana in 1968 was on the upswing, rising to about 25 percent. The following year, it skyrocketed. A Defense Department survey found that between 1969 and 1971 almost 50 percent of America's troops were using marijuana on either a regular or occasional basis. "All you have to do," said one GI, "is shuffle around until some mama-san offers it to you." A brigade officer confirmed his assessment: "When a man is in Vietnam, he can be sure that no matter where he is, who he is with, or who he is talking to, there are probably drugs within twenty-five feet of him."

MACV responded to the marijuana problem with a campaign to arrest and prosecute users. It set up a crime lab to assist in convicting servicemen suspected of drug use and requested a narcotics agent from the Justice Department. The first of a corps of dogs trained to be "marijuana sniffers" arrived in 1969 to uncover pot caches at U.S. installations. MACV even undertook a psychological operations program, distributing posters with messages like "Marijuana Means Trouble" to discourage potential offenders.

MACV's war on marijuana achieved substantial success in cutting the supply of marijuana available at American installations. But it could not control the ability of soldiers to purchase marijuana almost anywhere outside their base. In addition, military commanders made little progress in convincing the troops that smoking marijuana was harmful. The rise of a permissive attitude toward marijuana in the United States made it difficult to persuade soldiers that marijuana was "immoral" or posed any risk to their health. Moreover, many soldiers had experimented with drugs or used them regularly before entering the military.

The American drive against marijuana was well underway when heroin made its appearance in South Vietnam. The source was the mountainous region stretching across the borders of Laos, Burma, and Thailand, known as the "Golden Triangle." The CIA identified at least twenty-one opium refineries there, which produced 700 tons of opium annually or about half the world's supply. Heroin flowed into South Vietnam via several conduits: Royal Thai Air Force and army personnel, American soldiers returning from R&R in Bangkok, and corrupt South Vietnamese civilians and military officials. American pilots also participated in smuggling. The command pilot for Ambassador Ellsworth Bunker was arrested at Tan Son Nhut air base with $8 million worth of heroin in his aircraft. He was court-martialed and sentenced to Leavenworth.

Other drugs flowed through the virtually uninterrupted drug pipeline that brought American soldiers a smorgasbord of pot, heroin, opium, cocaine, and amphetamines at ridiculously low prices compared to the United States. Opium sold for one dollar per injection, morphine five dollars a vial. A heroin habit could be supported for as little as two dollars a day. An American drug expert, Alfred McCoy, noted: "Fourteen-year-old girls were selling heroin at roadside stands; Saigon street peddlers stuffed plastic vials of 95 percent pure heroin into the pockets of soldiers and marines as they strolled through downtown Saigon." By 1969 pot and heroin sales among GIs were booming. According to DOD statistics, an estimated 60 percent of U.S. soldiers in Vietnam were customers for marijuana and 25 to 30 percent for hard drugs like heroin.

Slowing time down

For many soldiers dope supplied an antidote to short-timer's fever. "Sure I used a lot more as I got shorter," said a soldier. "It turned things into a joke. You smoked dope, you avoided contact, you avoided patrol, you faked your way through. . . ." Soldiers with a bad case of short-timer's fever sometimes graduated to heroin, according to drug treatment specialist Dr. Norman Zinberg, after finding that, as a soldier told him, "marijuana slows time down" but "heroin speeds it up. The days go bip, bip, bip."

A Defense Department report cited the compulsion "to separate one's self from mental and physical pain" and the hope of "easing frustrations . . . of the military environment" as primary causes of widespread drug use. The demoralized state of the troops—evidenced by disobedience, fragging, and racial upheaval—contributed to the emotional pressures. "Vietnam is a very concentrated experience," commented one marijuana-smoking GI. "It's like a giant corporation where you can't quit and everybody

has gone crazy." Bill Karabaic, who counseled drug users in the 101st Airborne Division, described the link between the "unreal" world of the soldier where traditional values were turned topsy-turvy and the use of drugs as painkillers: "Many GIs find the war so confusing they feel they are in a dream. Life is unreal. Values are crazy [and] fragging officers is acceptable. . . . Vietnam is a bad place, and most people want to get through as . . . painlessly as possible."

Drugs were sometimes used by combat troops as well as by those in the rear. Although evidence shows that drugs in combat were the exception rather than the rule, a Congressional committee heard testimony that "American soldiers are smoking pot in combat [and] pilots smoke it before going on helicopter missions." An officer recounted how "one of the guys I worked with had been doing speed and they got into contact, and he flipped out . . . he was a basket case."

In the rear, away from many of the dangers of war, combat troops could partake of drugs freely and in large, powerful doses. A journalist saw "one young man who had just returned to base after thirteen days in the field pour a vial of heroin into a large pot of vodka and drink it." On November 10, 1970, CBS News presented a six-minute television broadcast of members of the 1st Air Cavalry Division conducting a "marijuana smoke-in" at a firebase. American viewers watched soldiers smoke pot through the barrel of a shotgun. Asked if he worried about getting high on the job, one rear area soldier from another unit replied, "As long as we do our jobs, we can get stoned from the minute we get up until the minute we hit the sack." For rear area troops, boredom, low morale, hostility toward the military, and peer pressure were the principal reasons for widespread drug use.

The use of drugs was primarily confined to enlisted ranks. A study on heroin use in Vietnam among the 1,100 enlisted men of the 23d Artillery Group at Phu Loi found that over 20 percent of them had used heroin at one time or another in Vietnam.

Many officers despaired of discipline or punishment as a solution. "If I caught a guy with marijuana and docked him half a month's pay, it wouldn't matter to him," remarked a master sergeant. "They all had money to burn. . . . If I booted them out, I wouldn't have any company left." Nevertheless, the military in South Vietnam used every weapon it could muster in a war on drugs. But despite 8,000 arrests in 1969 and 11,050 in 1970, the numbers of pot and heroin users increased. An amnesty program to rehabilitate soldiers with drug addictions provided help for some, but many refused to participate. A Defense De-

---

At a drug rehabilitation center in Can Tho in 1971, a doctor has put this GI to sleep for two or three days to ease the agony of withdrawing from heroin.

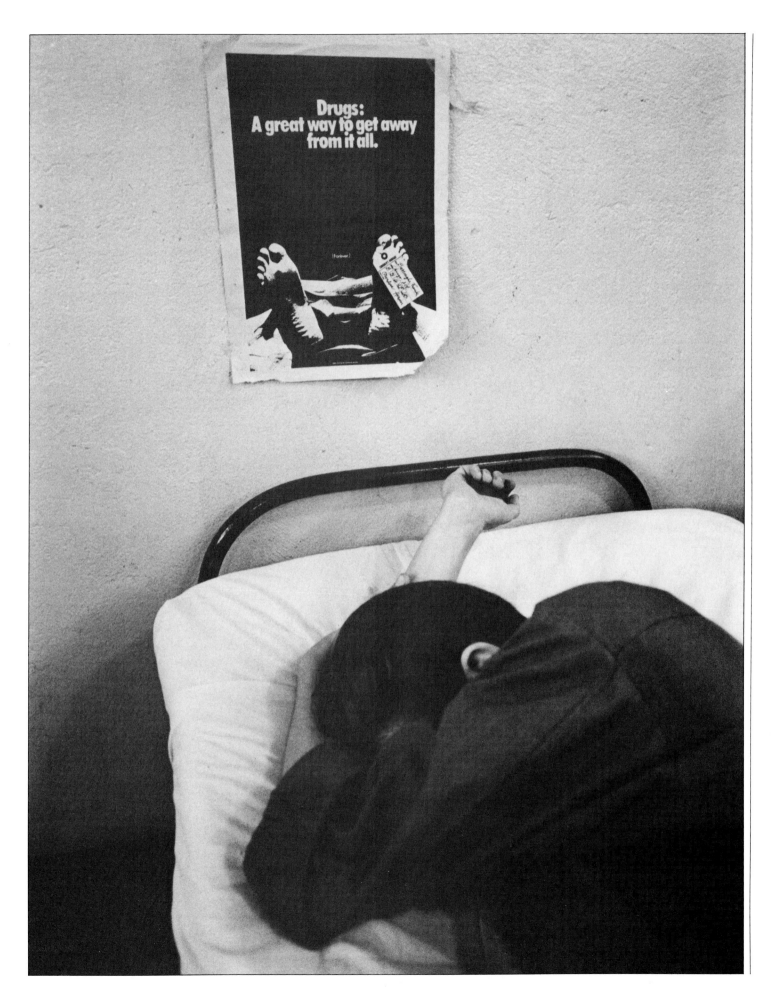

partment study evaluated the military's drug enforcement and rehabilitation programs in Vietnam as having "little effect because of failure to understand the basic causes for drug usage in Vietnam. . . . As a consequence of its failure to anticipate the drug abuse problem, the army initially had no effective activity/work programs to divert potential users from drugs, and the subsequent response to the drug epidemic in many cases was 'too little, too late.' "

Meanwhile, drug-related crimes proliferated. Drug-induced squabbles between enlisted men resulted in beatings, knifings, and fraggings. A military psychologist recalls a sentry, sky-high on drugs, "who shot his buddy at pointblank range in the belief that his buddy was Ho Chi Minh." The fragging of officers who tried to crack down on drugs was also known to occur.

The drug toll for American soldiers rose to a degree that throughout 1971, while fewer than 5,000 soldiers underwent hospital treatment for combat wounds, four times that number, 20,529, required treatment for serious drug abuse. A high-ranking military officer described Vietnam as "poison in the veins of the American military." Insofar as drugs were concerned, he was correct.

A question of honor

The declining discipline and morale affecting America's army during the withdrawal also contributed to worsening relations with the South Vietnamese. American troops were painfully aware that the timing of their redeployment depended to a considerable degree on the rate of progress achieved in Vietnamization. What Americans had observed of the performance of their ARVN allies did not inspire much respect or confidence. And in 1969 and 1970 the oft-repeated saying of soldiers became, "I don't want to die buying time for the gooks," or as an American army sergeant lamented, "ARVNs aren't worth a damn. Every time they get scared they run. . . ."

The contemptuous attitude of many American soldiers toward ARVN eventually distorted their perception of all South Vietnamese, soldiers and civilians alike. Language and cultural barriers had always obstructed communications between American soldiers and Vietnamese civilians. Soldiers, therefore, enjoyed few meaningful and regular contacts with the average Vietnamese. Unfortunately, the Vietnamese they did have regular contact with were those trying to make a profit from the American presence, a crowd of pimps, prostitutes, and drug pushers. American troops, their negative impressions daily compounded, branded all Vietnamese—VC, ARVN, or civilians—in derogatory slang as "slopes," "dinks," and "gooks." The potentially violent ramifications of such acute prejudice, tinged with more than a streak of racism, were pointed out by a U.S. official: "Psychologically and morally, it's much easier to kill a 'dink' than to shoot a Vietnamese."

It had sparked friction between Americans and South Vietnamese since 1965. But during redeployment, the so-called "dink complex," with all its antipathy and mistrust toward Vietnamese, severely altered American behavior. The U.S. military experienced a dramatic increase in the number and type of American criminal offenses against Vietnamese. The list included drunken and disorderly conduct, theft and destruction of property, like the joy-killing of water buffaloes and cattle, and running Vietnamese cyclists and pedestrians off the road or tossing rocks and cans at them.

According to MACV statistics, more violent crimes like assault, rape, and murder also multiplied. The occasions for these ranged from drug hassles to robbery to simple revenge. Sometimes there was no motive, just a mindless impulse. Soldiers fired aimlessly into villages from passing vehicles. One American soldier was arrested, court-martialed, and sentenced to five years in prison after he took a pot shot at a Vietnamese farmer's hat, missed, and blew the man's head off. The withdrawal itself worsened the situation by concentrating large numbers of American troops in densely populated rear areas.

Irate Vietnamese responded in kind to American harassment and violence. Beginning in 1969, a wave of anti-Americanism escalated into attacks on American civilians and servicemen. Vietnamese teen-agers on speeding motorcycles tried to run down American pedestrians. Outside Tan Son Nhut air base in July 1970 a gang of Vietnamese youths assaulted and attempted to castrate some Americans.

The anti-Americanism also had political overtones because the U.S. was withdrawing. If Americans were disenchanted with their allies, the South Vietnamese were growing equally so with them. A Vietnamese civilian sounded off to an American journalist, "You came in, shoved us aside and said, 'We'll win this war for you.' Well, you didn't win the war and now you're leaving and trying to put all the blame on us." American soldiers, bristling at demonstrations of South Vietnamese anti-Americanism, interpreted them as betrayal. "It makes me angry," wrote one GI, "to see my friends killed and wounded here and put my own life on the line daily when you see the Vietnamese . . . don't give a damn for your efforts and sacrifices." It was a vicious cycle.

Out in the countryside, the unbridled enmity of some Americans toward the Vietnamese was likely to have violent consequences for civilians as well as VC and NVA soldiers. Telling friend from foe in a guerrilla war fought among civilians would tax the moral and psychological resources of any army. At best, rules of engagement, no matter how strict and clear, could serve only as guidelines, not absolute instructions for every combat contingency. But the malevolence evoked by the "dink complex" led a small, unrepresentative minority of American troops to identify all Vietnamese villagers as the enemy. The

The "ugly American." A young Vietnamese picks the pocket of an unwary American soldier.

"mere gook rule" some soldiers followed eroded the restraint on shooting first and asking questions later. Reasoned one soldier, "No one has any feelings for the Vietnamese. . . . They're not people. Therefore, it doesn't matter what you do to them."

On the evening of February 19, 1970, five young marines, a roving patrol called a killer-team, from Company B, 1st Battalion, 7th Marines, went to seek out the enemy in a series of hamlets in the Queson Valley in Quang Nam Province. After enduring a month of casualties from mines and booby traps, the marines' nerves were strung tight. Company commander First Lieutenant Louis Ambort urged the patrol, led by Lance Corporal Randall Herrod, to "get some damned gooks tonight" and avenge their buddies. That night the killer-team entered Son Thang Village. The marines went to a hut and called out the occupants, all women and children. Suddenly one of the women dashed toward a nearby tree line. A marine shot her and then, at Herrod's command, killed all the others. The marines moved to two more huts, ordered the occu-

pants out and then gunned them down. Sixteen women and eleven children died that night in Son Thang. In its report, the patrol claimed an impressive tally of armed VC killed. The next morning, however, another 1st Battalion patrol, at the request of Vietnamese villagers nearby, unearthed the truth. Although Lieutenant Ambort tried to cover up the killings with a false report to his superiors about a VC firefight, all five marines were charged with premeditated murder. Two were convicted of murder. One received a life sentence, the other five years.

These crimes of violence—how many were never reported or uncovered is not known—against Vietnamese civilians in combat areas were not totally isolated. From 1965 through 1971, twenty-seven marines were convicted of various instances of murdering Vietnamese civilians and fifteen of manslaughter. Ninety-five army personnel were also convicted of murder and manslaughter; a quarter of these transpired during the course of combat but were found to be not justified by necessity. The most appalling episode of this nature happened, in fact, before the

American withdrawal policy went into effect, but the American public did not learn about it until a year and a half after it occurred.

"Tragedy of major proportions"

On the morning of March 16, Charlie Company of Task Force Barker, 11th Brigade, Americal Division, hit an LZ near My Lai and My Khe in the village of Son My in I Corps to strike a Vietcong unit reported operating in and around the hamlets. The tired men of Charlie Company had been fired up by their officers. One GI recalled being told, "This is what you've been waiting for, search and destroy, and you got it." A few VC were spotted as they fled the hamlet but they were the only enemy Charlie Company contacted. Yet there was much killing and destruction in My Lai that day. For the frustrated, agitated troops of Charlie Company, commanded by a young Lieutenant William Calley, the search and destroy mission degenerated into the massacre of Vietnamese civilians: old men, women, and children.

At nearby My Khe hamlet, where Bravo Company, Task Force Barker, was acting on similar orders, this brutal scenario was repeated. Terry Reid of Bravo Company will never forget what happened there: "As soon as they [the soldiers] started opening up, it hit me that it was insanity, I walked to the rear. Pandemonium broke loose. It sounded insane—machine guns, grenades. One of the guys walked back, and I remember him saying, 'We got 60 women, kids, and some old men.' " By day's end at My Khe the total dead would be higher. A GI who kept a count said he knew of 155 killings; others spoke of 90. Charlie and Bravo companies officially reported victory at My Lai and My Khe—178 VC killed.

Despite a minimum of supportive evidence (for example, the Americans captured an extraordinarily low number of weapons), no one at the Americal Division challenged the report. In fact, division officers suppressed and obfuscated the details of the My Lai and My Khe operations. Moreover, nearly two weeks after My Lai, Captain Ernest Medina of Charlie Company was awarded a special commendation from Colonel Oran Henderson, 11th Brigade commander, as well as congratulations from Americal Division commander Major General Samuel Koster. Henderson told Medina "to convey my sincere appreciation to those personnel responsible for a job well

Victims of the My Lai massacre, March 16, 1968.

"Guys were about to shoot these people," army photographer Ron Haeberle told Life magazine reporters. "I yelled 'hold it,' and shot my picture. As I walked away I heard M16s open up. From the corner of my eye I saw bodies falling, but I didn't turn to look. . . ."

The Shock of My Lai

by Ward Just

There had always been atrocities, a prisoner beaten and killed, a rape, a murder, a body mutilated, a village burned, the casual violence that accompanies any war. But by 1968, things had begun to fall apart. Discipline was going to pieces, partly because of the clamor at home, partly because the war was not being won and showed no signs of ending. And partly because so many of the army's most experienced professionals were either dead, wounded, missing, or rotated back to the Pentagon or to Europe. Tet had come and gone in a tide of blood and while the command insisted that a great victory had been won, others further down the ranks were not so sure; the losses, on both sides, had been terrible and the fury of the enemy's attack astonishing. The drug problem, insignificant in 1966, was by 1968 a threat to the combat effectiveness of the army. Still, more troops poured into the country in support of the strategy of attrition.

No war ever tested the professionalism of a soldier more than the war in Vietnam. It was always nasty and ambiguous, dwelling in a kind of political and moral half-light. Legally, there was some question whether it was a "war" at all since Congress had never declared one, though that made scant difference to anyone in the field. The rules of engagement were continually revised, always made looser as the light at the end of the tunnel receded; and the measurement of progress was the body count, and the body

didn't necessarily have to be in uniform, or carrying a weapon. In the beginning, the army assigned its best men to the effort—the only war there was—and all the professionals wanted to be there. Until 1965 it was an advisory effort with heavy support from Green Berets—the U.S. Special Forces—who had been exactingly trained for counterrevolutionary warfare, though it was called counterinsurgency. The Green Berets liked to think of themselves as a new breed of soldier, sophisticated, well read in the works of Giap and Guevara, as much diplomat as warrior. One of the canons of the training was "never harm the civilian population," for their support was vital to the war effort. Indeed it was what the war was all about, in the phrase that is now breathtaking in its innocence: "the hearts and the minds of the people."

But by 1968 all this was by the way. The Americans had taken over and the Vietnamese were spectators at their own war. The methods of the Green Berets had been overtaken by events, as the war of attrition had replaced counterinsurgency. And draftees had replaced professionals at the head of platoons and companies. The war zone itself had become a kind of never-never land, teeming with fantastic stories, some of them true. Every GI knew the story of the teen-age Vietnamese girl who lobbed a hand grenade into the mess hall, of ground glass found in a bottle of Coke, mama-sans with Kalashnikovs in their laundry bags, booby traps everywhere. No Vietnamese could be trusted. As it was indisputably true that all Communists in Vietnam were Vietnamese, so it seemed to Americans in their fear, frustration, and ignorance that all Vietnamese were Communists. And by 1968 there was no restraint. The war, though geographically restricted, was otherwise total: strategic bombing, naval gunfire, division-sized sweeps, the indiscriminate destruction of villages, the Phoenix Program, the defoliation of forests—whatever was required to do the job. So much seemed at stake.

When reports of a massacre at a village called My Lai began to circulate in 1969, most professional soldiers discounted it as the fantasy of a journalist. There were mistakes, everyone knew that; but not a massacre. And it was true that the Americal Division was not the army's best, but not a *massacre;* not Americans, and not a unit of the American army. A subcommittee of the Congress, so chaste and remote from the craziness of the zone, reported after it had sifted the facts, indisputably true now: ". . . it was so wrong and so foreign to the normal character and actions of our military forces as to immediately raise a question as to the legal sanity at the time of those men involved." Alas, as testimony was later to show, there was no question at all. In Lieutenant Calley's words, the operation at My Lai was "no big deal." Yet the pictures were there, more than a hundred dead. Exactly how many was never determined. They were old men, women, children, babies. Civilians, noncombatants, massacred in a ditch. This, in the name of security.

The professional army, appalled and defensive, moved in its ponderous way to name a commission to investigate and clean house. That the commission, and its report, would be taken seriously seemed to be guaranteed by the identity of its chairman, Lieutenant General William R. Peers, himself a former division commander in Vietnam and a well-respected soldier of the old school. Significantly, he was not a graduate of West Point. The army knew that the report would be bad news; the question was how bad. In the end, the Peers Commission recommended that two generals and twelve lesser officers be charged in connection with the incident at My Lai. But neither the commission nor the courts was able definitively to assign responsibility. It was the dilemma of the overcrowded boat and who to throw over the side. Lieutenant Calley was such a limited man, limited intelligence, weak character, an amateur, he could never bear the real weight of the

My Lai disgrace. Calley-as-scapegoat might appeal to a civilian, never to a serious professional soldier. Almost to a man, the professionals maintained that if the educated middle class ("the Harvards") had fought instead of run, a flake like Calley never would have become an officer in the U.S. Army.

The charges against the two generals were harder to blink away. One of them, Major General Samuel Koster, commanded the Americal Division at the time of the massacre. In 1970, when the Peers Commission issued its report, Koster held the most esteemed two-star billet in the army: superintendent of the military academy at West Point. And he was there in the superintendent's office when charged with violations of Article 92, Uniform Code of Military Justice, failure to obey lawful regulations and dereliction in the performance of duty. Sam Koster had been one of the army's comers, and now the cadets had to watch as the superintendent left the academy for trial at Fort Meade. I visited West Point at the time, expecting to find outrage, one way or another. Instead, there was only a kind of embarrassed silence. What was there to say? *The superintendent had been charged with dereliction in the performance of duty.* Later, I remembered talking with officers at West Point and elsewhere and it seemed to me that My Lai marked a kind of turning point for the army. It was when the army itself began to lose faith in the war, seeing Vietnam at last as a terrible corruption. A senior general bitterly justified his own swing from hawk to dove: "I will be damned if I will permit the U.S. Army, its institutions, its doctrines, and its traditions, to be destroyed just to win this lousy war."

Ward Just is a novelist and short story writer. As a reporter, he wrote about the war in Vietnam for Newsweek *and The Washington Post.*

The revelation in 1969 that a unit of American soldiers had massacred several hundred Vietnamese civilians at the hamlet of My Lai aroused heated controversy throughout the United States. Some Americans expressed outrage, others disbelief, and still others the grim conviction that what had occurred at My Lai was inevitable given the kind of guerrilla war being waged in South Vietnam. The My Lai incident evoked a similar range of responses within the American military establishment, particularly among the corps of officers—from the Pentagon down to platoon leaders responsible for conducting the fighting by U.S. troops. The following are the reactions to My Lai of four American officers:

Captain James Cain, *U.S. Army 525th Military Intelligence Group, three tours in South Vietnam, 1968-69, 1972-73, and 1973-74*
We didn't teach anybody about the Vietnamese; we didn't teach them history; we didn't explain. In turn, we developed a general attitude where all the South Vietnamese were bad, all Vietnamese were bad, and it didn't matter if you shot men, women, or children. If they were dead, they must be VC, you know, and it just kind of deteriorated from there. You'd go out to a village and knew that the villagers were feeding the VC but you couldn't prove it. You know, frustration and rage would just reach the point where you had to do something and from that point of view I can see it. And, even to me, it was sometimes hard, you wanted to get even, you wanted to get even with somebody for blowing your best friends away. I think you can get a general consensus from the ones that were out there—they know. They know how it could have happened.

Lieutenant Colonel Edward King, *U.S. Joint Chiefs of Staff, 1966-69*
What happened at My Lai did not con-

stitute for the "professional" officer or noncommissioned officer the same sort of tragedy that it represented to the American public. My Lai represented to the average professional soldier nothing more than being caught in a cover-up of something which he knew had been going on for a long time on a smaller scale.

Colonel Zane Finkelstein, *Judge Advocate General's Office, South Vietnam, 1970*
As an American soldier I didn't want to believe it. I had all kinds of built-in biases that would lead me away from believing. My training, my education, my own ethical background, my belief in the genuine professionalism of the United States Army, all those things led me away from beginning to even accept this until the evidence began to be marshaled. I was appalled at the lack of professionalism, but when you look at the way we fought Vietnam kind of on the cheap, it didn't surprise me that people like Calley might get a commission. Yeah, I was shocked, I was appalled. And it did—it shook my faith.

Lieutenant Paul Lapointe, *Company D, 198th Infantry Brigade (Light), Chu Lai, 1969-70*
I don't remember any conversations about it. I do recall myself thinking about the My Lai situation one day when we had three casualties in my platoon from booby traps. I remember that day very well and I think I could envision a situation where if a platoon had been through a succession of those kinds of days where people were getting limbs blown off, and were tired and fatigued, you could have reached a point where you could have been involved in something like that yourself. I think I felt a little bit differently about it after I'd been over there for awhile than I did when I had heard about it stateside before I wound up in Vietnam.

111

done." A subcommittee of the House Armed Services Committee would later characterize My Lai and My Khe as "a tragedy of major proportions." That "tragedy" remained buried for many months beneath a "blanket of silence."

What really took place at My Lai and My Khe surfaced on November 13, 1969, when about thirty newspapers published a story written by journalist Seymour Hersh. Hersh had compiled his information from an ex-GI and Vietnam veteran, Ron Ridenhour. Eight months earlier, Ridenhour, who had learned about the My Lai massacre from conversations with members of Charlie Company, had written a letter to officials in the Pentagon, the White House, and Congress about what he had heard. His letter focused on the role at My Lai of Lieutenant Calley. "Exactly what did, in fact, occur in the village of Son My in March 1968," he wrote, "I do not know for certain, but I am convinced that it was something very black indeed." An initial army inquiry into My Lai during the spring and summer turned up enough evidence to charge Calley with murder in September 1969. But it was not until November that the Hersh story made public the full account of the killings at My Lai.

Although My Lai occurred in 1968, before the start of redeployment, the factors that caused the massacre had particular relevance to the ills of America's disengaging forces. The official military inquiry set up in November 1969 to investigate My Lai, headed by Lieutenant General William Peers, disclosed during its sixteen months of research and hearings that the responsibility for My Lai extended beyond the wanton acts of violence committed by the individual members of Charlie and Bravo companies. Delving into the causes of the massacre, the Peers inquiry and the press detected critical failures of leadership, discipline, and morale, some attributable solely to the American Division and some to the institution of the army itself.

Peers's inquiry concluded that the most glaring absence of leadership was at the junior officer level. Both Lieutenant Calley and Captain Medina failed to control their men in a combat situation and to keep their actions within the bounds of the rules of engagement. Lieutenant Calley was a striking example of how the six-month tour and the deficiency of qualified officer candidates was already impairing the officer corps in South Vietnam as early as 1968. Calley, a chronically unemployed college dropout, graduated from Officers' Candidate School at Fort Benning, Georgia, in 1967 even though he "had never learned to read a map." He was not unique among OCS candidates for his ineptness. A colonel at Fort Benning made the disturbing prognosis that "we have at least two or three thousand Calleys in the army just waiting for the next calamity."

The American Division cover-up itself bared another institutional weak link in the military: the "ticket-punching," career-minded officer whose primary goal when commanding a combat unit is to "earn good marks." The officers' emphasis on body count and their continual exhortations to "get some gooks" inflamed their troops' already violent mood. At the time of My Lai the men of Charlie and Bravo companies suffered from depressed morale, but their malice toward the Vietnamese was intensified by recent casualties they had suffered from mines and booby traps in the Son My area. They were poorly disciplined and trained, the products of the military's manpower pinch. Yet from Lieutenant Calley up through Captain Medina and his superiors in the American Division— Lieutenant Colonel Frank Barker, Colonel Oran Henderson, and division commander Major General Samuel Koster himself—the truth about the atrocities at My Lai and My Khe was suppressed to protect both the officers and their careers. The Peers inquiry ascertained that "some [officers] actively suppressed information, others withheld it, and still others were responsible by not wanting to get involved."

In these and other ways the elements that led to the My Lai and My Khe massacres foreshadowed those that crippled leadership, discipline, and morale during the American withdrawal. Had there been no cover-up, America might have had some forewarning that its military forces in South Vietnam were becoming increasingly vulnerable to such a breakdown. Instead the revelation of later atrocities in 1969 and 1970 and the furor it incited dealt a hard blow to an army already in the throes of a crisis. The maladies of U.S. troops in South Vietnam in those years, combined with the jolt of the My Lai disclosures, finally prompted Americans to question the health and effectiveness of their fighting men. Colonel Robert D. Heinl, a marine combat veteran and specialist on military strategy and organization, wrote that by "every conceivable indicator, our army that now remains in Vietnam is in a state approaching collapse, with individual units avoiding or having refused combat, murdering their officers and noncommissioned officers, drug-ridden, and dispirited where not near-mutinous."

General William Westmoreland, by then serving as the army's chief of staff, felt that, if such a collapse were not prevented, the results could be calamitous for the nation: "An army without discipline, morale, and pride is a menace to the country that it is sworn to defend." Former national security adviser to President Johnson, McGeorge Bundy, declared that only a swift and total withdrawal could forestall that calamity: "Extrication from Vietnam is now the necessary precondition for the renewal of the Army as an institution." But before that withdrawal would end the ordeal of U.S. armed forces, the battlefield would widen and bring more years of fighting.

A GI reflects over a drink, Da Nang, July 21, 1970.

Saigon's Warriors

by Brian Nicol

Marijuana, long hair, love beads, the peace sign—the symbols of American youth in the 1960s—all made it to Vietnam. To the commanders, they were problems, representative of poor morale. But for the men in the ranks—and especially those in the rear areas away from combat—smoking marijuana and flashing the peace sign were ways of staying sane, of easing the tension, and of passing time. Brian Nicol spent 1970 in Saigon, where he served as a personnel specialist with the United States Army Headquarters Area Command. Here he tells of how he and his friends passed the time that year in Saigon.

It was my first trip to Mom's. Three of us walked slowly down the alley—a twisting, narrow path that wound between and among the tin houses, shacks, and shanties. The traffic sounds of Le Loi Boulevard faded away behind us and the alley sounds took over: mama-sans arguing, dogs barking, children yelling, radios playing. The awful aroma of *nuoc mam* shot down my nostrils and nearly turned my stomach inside out. As we passed open doorways, papa-sans and mama-sans stopped and stared, then went about their business. We were intruding, but they had gotten used to it. I tried to memorize each twist and turn in our route. Even though it was afternoon, the confining alley was nearly dark, with the only light coming from the gray sky above. I followed the guy in front of me

and wished I were back at the compound.

"Hey BudDAH! Hey BudDAH!" A small but loud voice down at my right was shouting up at me. A tiny hand grabbed mine and the voice laughed. The baby-san pointed at my bald head and said "BudDAH, same-same BudDAH." My two companions, ever eager to kid me about my premature hair loss, also laughed. I smiled a bit nervously. The baby-san, dressed only in a dirty green T-shirt, held onto my hand and escorted us the rest of the way.

My friends introduced me to Mom and some of the regulars at her "magic shop." Mom—a middle-aged woman with a tired face and teeth stained by betel nut juice—forced a smile and nodded. We bought a bag of her special grass—pre-rolled *canh sa*—and sat down on the stone wall outside. We smoked, talked, and sipped warm Schlitz, which Mom also sold. I started to relax. Other GIs came along and made purchases and then went on their way. Neighborhood mama-sans bustled in and out and sometimes stopped to flirt with us visitors. A teen-age girl played "Let It Bleed," a song by the Rolling Stones, on her cassette tape recorder. We sang along.

Finally, after about an hour, it was time to leave. The baby-san in the T-shirt appeared again and climbed up on my shoulders for the walk out to the street. He slapped my stoned head like it was a conga drum. Soon we were back on Le Loi, then riding in a cyclo to our compound, and, finally, safe within its walls. My first trip to an alley had been uneventful, yet somehow exciting. I had been in-country, in Saigon, about four weeks. Up until this visit to Mom's, I had played it safe. But no more.

We could always play it safe. After all, the United States Army takes care of its own. Our small compound, at 27A Vo Tanh Street, a few blocks from the Tan Son Nhut main gate, was surrounded by a high wall topped with concertina wire

and watched over from a guard tower in a back corner. An MP manned the front gate twenty-four hours a day.

We clerks pounded ancient Underwoods for ten hours a day. Officially, we concerned ourselves with all kinds of forms—MACV forms, USARV forms, USAHAC forms—and other military minutiae. Realistically, we finished our daily chores in about an hour and then spent the rest of the time drinking coffee, listening to the radio, reading magazines, and writing letters.

At about 5:30 P.M. we'd amble over to the mess hall for chow, then watch a movie in the Quonset hut theater, or suck up ten-cent beers (only five cents during happy hour) in the enlisted men's club. A couple of nights a week the club featured live entertainment—Filipino bands banging out their own renditions of our favorite rock hits ("Don't Let Me Down," "Rolling on the River," and so on). If we wanted a little less noise, we crowded into the TV room to watch two-week-old baseball games and ten-year-old sitcoms. In many ways army life inside our compound wasn't much different from army life inside Leonard Wood, Dix, or Campbell.

In Vietnam, of course, there was no true sanctuary. We were constantly reminded that "any gook might be VC": the maid who starched (and stole) our underwear, the club waitress who served us warm beer and cold steaks, the KPs who clattered pots and pans at the crack of dawn, the honeywagon drivers who drained the cesspool twice a week, even the papa-san at the front gate who smoked opium all day. If we were reasonably careful, however, and avoided the streets and stayed inside the walls, we could watch our year slip comfortably by. Or we could approach it a little differently: As long as we were here, as long as this was the only war we had, why not get out and enjoy it?

Our apartment had that basic quality

114

of any good piece of real estate: location. It was on a quiet side street off Tru Minh Ky, a short cyclo ride—or long walk—from our compound. There was a sauna/massage parlor ("steam and cream") on the corner and two reasonably priced hookers next door. A small refreshment stand out front sold beer, soda, French bread, and cigarettes. Our building's roof top was a perfect open-air veranda. Four of us shared the rent and spent many of our evenings and a few of our days there, far away from the army.

We weren't supposed to have an apartment, of course, but then, we weren't supposed to wear beads instead of dog tags, or let our sideburns and mustaches get long and shaggy. We considered ourselves revolutionaries in the ranks. We flashed the peace sign and shook hands in the now-familiar thumb grasp. We faithfully listened to a late night hour of acid rock music on AFVN called "Love Radio." We cheered virtually every line in the movie *M.A.S.H.*, especially since the brass had tried unsuccessfully to ban it from the military movie circuit. The lifers called us "heads"; we called them "juicers." When the Kent State students were gunned down that May, we thought the real revolution had come and we wondered which side we were on.

From our convenient apartment or our secure compound we ventured forth on "search and delight" missions. We'd stroll along the downtown waterfront or wend our way through the central marketplace. We'd fight off the beggars and money-changers, watch for those camera-snatching cowboys (Vietnamese teenagers on Hondas), and haggle with the black marketeers for PX Salems and watered-down booze. Then we'd join the civilian Graham Greenes and Ernest Hemingways on the terrace of the Continental Palace Hotel and watch the Orient unfold before us. Waiters brought us Pernod ("tastes like licorice") and "33" beer ("tastes like formaldehyde") and chased away the smiling old men who brought us

"dirty picture." After a drink or two we'd visit the Tu Do Street bars and fondle the bar girls while they repeated over and over, "You buy me tea?"

A couple of evenings a week, five or six of us would pile into an army pickup and drive past MACV headquarters ("Fat City") out to the Tan Son Nhut airfield's perimeter road. The Rolling Stones, the Beatles, or Crosby, Stills, Nash, and Young provided the music, via cassette tapes, and Mom provided the mood, via a bag of her *canh sa.* We called these excursions "perimeter runs." We'd stop at a spot alongside the main runway where other vehicles—army or air force and filled with other perimeter runners—were parked in a row. We smoked, talked, and drank until the first Phantom F-4 eased out of the hangar far across the field. We silently watched as, one at a time, each sleek death bird positioned itself at the end of the runway, revved its engines to a sustained, high-pitched roar, then suddenly, at a signal from somewhere, shot off down the tarmac and disappeared into the black sky. The heat wave from the jet blast blew across us like a desert wind. Invariably, someone muttered, "Wow."

After the Phantoms, usually at about eight, the daily Pan Am freedom bird came creeping over from the main terminal. The 707 was filled with the shortest of short-timers, those who had put in their 365 days and were on their way back to the world. When it finally lumbered on down the runway, we perimeter runners raised both arms high and flashed peace signs at the faces behind the tiny fuselage windows. Someday it would be our turn.

Our days may have been routine and our nights playful, but occasionally we earned our combat pay. One typical party evening in November was interrupted by an explosion that shook the apartment's walls and knocked the beer cans off the table. We froze for a second. "Rocket," somebody whispered. We scrambled down the stairs and out into

the street. The yellow, dust-filled air was still shimmering from the concussion. The refreshment stand a few yards away was on its side; a nearby car's windows were blown out, its tires flattened. Bodies were everywhere. Instinctively, but numbly, we moved in to help. We tried to clamp spurting arteries with our hands. We scraped smashed faces off the pavement. We pushed protruding intestines back into torn stomachs. We smelled the aroma of warm blood. Most of the wounded moaned and twitched; some lay still and staring. We yelled for help, but the crowd stood far back, watching our frantic efforts and waiting for the next explosion. Finally, with the aid of some American MPs and Vietnamese police, the carnage was cleared. The next day we learned that the rocket had been merely a grenade tossed from a speeding Honda—typical Saigon insanity. The official score: three dead and twenty-one wounded. We had gotten a taste of it.

That grenade robbed our quiet side street of its charm. As our days in-country became fewer, so did our trips to the apartment, to Mom's, to the perimeter, to the whorehouses and strip joints, to the Tu Do Street bars. We ended as we had begun: concerned about safety.

Soon I had colored in all the spaces on my short-timer's calendar. It was time to go. I packed most of my gear, gave some of it away, paid off my mama-san maid, said farewell to friends, and made my final trip to Tan Son Nhut. When the 707's wheels left the ground, the others in the plane cheered, but I stared out the window at four GIs sitting on the cab of a truck, waving me home with a peace sign.

Brian Nicol was drafted in June 1969 and spent the year 1970 in Saigon, where he served as a personnel specialist (clerk) with the United States Army Headquarters Area Command (USAHAC). Today he is editor of Hono-lulu magazine.

Cambodia: The Politics of Survival

It is a small country, not much larger than the state of Missouri. When Cambodia's full independence after seventy-five years of French colonial rule was recognized at the Geneva Conference in 1954, the world took little notice. International attention during the Indochina War had been centered on the fighting in Vietnam between the French and Vietminh. To Americans at that time, Vietnam—its people and culture—was still a remote, unfamiliar country. While they knew little about Vietnam, Americans knew even less about Cambodia. Yet Cambodia, like Vietnam, was destined to play a significant role in the American-led struggle to halt the advance of communism in Southeast Asia. During the cold war years of the 1950s and early 1960s the United States poured hundreds of millions of dollars into Cambodia to build up its economy and strengthen its armed forces. And U.S. agencies like the CIA, the U.S. Information Service, and Aid for International Development exerted their

influence to bring Cambodia into the "Free World" alliance.

But the dynamics of international politics and long-standing rivalries among the Cambodians, Thais, and Vietnamese dashed Washington's hopes for a united front in Indochina against Communist aggression. Cambodia's adoption in 1955 of a neutral stance between the Communist and anti-Communist blocs cooled its relations with the United States. Cambodia later estranged itself from the United States during the mid-1960s following a long series of bitter territorial disputes with South Vietnam and Thailand, America's two closest allies. As a result, instead of the ally Washington had sought, Cambodia in 1965 not only became openly sympathetic to the Communist cause in Southeast Asia but also began allowing the North Vietnamese to use its territory adjacent to the South Vietnamese border as a vital supply corridor and sanctuary. American attempts to persuade Cambodia to forbid Communist exploitation of its territory proved fruitless. Ultimately, Cambodia itself became a major theater of war in 1970 when U.S. and ARVN forces began fighting and dying there in an effort to destroy the enemy's sanctuaries.

Amid the furor raised at home and abroad by this allied invasion Americans began asking the same questions about Cambodia that they had already come to ask about Vietnam. Who are the Cambodians? Why had they become entangled in a conflict their leaders had so long and desperately sought to avoid? And what would be the outcome of Cambodia's fighting a war in which, like South Vietnam, its very survival was at stake? The answers to these questions were rooted in Cambodia's recent past.

Cambodia's 4 million people, as they celebrated independence in 1954, felt their country's worst adversity was behind them. They looked toward freedom to chart their own course without foreign interference. No one was more identified with that freedom than Cambodia's king, Norodom Sihanouk. Following his accession to the throne in 1941, Sihanouk had traveled widely about his kingdom, addressing and mingling with the people, particularly the peasant farmers who comprised the majority of the population. These contacts impressed upon him the extent of nationalist impatience with French control. They also taught him how his kingship, as a focus for national identity, could be used to galvanize opposition to the French and support for independence.

After World War II, Sihanouk undertook an unrelenting campaign for independence, forcing Paris to recognize Cambodia's awakening nationalism by granting him broad responsibility for the country's internal affairs. When the French rejected his proposals for further independence, Sihanouk, in 1953, launched an anti-French propaganda crusade around the world. His well-publicized pleas for support in Canada, the United States, and Japan employed every trick that might embarrass the French: threats, tirades, insolence, and ultimatums. His crusade so disconcerted the French, hard-pressed by their war in Vietnam, that they finally acceded to all the troublesome king's demands. On November 9, 1953, Sihanouk returned triumphantly to Phnom Penh to proclaim his country's unconditional independence from France.

Past and present

Cambodia's new era of independence compelled the nation to confront an issue that it had not had to face for almost a century: national survival. By the mid-1800s Cambodia's glorious age of conquest and prosperity under the Angkor kings was but a memory. Centuries of economic and military decline had so weakened Cambodia that its expansionist neighbors, Thailand and Vietnam, were able to gobble up large chunks of its territory. It was the French protectorate over Cambodia in 1864 that had saved the country from imminent extinction and preserved its monarchy.

The French withdrawal from Indochina in 1954 once more exposed Cambodia to the potentially aggressive military and political ambitions of its neighbors. When Sihanouk gazed across his borders in the 1950s, it was with much trepidation. The Thais, allies of the Japanese in World War II, had exploited the weakness of the French in 1941 by trying to annex Cambodia's northwestern provinces of Battambang and Siem Reap. After the Japanese defeat, the French had secured the provinces' return to Cambodia. With the French gone, however, Thailand appeared intent on reverting to business as usual. In 1956, for example, Thai troops occupied the Cambodians' sacred temple of Preah Vihear in the Dangrek Mountains along Cambodia's northern border.

To the east, Sihanouk eyed Vietnam with equal anxiety. In the wake of the Geneva accords of 1954, North Vietnam and South Vietnam were preoccupied with the question of reunification. But Cambodia's wary king entertained no doubt that the Vietnamese would ultimately cause problems for his country. The Vietminh, as prescribed at Geneva, had withdrawn the thousands of troops they had sent against the French in Cambodia. But Sihanouk did not forget Ho Chi Minh's long-time determination to establish Communist hegemony over Vietnam, Cambodia, and Laos. He knew that in 1954 Ho had ordered Cambodian Communists to remain in their jungle hideouts to form an infrastructure for the eventual continuation of his Indochinese revolution.

If North Vietnamese plans for Cambodia looked ominous, Sihanouk drew no comfort from the policies of the Diem regime in South Vietnam. It might have been difficult in any circumstance for Cambodia and South Viet-

As Cambodia's king Norodom Sihanouk and his ministers enter the crown room, an umbrella is swung to the right to signify the protection of heaven.

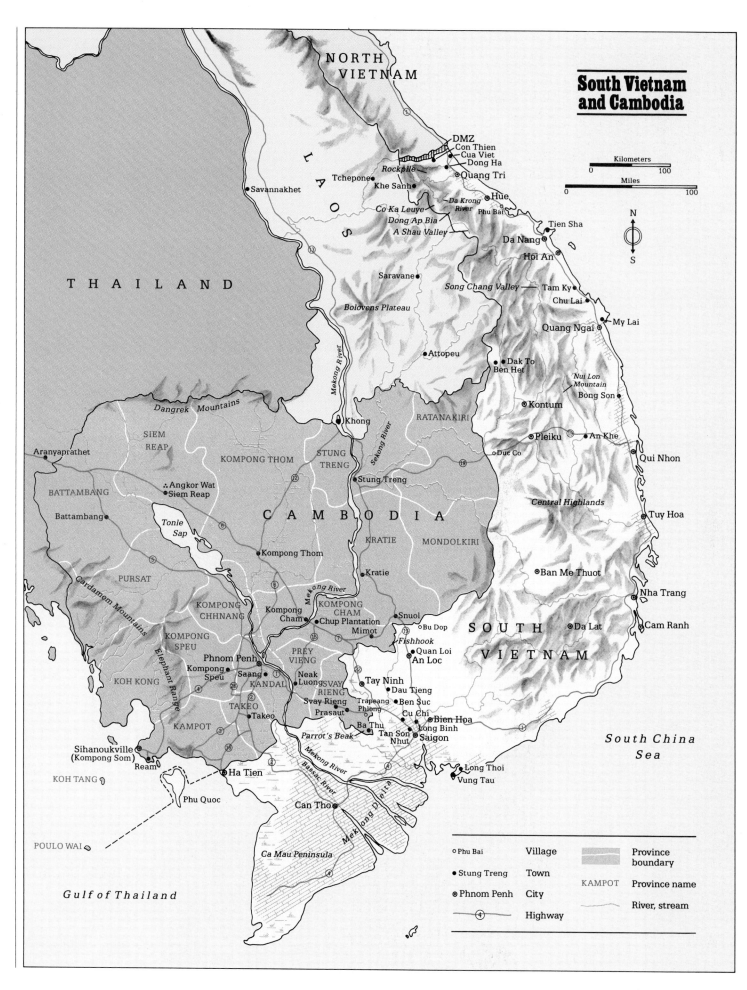

South Vietnam and Cambodia

NORTH VIETNAM

LAOS

THAILAND

Savannakhet

Tchepone

DMZ
Con Thien
Cua Viet
Dong Ha
Rockpile
Quang Tri
Khe Sanh
Co Ka Leuye
Da Krong River
Hue
Dong Ap Bia
Phu Bai
A Shau Valley
Tien Sha
Da Nang
Hoi An

Saravane

Song Chang Valley
Tam Ky
Chu Lai
Bolovens Plateau
Quang Ngai
My Lai

Attopeu

Dak To
Ben Het
Nui Lon Mountain
Bong Son
Kontum

Pleiku
An Khe
Duc Co
Qui Nhon

Dangrek Mountains

SIEM REAP

Aranyaprathet

KOMPONG THOM

STUNG TRENG

RATANAKIRI

Khong

Sekong River

Stung Treng

Mekong River

Angkor Wat
Siem Reap

BATTAMBANG

Battambang

Tonle Sap

Central Highlands

Tuy Hoa

CAMBODIA

KRATIE

MONDOLKIRI

PURSAT

Cardamom Mountains

Kompong Thom

Kratie

Ban Me Thuot

Nha Trang

KOMPONG CHHNANG

KOMPONG CHAM

Snuol

Bu Dop

SOUTH

Mekong River

Kompong Cham
Chup Plantation
Mimot

Fishhook
Quan Loi
An Loc

Da Lat

VIETNAM

Cam Ranh

KOMPONG SPEU

Elephant Range

KOH KONG

PREY VIENG

Phnom Penh
Kompong Speu
Saang

Neak
Luong
SVAY RIENG

Tay Ninh
Dau Tieng

Trapeang
Phlong

Ben Suc
Cu Chi
Bien Hoa

KANDAL

Svay Rieng
Prasaut

TAKEO

Takeo

Ba Thu

Tan Son Nhut
Long Binh
Saigon

Parrot's Beak

KAMPOT

Sihanoukville
(Kompong Som)
Ream

Ha Tien

South China Sea

Long Thoi
Vung Tau

KOH TANG

POULO WAI

Phu Quoc

Mekong River

Bassac River

Can Tho

Mekong Delta

Ca Mau Peninsula

Gulf of Thailand

○ Phu Bai	Village		Province boundary
● Stung Treng	Town		
◉ Phnom Penh	City	KAMPOT	Province name
—④—	Highway		River, stream

120

nam to develop friendly relations, since much of South Vietnam consisted of territory that once belonged to Cambodia. Hope for improvement, however, diminished when South Vietnam laid claim in the late 1950s to two offshore islands inhabited entirely by Cambodians, as well as to several disputed villages on the Cambodian frontier.

For help in insuring Cambodia's survival, Sihanouk turned to other countries. The United States was his first choice. France's departure from Indochina had left the United States the most important military power in Southeast Asia and the Pacific. The U.S., however, was not eager to become Cambodia's "protector." In formulating the SEATO defense treaty, American diplomats refrained from offering Cambodia a more substantive defense than an "umbrella of protection" against only Communist aggression. This would not protect Cambodia from Thai expansionism, for example. The U.S. had justification for withholding unqualified commitment to Cambodia, hesitant as it was to overextend its political obligations and military resources in Southeast Asia.

Unable to elicit an absolute defense commitment from the United States, Sihanouk chose a different course for his country in 1955, a policy of neutrality, in order to steer a middle course between the Communist and non-Communist blocs. "Our neutrality" he said,

has been imposed on us by necessity. A glance at a map of our part of the world will show that we are wedged in between two medium-sized nations of the Western bloc and only thinly screened by Laos from the scrutiny of two countries of the Eastern bloc, North Vietnam and the vast People's Republic of China. What choice have we but to try and maintain an equal balance between the blocs?

Sihanouk's neutrality did not go over well with American policy makers. According to the uncompromising logic of the Cold War, America and its allies lined up on the principle of "you're either with me or against me." Thus, American secretary of state John Foster Dulles, railed against Sihanouk's posture as "immoral" and an "obsolete conception." For him "neutral" was nothing but a euphemism for "pro-Communist."

Sihanouk's personality and leadership style also hampered understanding between himself and American officials. The prince was given to long, loud speeches in a high-pitched voice. He poured vitriol on critics, charm on admirers. He relished the kingly life—fine wines, sumptuous dining, and luxurious accommodations—and was vain to excess. He boasted of his sexual exploits and was every bit the showman as band leader, film director, and actor. Such erratic behavior baffled America's stern cold warriors. Richard Nixon, who as vice president traveled to Cambodia in 1957, described Sihanouk in his memoirs as "vain and flighty. He seemed prouder of his musical talents than of his political leadership, and he appeared to me to be totally unrealistic about the problems his country faced."

A National Security Council study in 1956 recommended that the United States exert every effort to "reverse the drift [in Cambodia] toward pro-Communist neutrality [and] encourage individuals and groups in Cambodia who oppose dealing with the Communist bloc." Washington's primary lever of influence on Cambodia was its aid program. Sihanouk had expressed his willingness "to accept aid from any country," but the United States was his largest benefactor. Between 1955 and 1960, U.S. economic and military aid to Cambodia amounted to $179.2 million and $64 million, respectively.

The U.S. military program was confined to funds for equipping Cambodia's 30,000-man army with modern arms and logistical facilities. American economic assistance consisted of industrial development loans to small private enterprises and long-range programs for improving Cambodia's educational and medical institutions. The showcase of U.S. aid became the $32 million, 130-mile highway connecting Phnom Penh to the port being constructed by French engineers at Sihanoukville.

Sihanouk, fearful that overreliance on American aid made his neutrality vulnerable to outside pressure, sought balance by vigorously soliciting economic assistance from Communist bloc nations. After the U.S., the Soviet Union and the People's Republic of China soon became Cambodia's principal sources of assistance. Soviet and Chinese aid between 1955 and 1960 totaled about $50 million. The Soviet Union, set on a policy of economic competition with capitalist nations in developing countries, contributed funds for nonmilitary industrial, and agricultural projects. China also had an ulterior motive for assisting Cambodia. It hoped to win the friendship of Southeast Asian countries, in part to check Soviet efforts to trespass on an area it considered China's private preserve. Chinese aid was likewise limited to economic purposes, such as the construction of plywood, cement, paper, and textile factories.

Neutrality begins at home

For Sihanouk, the task of navigating the narrow straits of political factionalism was a matter of domestic as well as foreign policy. Internally he found himself pulled in opposite directions by right- and left-wing parties whose advocacy of alignment with either Communist or non-Communist countries threatened to upset Cambodia's precarious neutrality. The most powerful were the right-wing Democrats, many of whom adhered to republican ideas about abolishing the monarchy. Fewer and less influential were the leftist members of the Pracheachon, Cambodia's Communist party. The Pracheachon had links to the Vietnamese Communists and was as unfriendly toward Sihanouk and the monarchy as the Democrats.

While Cambodian society was almost entirely rural and peasant, the parties of the right and left were comprised of a politically active urban elite. The right drew

A crowd greets Sihanouk with a traditional Cambodian welcome during his 1955 campaign tour.

support mostly from civil servants, the military, wealthy landowners, and businessmen; the left from intellectuals, academics, journalists, and former anti-French, Marxist revolutionaries. In the national elections mandated by the Geneva Conference for September 1955, Sihanouk could not let either party prevail. A victory by right or left could not only endanger his position as Cambodia's leader but could also destroy the country's neutrality.

So, in March 1955, Sihanouk decided to enter the political fray. He abdicated his throne in favor of his father, Norodom Suramarit, and became a candidate for premier. Sihanouk campaigned on the principle of establishing a democratic government. He formed a movement, the Sangkum Reastr Niyum (People's Socialist Community). The Sangkum cut across party lines and adopted as its themes "loyalty to nation, Buddhism, and monarchy." The Sangkum was created, he said, to end "the quarrels and rivalries among parties and political groupings." His appeal to the peasantry was irresistible. The Sangkum won overwhelmingly, capturing all the seats in the National Assembly and more than 80 percent of the vote.

Sihanouk's "Buddhist Socialism" matched the neutral cast of his foreign policy, borrowing ideas from both the right and the left. Besides inviting American aid, the prince promoted capitalist projects attractive to the right: intensive development of tourism, a free trade zone in Sihanoukville, the country's new port, and limited free trade along the Cambodian–South Vietnamese border. For the left Sihanouk encouraged state-owned enterprises and imposed government price controls on agricultural goods. Sihanouk's fragmented economic initiatives ultimately satisfied neither side, so rivalry between them persisted, sundering the unity achieved by the Sangkum.

To fend off continued criticisms and challenges, Sihanouk cultivated his extensive popularity among the peasants. Like the ancient monarchs of Angkor, he held popular audiences where the peasants could both pay homage to their "king" and seek redress of grievances. In the courtyard of his palace in Phnom Penh, Sihanouk attempted to solve his people's problems and disputes. His shrill voice could be heard above the din of excited villagers, shouting "Water shortage in Mondolkiri, corruption in Kompong Cham? I'll deal with it, where is the minister?" At other times Sihanouk would rush about the country with the zeal of a politician seeking reelection. One day he

sonnel carrier was attacked and destroyed by Cambodian troops after it penetrated half a kilometer into Cambodia. When three South Vietnamese aircraft chasing Vietcong soldiers bombed the village of Anlong Kres one kilometer inside Cambodian territory, killing eight people and wounding eight more, Sihanouk accused the United States of having not only approved but encouraged the cross-border incursions. "The dead," he said, "have fallen under the bullets and bombs of modern barbarians . . . [who came] from the mountains of Mississippi, Ohio, or Missouri to exterminate people who would resist them."

The South Vietnamese leveled accusations of their own at Cambodia. Cambodian forces were reportedly assaulting ARVN troops and installations within South Vietnam. The South Vietnamese Defense Ministry announced on September 7, 1964, that an ARVN soldier was killed when ten Cambodian gun boats on a Mekong River tributary fired upon a South Vietnamese outpost about one kilometer from the border. Over the next few months the ministry publicized similar clashes. Sihanouk called Cambodian attacks on ARVN self-defense: "It is impossible for us not to strike back, whatever the consequences."

The ARVN cross-border air and ground sallies continued. On April 10, 1965, four South Vietnamese air force A-4 Skyraider jets strafed and rocketed two Cambodian border villages suspected of being used by VC guerrillas. Neither U.S. and South Vietnamese apologies nor explanations that the pilots thought they were firing at VC could assuage an enraged Sihanouk. He promptly dissolved diplomatic ties with the United States and openly adopted what he called a "pro-Communist neutrality," which dictated warm diplomatic relations with the People's Republic of China. He also moved toward establishing full diplomatic connections with North Vietnam and the National Liberation Front. To alarmed and angry U.S. State Department officials, as they shut down the embassy in Phnom Penh on May 3, 1965, Cambodia appeared to have aligned itself, formally and permanently, with the Communist camp.

The price of "neutrality"

The People's Republic of China welcomed Sihanouk's diplomatic advances and requests for increased economic assistance and a military arms agreement. Sihanouk capped off a new military assistance agreement with China by affirming that "countries which firmly oppose United States imperialist provocations like [Communist China] would help Cambodia resist criminal acts of oppression." Cambodia's foreign policy shift toward China, however, represented more than a temporary expedient for striking back at the United States. Behind the Cambodian leader's determined tilt to the left was his growing conviction that of the world's three major powers, China,

not the United States or the Soviet Union, would ultimately dominate Southeast Asia. Sihanouk concluded that "our interests are served by dealing with the [Chinese] camp that one day will dominate the whole of Asia—and by coming to terms before its victory—in order to obtain the best terms possible."

For Sihanouk the "best terms possible" meant Cambodia's continued existence as a nation. His prediction of Chinese suzerainty over Southeast Asia also assumed a Communist victory that would put a united Vietnam under Ho Chi Minh's control. Like most Cambodians, Sihanouk always feared the Vietnamese, Communist or non-Communist. But he feared most an undivided, Communist-ruled Vietnam. As early as 1961 he had contemplated having to "entreat China to make North Vietnam confine itself to South Vietnam." Now he would begin bargaining in earnest with China to achieve that purpose.

Chinese leaders promised Sihanouk what he so far had not obtained from the United States. They affirmed their recognition of Cambodia's territorial integrity and pledged to protect it against any and all "acts of agression endangering [its] security." In return for his Chinese "guarantor," Sihanouk owed his cooperation in China's efforts to support the Communist struggle against the United States in South Vietnam. North Vietnam's prosecution of the war, after the introduction of American troops in 1965, required more extensive supply routes into South Vietnam. Sihanouk, resigned to the inevitability of Communist victory, fulfilled his part of the bargain with China by allowing NVA and VC troops to use sections of Cambodia's eastern provinces.

At first the North Vietnamese infiltrated men, arms, and supplies down the Ho Chi Minh Trail through Laos, across northeastern Cambodia, and into South Vietnam. When the American bombings, starting in 1965, constricted the flow of material transported down the trail, Chinese premier Chou En-lai personally asked Sihanouk to permit the completed Cambodian port of Sihanoukville to be used as an alternate supply conduit. Sihanouk did not like the idea but felt he had no option. The Chinese assured him some profit on the deal. "Two-thirds for the Viet Cong, one-third for yourself. At that rate one sells oneself," Sihanouk later commented.

Soon thousands of tons of Communist supplies and equipment were being unloaded at Sihanoukville. According to MACV commander General William Westmoreland, "From 1966 through 1969 the VC received 21,600 metric tons of military supplies such as arms and ammunition, including almost 600 tons of Soviet rockets, and over 5,000 metric tons of nonmilitary supplies such as food, clothing, and medicine." From Sihanoukville a Chinese firm called Haklee trucked the Communists' goods down the American-built "Friendship Highway" through Phnom Penh to supply depots near the South Vietnamese border. The Communists' "Sihanoukville connection" infuriated American officials. One American complained that Sihanouk "may not know the full extent of the North Vietnamese activities in his remote border areas. But he could very well control what moves through his port."

Communist demands on Cambodian hospitality increased with the escalation of the war in South Vietnam. Through 1966 the VC and NVA had been able to maintain bases and troop concentrations on the large stretches of South Vietnamese territory they controlled. Until 1967, Cambodia served principally as a logistical base and supply passageway. Communist facilities there—hospitals, barracks, and training areas—were used primarily by logistical personnel and support troops. Communist combat forces continued to use Cambodia mainly as a temporary haven or escape hatch when battered or cornered by U.S. or ARVN units.

After the Americans brought their superior firepower and division-sized search and destroy operations in 1967 to previously inviolate enemy enclaves in War Zones C and D, the Communists started expanding their border sanctuaries into semipermanent base installations. The Cambodian bases now served not only logistical units but also increasing numbers of combat troops. Intelligence analysis of Operation Junction City in War Zone C during early 1967 disclosed that "Junction City convinced the enemy command that continuing to base Main Force combat units in close proximity to the key population areas would be increasingly foolhardy. From that time on the enemy made increasing use of Cambodian sanctuaries for his bases, hospitals, training centers, and supply depots." The Communists were not abandoning their bases in South Vietnam, but Cambodia was becoming a major component of their tactical as well as logistical apparatus.

Beyond reach

American concern about the Cambodian sanctuaries and proposals to eradicate them began from the time the U.S. entered the war. On December 21, 1965, however, the U.S. State Department announced a decision made by the White House not to authorize American commanders, as they had requested, to pursue NVA and VC troops into Cambodia. State Department press officer Marshall Wright said that U.S. policy continued "to respect the sovereignty, the independence, and territorial integrity of Cambodia."

Still, sporadic incidents of "hot pursuit" border crossings by U.S. and ARVN air and ground forces did occur. And they proved politically damaging. Although the U.S. insisted "hot pursuit"—that is, the pursuit of enemy units fleeing from battle across the border—was not authorized and claimed allied border crossings were accidental, these incidents consistently hindered Washington's attempts to improve relations with Sihanouk and coax him to curtail, if not ban, the sanctuaries. In the summer of 1966,

the American journalist Robert Shaplen conveyed a letter to Sihanouk from President Johnson's roving ambassador, Averell Harriman. It requested an opportunity "to resume amicable conversations to which I have always attached the greatest interest." Sihanouk replied that Harriman would "be welcome in Cambodia on a date of your choosing." But on July 31, U.S. aircraft bombed the village of Thlok Trach, just inside the Cambodian border. Then, on August 2, while foreign diplomats and military attachés were surveying the damage, U.S. helicopters and jets twice assailed Thlok Trach. An old woman and two children were killed. "This touched Sihanouk on the raw," Shaplen noted. "He angrily declared that there was no sense in holding any talks because the United States must first recognize that Cambodia is a country that has frontiers."

The Communists' untrammeled access to Cambodia exasperated American officers from 1965 to 1970. General Westmoreland wrote in his memoirs that in 1966 he had asked "specific approval to move a few miles inside Cambodian jungles to cut in behind the Chu Pong Mountain massif and trap North Vietnamese that had crossed into South Vietnam." Nothing came of it. Later Westmoreland had his staff "prepare a contingency plan for limited air and ground operations against the enemy bases . . . but the State Department opposed the plan and the President disapproved it."

President Johnson was steadfast in his opposition to offensive operations against the sanctuaries. Despite exhortations from ex-President Eisenhower to "Tell 'em they have no sanctuaries," Johnson feared the consequences of widening the war: "With an unfriendly Prince Sihanouk still in power in Cambodia we feared that any action there would lead him to ask Peking for help." So obdurate was Johnson about keeping Cambodia out of the war policy debate that General Westmoreland's request to tell the world press of the Communists' use of Cambodia was denied until late 1967.

Since Sihanouk refused to acknowledge North Vietnam's use of his country for sanctuary and supply and barred Western journalists from Cambodia until autumn 1967, concrete evidence of the sanctuaries was not made public until two American journalists uncovered one in November. George MacArthur of the Associated Press and his colleague, photographer Horst Faas, investigated a wooded area of Cambodia north of Tay Ninh. "We didn't get into that area more than 500 yards," MacArthur remembers, "when we began to find the first signs that somebody was there. A road had been carved . . . then we went in another 300 to 400 yards and found an area for the storage of rice . . . that was VC, there was no question about it." MacArthur and Faas proceeded 200 yards farther until "Horst smelled their latrine. There was a military camp. Thank God, it was abandoned."

Because President Johnson would not permit attacks on

Threat from the west. In fall 1965, at the Special Forces outpost at Bu Dop, South Vietnam, near the Cambodian frontier, Communist forces attacked and then retreated across the border. Here, some of the 150 enemy dead from the skirmish lie along a trench inside the post.

At Duc Co, a border post west of Pleiku, a helicopter arrives to evacuate dead and wounded from a Communist mortar attack in mid–1965. The smoke is from American tanks, which came to the rescue of the camp.

the sanctuaries, MACV had to make do with stopgap defensive measures to cut the flow of men and materiel from the sanctuaries into South Vietnam. The U.S. Special Forces and the CIA dotted the South Vietnamese side of the Cambodian border with camps to monitor enemy infiltration. To man them they recruited mercenaries from mountain tribesmen and ethnic Cambodians living in South Vietnam and organized them into the Civilian Irregular Defense Group (CIDG). Many were former members of Son Ngoc Thanh's Khmer Serei. MACV also established the Studies and Observations Group, which conducted clandestine reconnaissance missions into Cambodia. Their job was primarily intelligence gathering. SOG teams (under the code name Daniel Boone, later Salem House) quietly slipped across the frontier in search of Communist trails or bases.*

General Westmoreland had described the countermeasures allowed him against the sanctuaries as "few and feeble." Together they did little to stem infiltration. Remonstrating with Sihanouk was useless. Besides, as an American officer indicated, Sihanouk "wouldn't be able to do much with his 40,000 man army even if he wanted to." When Westmoreland relinquished command in 1968, Cambodia was still "off limits." That would change someday. The impetus, however, would not come from the U.S. or its allies but from within Cambodia itself.

Reds and blues

Sihanouk managed to conceal the Communist intrusion into Cambodia from the outside world beneath a cloak of "sincere" disavowals and coy evasions. But the economic and political effects of his Communist guests could not be hidden from Cambodians. The Vietnamese Communists in border areas encouraged rice merchants and farmers to smuggle them at least 100,000 tons of rice a year by offering payment in American dollars at the world market price instead of the government's lower fixed price. This deprived the government of both taxes and profits from the legitimate export trade. Communist cadres also siphoned off government revenues by taxing peasants in the vicinity of their bases, in the form of "donations." They even contrived a counterfeiting scam. They forged Cambodian currency to purchase rice and to cover the cost of shipping war materiel to their sanctuaries.

Certain members of Sihanouk's royal family engaged in the illicit Communist trade. His half-Italian, half-Cambodian wife, Monique, and her conniving relatives used their positions to fatten their foreign bank accounts. Rumor had it that Monique elicited enormous "gifts" from the Vietnamese and Chinese Communists in return for

prevailing upon Sihanouk to refrain from clamping down on the illegal rice market. Monique's half brother, Oum Manorine, secretary of state for surface defense, collaborated in rice smuggling with Colonel Sosthene Fernandez, secretary of state for national security. They also exacted bribes from the Communists for shipping arms and ammunition to the sanctuaries.

Sihanouk's biggest concern was that the Communists might sow leftist dissension. Back in 1955 he had protested propaganda broadcasts from Hanoi as a "campaign of interference in the internal affairs of Cambodia." With the Vietnamese Communists now operating in his own backyard, he worried that the Pracheachon might be emboldened to rise against him. He labeled the Pracheachon's members the "Khmers Rouges," or "reds," in contrast to members of the right-wing party, or the "blues." Since the early 1960s Pracheachon cadres had been active in Cambodia's rural areas building a power base among peasants. They fanned discontent over high interest rates on credit, oppressive taxes, inflation, and low prices for rice crops. Communist organizing focused on rice-rich Battambang Province, which had a history of peasant unrest and economic turmoil. From there the Khmers Rouges made their bid to displace Sihanouk.

On March 11, 1967, Battambang erupted in open revolt against the government. Agrarian riots also broke out in other provinces. At the urging of his "blue" defense minister, Lon Nol, Sihanouk moved swiftly and harshly to quell the rebellion. Cambodian troops, in a brutal campaign to smash the rebels, razed scores of villages, killed hundreds of peasants, and arrested thousands more. The soldiers clubbed some villagers to death and beheaded others to collect government bounties. Martial law was imposed before several thousand rebels finally retreated to their forest havens in mid-April. In Phnom Penh, Sihanouk imprisoned five former leftist cabinet members, including Khieu Sampan, for allegedly organizing the revolt. Sampan and two others disappeared; they were reported to have been secretly executed, but this could not be confirmed, and Sampan would later emerge as Pol Pot's right-hand man.

Sihanouk blamed Vietnamese and Chinese "provocateurs" in addition to the Cambodian leftists for the Battambang rebellion. It was a rude shock to Cambodia's wheeling-and-dealing chief of state, for Sihanouk's pro-Chinese tilt had gained him nothing. For all his pro-Chinese rhetoric and his accommodation of the sanctuaries, China had not only failed to restrain the Vietnamese Communists but had involved itself in revolutionary subversion against his government. Sihanouk's Chinese guarantor had been a fraud. A sense of fatalism overtook him. His last objective, as he glumly described it, became "to push away as long as possible the death of our country and people." In turning to China Sihanouk had seriously miscalculated. Now it appeared to be time for a turn to a different direction.

---

* For more information on SOG, see chapter 7 of *Raising the Stakes* and chapter 6 of *A Contagion of War,* two other volumes in "The Vietnam Experience."

Cambodia Portraits

Before the beginning of American involvement in Southeast Asia following World War II, most Americans knew almost nothing about Cambodia, its people, history, and culture. To those few Americans who traveled there, Cambodia seemed a serene, exotic land of peasant farmers and fishermen, Buddhist temples and royal pageantry, as depicted in the photographs shown on the next two pages. The French financier Alfred Kahn commissioned these pictures, some of the first examples of color photography, in 1915. But these images of a tranquil Cambodia masked the oppression its people experienced under French colonial rule and their nationalist struggle to overthrow it.

After acquiring independence from France in 1954, Cambodians looked to a future of genuine peace and freedom. However, the efforts of Cambodia's leader, Prince Norodom Sihanouk, to preserve that country's neutrality during the bitter conflict in nearby South Vietnam and Laos were to no avail. By the late 1960s Cambodia, beset by military and political forces beyond its control, had become engulfed in an Indochina war.

A peasant woman interrupts her work to pose for Kahn's photographer.

The elephant was not only a symbol of the ancient Khmer empire, it was also an important form of transportation.

Cambodians stand before their home, built on stilts to protect it against seasonal flooding.

Remnants of a kingdom that was. In 1915, royal dancers pose before depictions of their earlier counterparts sculpted on a wall at the ancient Khmer capital, Angkor Wat.

Boys with fishing baskets, Angkor Wat, 1915.

A peaceful people in the shadow of war. Cambodian bonzes stand near a self-propelled artillery piece of the Cambodian army in 1970.

A boy no longer, this Cambodian youth totes an M16.

The Vietcong held Saang, Cambodia, in early 1970 and then evacuated it in April to a disorganized Cambodian force, which looted the town. Here, Cambodian soldiers have stolen a dog and are breaking into a store.

Preparing for war: a Cambodian soldier outside of Phnom Penh.

Near Highway 1, two Cambodian soldiers carry their Chinese-made 12.7MM machine guns across a field.

Aboard a truck bound for Phnom Penh carrying the casualties of fighting at Setbo in April 1970, two Cambodians comfort a suffering comrade. The photographer, Don McCullin, was also wounded during the battle.

A Haven of Peace

When she was in college, Jacqueline Bouvier was enchanted by accounts she read of the magnificent Khmer temple-city of Angkor in northwestern Cambodia and hoped one day to visit there. Many years later, in 1967, Prince Norodom Sihanouk invited the widow of President John F. Kennedy to fulfill her dream with a tour of Angkor's ancient ruins. On November 3, Mrs. Kennedy, with a jumble of American journalists and television camera crews around her, strolled through Angkor's huge temples and along its long colonnades and pillared galleries, lunched at tables set out under giant banyon trees, and watched traditional Khmer dances.

This was more than an occasion for entertaining a famous visitor. It was the beginning of an effort by Cambodian officials to bring about a rapprochement with the United States. A month later Chester Bowles, the U.S. ambassador to India, visited Phnom Penh for talks. On January 12, 1968, the two nations, while not resuming diplo-

matic relations, agreed on means to prevent Cambodia from being caught up in the Vietnamese war. In a joint communiqué Bowles stressed that the U.S. would "do everything possible to avoid acts of aggression against Cambodia as well as incidents and accidents which may cause losses and damages to the inhabitants of Cambodia." In turn, Sihanouk agreed "to request the Vietcong to leave Cambodia" if the U.S. would "inform Cambodia of all information she possesses of Communist Vietnamese infiltration [to] enable Cambodia to perform its duties as a neutral country." To facilitate this transfer of information, the U.S. started an intelligence operation code-named "Vesuvius." This operation called for American intelligence analysts in Saigon to prepare reports of what U.S. air and ground reconnaissance learned about the Communist sanctuaries. This documented evidence would then be periodically supplied to Sihanouk.

While the Americans supplied much evidence, Sihanouk reneged on his promise. For reasons he has never explained, Sihanouk was still unwilling to take action against the Vietnamese Communists. To make matters worse, not long after the joint agreement, he charged the U.S. with unwarranted U.S. air and ground intrusions into Cambodia.

By late 1968, the erratic Sihanouk found the hard realities of the war in Vietnam catching up to him. After the Tet offensive, the NVA and VC had found it necessary to rely more than ever on their Cambodian sanctuaries in order to sustain their operations in South Vietnam. Cambodia's State Security Secretary Sosthene Fernandez reported "armed Vietnamese are continuing to install themselves in Khmer territory near the frontier." American intelligence indicated that NVA/VC military activity "in the area of Cambodia closest to Saigon" had "increased three-fold" after November 1967. "They now have munitions, workshops, hospitals, prisoner-of-war camps, supply depots and training centers in the area."

Still Sihanouk refused to address the problem of the sanctuaries. Despite his own intelligence reports that "the Vietnamese are becoming increasingly hostile to the local people and authorities," Sihanouk ordered Cambodian military officers to stay out of areas where they might contact Communist troops, because he feared the consequences of confrontation.

Sihanouk did, however, take economic measures against the Communists. He foiled their counterfeiting operation by replacing old-series 500-riel notes with new ones. As old bills were taken in, some $70 million in notes forged by the Communists were not redeemed.

Preceding page. Cambodian troops survey the ruins of a border outpost near Trapeang Phlong destroyed by the VC in April 1970. After Lon Nol broke off relations with North Vietnam, Communist attacks in Cambodia's border region increased markedly.

Also, at the suggestion of Lon Nol and other rightist politicians, on May 11, 1969, Sihanouk welcomed a return to full diplomatic relations with the United States, in order "to play a new card since Asian Communists are already attacking us before the end of the Vietnam War." A U.S. official said on the occasion of the resumption of relations: "Maybe, they're just a silly millimeter closer to the U.S. now. But for Cambodia that's a major change."

That "silly millimeter closer" meant much more to the Nixon administration than seemed apparent at that time. During the several months it took to arrange diplomatic reconciliation, the White House was authorizing secret bombings of Communist sanctuaries in Cambodia. Neither the U.S. Congress nor the American people knew about it, but the bombings had begun shortly after Nixon took office. The bombing raids were the Pentagon's way of responding to Nixon's wish to "quarantine" Cambodia. From Saigon, General Abrams proposed that the best approach would be to direct a B-52 raid against a border section of Cambodia (labeled Base Area 353 on U.S. military maps) that was thought to be the location of headquarters for the Communist Central Office for South Vietnam (COSVN). Nixon approved a proposal for forty-eight B-52 bombing sorties to be flown against Area 353. The Joint Chiefs of Staff code-named this bombing operation Breakfast, and on March 18, 1969, the first American B-52s took off from Anderson Air Force Base in Guam.

Menu

President Nixon wanted nobody to know about Breakfast. Although, of course, the North Vietnamese and those Cambodians living in the target area would know a bombing operation had begun, the president reasoned that Hanoi could not publicly disclose or protest it without admitting the presence of its troops in Cambodia. The chairman of the Joint Chiefs of Staff, General Earle Wheeler, explained: "In the event press inquiries are received following the execution of the Breakfast Plan as to whether or not U.S. B-52s have struck in Cambodia U.S. spokesman will confirm that B-52s did strike on routine missions adjacent to the Cambodian border but state that he has no details and will look into this question."

The emphasis on secrecy was so intense that U.S. Strategic Air Command records were falsified. Major Hal McKnight, who directed radar crews at Bien Hoa airfield for the tactical region between Saigon and the Cambodian border, later described the subterfuge: "The site commander [at Bien Hoa] called me in and said 'From time to time, we have special missions that we run off here.' " McKnight was then ordered to meet a Strategic Air Command courier on board an airplane at Bien Hoa. From the courier he was to receive an envelope containing the coordinates for the bombing targets. After directing the bombers on the mission, McKnight said, he would

The Columbia Incident

The American merchant freighter the SS *Columbia Eagle* was steaming through the Gulf of Siam on March 13, 1970, when an alarm sounded and a voice over the ship's loud-speaker ordered the crew to abandon ship, warning that a bomb was about to explode: "Do it now ... Hurry ... Get those boats away!" The crew needed little urging, for the *Eagle* was loaded to the gunwales with munitions for American B-52s in Thailand.

Within minutes twenty-four of the ship's thirty-nine crewmen tumbled into two lifeboats and pushed off from the ship to wait for what they were sure would be a shattering explosion. None came. After an hour, to the amazement of the stranded crewmen, smoke belched from the *Eagle's* stack and the ship sped off at full steam. "We didn't know what was happening," recalled second mate Robert Stevenson, "some of the men joked that maybe we were being hijacked, but we thought it was just that—a joke."

Though it may have seemed farcical, the seizure was no joke. The bomb scare had been engineered by two crewmen, steward Clyde McKay and stoker Alvin Glatkowski. They had taken the bridge at gun point, ordering Captain Donald Swann to sound the alarm and then to shift course for Cambodia. If Swann did not obey, they threatened to blow up the ship. McKay and Glatkowski later said they had commandeered the ship "to help President Nixon deescalate the war by removing 10,000 tons of napalm from circulation." Newspapers reported the captain was told this was "the first in a series of mutinies" that would be staged to "impede" the war in Vietnam.

Hours later, after another munitions ship, the SS *Rappahanock*, spotted the stranded lifeboats, word of the hijacking got out. By the time Americans knew of the hijacking, the *Columbia Eagle* had almost reached the waters of neutral Cambodia. Late on March 15 it anchored five miles off the port of Sihanoukville. McKay and Glatkowski then requested, and were granted, political asylum by Prince Sihanouk's government.

At first it seemed more an impulsive act than a political gesture. Neither of the hijackers had a history of political militancy. Both came from military families; each of their mothers had divorced and remarried servicemen. McKay, twenty-five, had tried to join the army, was rejected for medical reasons, and instead went to sea. Glatkowski, twenty, had been a merchant mariner off and on for four years. In 1969 he had married and taken an on-shore job as a maintenance man. After his wife became pregnant the couple needed money so he signed back on for a short tour with the *Eagle*. During and after the hijacking it was McKay who took the lead. He said he'd felt himself "in the position of a German sailor during World War II. . . . I should feel myself guilty if I were just to comply and be a part of threatening the people of Asia."

No one knew what to make of the hijacking. From the *Rappahanock*, *Eagle* crewmen denounced it as an act of "hippies" high on pot and pills. "Hell, they wouldn't know Marx from Lenin," one sailor scoffed. The hijackers' relatives were baffled. Glatkowski's wife revealed that while her husband disapproved of the war, "He was not the type to march in peace parades or anything like that." Even American authorities were uncertain how to deal with the incident. State and Defense Department officials debated whether it constituted a mutiny. Meanwhile, five American vessels were sent to the area, ordered to wait outside Cambodian waters and maintain surveillance over the *Eagle*. A plan to pursue the *Eagle* into Cambodian waters and retake it by force was then authorized but scratched. Finally, the government began negotiating for the *Eagle's* release.

The *Eagle* affair might soon have faded had it not been for its timing. The coincidence of the *Eagle's* arrival in Sihanoukville, just days before the March 18 coup against Sihanouk, prompted speculation that the hijacking was an elaborate American ruse to smuggle arms to Lon Nol's right-wing, anti-Sihanouk group. The Communist press around the world suggested that the mutineers were acting as agents of the CIA. McKay and Glatkowski insisted, however, that the hijacking was an antiwar protest. Whatever their motives, it is doubtful the two hijackers had any connection with the ousting of Sihanouk. The *Eagle's* load of 500- and 750-pound bombs would have been useless to Lon Nol's troops.

Even though the charges of a CIA plot were never proven, they did help to secure the *Eagle's* release. After having first refused to hand over the ship, Lon Nol reversed himself. On March 28 he announced he would return the *Eagle*, its crew, and its cargo to the United States. His new government was eager to quash allegations that the hijacking had been staged to furnish arms for the coup. Lon Nol even invited a group of journalists to inspect the *Eagle's* hold, to verify that none of the cargo had been touched. In early April, after a brief ceremony, the *Eagle* was turned back over to the U.S. Captain Swann quickly sailed it out of Cambodian waters.

As for McKay and Glatkowski, for months they were held under guard in Phnom Penh, their asylum having turned into a loose arrest. The U.S. Coast Guard—which has limited jurisdiction over the merchant marine—turned the case over to federal authorities, and in June a federal grand jury in Los Angeles indicted the two, in absentia, on charges of mutiny, kidnaping, and assault. In October 1970, McKay escaped from his Cambodian guards and supposedly headed north to try to join the Communist forces at Siem Reap. His whereabouts since are unknown. Glatkowski suffered a nervous breakdown and, after unsuccessfully seeking asylum at the Chinese and Russian embassies, surrendered to the American embassy in Phnom Penh. In 1972 he was found guilty in a Los Angeles federal court on two counts of assault and mutiny and sentenced to ten years at the U.S. penitentiary at Lompoc, California. Five years later he was paroled and released to a halfway house. Though events had turned against him, Glatkowski was not sorry for his role in the *Eagle* affair: "I only regret," he told reporters in 1970, "I didn't sink the ship."

take "all the paperwork" [containing the secret Cambodian targets] and lock it in his desk "until daylight came." Only then, because his superiors feared that pieces of paper might be dropped in the dark, would he take the paperwork outside and "burn it."

Even the effort to check the results of the bombing raids was clandestine. On March 18 Special Forces Lieutenant Randolph Harrison received orders to send a reconnaissance team into Base Area 353 by helicopter and to pick up enemy survivors. It was supposed to be easy, recalled Harrison: "We had been told . . . that those carpet bombing attacks by B–52s were totally devastating, that nothing could survive and if there was anybody still alive out there they would be so stunned that all we would have to do was walk over and lead him by the arm to the helicopter."

Captain Bill Orthman led a thirteen-man Daniel Boone team into Cambodia. The men were confident and excited. Dropped amid the rubble and craters, they began searching for enemy soldiers killed or dazed by the bombing. The enemy were neither dead nor dazed. As Harrison tells it, "The only visible effect on the North Vietnamese who were there was the same as taking a beehive the size of a basketball and poking it with a stick—they were mad." The Communists trapped Orthman's team in withering crossfire. Their rescue call for helicopters reported "that everybody is getting hit." When a helicopter arrived, only two Daniel Boone members were alive. In Harrison's words, the others were "slaughtered."

Despite this inauspicious start, President Nixon continued the bombings on suspected Communist sanctuaries in Cambodia for fourteen months. Breakfast was followed by Lunch, Lunch by Snack, Snack by Dinner, Dinner by Dessert, Dessert by Supper. The composite name for these many operations was Menu. The administration defended the secrecy of Menu on the grounds that Sihanouk had approved it with the provision that the bombing be concealed to protect his "neutral" position. Henry Kissinger subsequently stated, "It was not a bombing of Cambodia, but it was a bombing of North Vietnamese in Cambodia. The prince at a minimum acquiesced in the bombing of unpopulated areas [and] told us that if we bombed unpopulated areas they would not notice." Sihanouk later denied that he had ever been informed about or granted his approval for the Menu raids. The details of whatever understanding, if any, the administration may have had with Sihanouk remain obscure. One thing about Menu was clear, as Harrison's Daniel Boone team discovered. It was going to take much more than B–52s to drive the NVA and VC from their Cambodian sanctuaries.

The end of an era

As 1970 began, Cambodia was a seriously troubled country. Its economy was in shambles. Industrial output and agricultural production were at all-time lows. Imports to-

taled $77 million, $27 million more than exports, the worst balance of payments deficit in Cambodian history. Inflation was rampant and taxes exorbitant.

The political situation was even worse. Lon Nol, whom Sihanouk had appointed prime minister in 1969, calculated at the time that the number of foreign troops in Cambodia was 35,000 to 40,000 and concluded, "nothing indicates that the foreign units will soon leave our soil." Not only were the Communists occupying long stretches of Cambodia's border regions, but they were creeping inland toward the central Cambodian provinces of Kompong Cham, Prey Veng, and Svay Rieng, all within a short driving distance from Phnom Penh. In a protest to the North Vietnamese and NLF ambassadors, Lon Nol charged "occupation is also in effect, not only in the border areas, but also in the interior," where Communist cadres "actively organized the population to deal in contraband." Also of concern were overt North Vietnamese efforts to organize and control Khmers Rouges rebels in outlying northeastern provinces.

Sihanouk's inability to bridle the Vietnamese induced mounting dissatisfaction among his people. Lon Nol realized that Cambodia was unable to apply offensive force against the Communists but wanted Sihanouk to press them more firmly to reduce their activities. On March 11, 1970, when Sihanouk was in France for a rest cure and vacation, a crowd of 10,000 students, Buddhist monks, and soldiers in civilian clothes, carrying anti-Communist banners and placards, sacked the North Vietnamese and Vietcong embassies. Shortly thereafter Lon Nol's cabinet called the demonstrators "worthy of praise." And in a terse one-sentence apology to the Vietnamese, the prime minister called the attacks "an expression of the real sentiments of the Cambodian people exasperated by the persistence of violations, encroachments, and occupation of Cambodian territory."

In France Sihanouk expressed outrage that the pro-American Lon Nol had gone so far as to disturb his "modus vivendi" with the Communists. He blamed the riots on "persons seeking to destroy unequivocally Cambodia's friendship with the socialist camp." Sihanouk then arranged to visit Moscow and Peking in an effort to persuade Russian and Chinese leaders to restrain the North Vietnamese from encroaching any further on Cambodian territory. Arriving in Moscow on March 13, he haughtily dismissed Lon Nol's emissaries who came to brief him on the deteriorating security of Cambodia. Sihanouk warned them that he would deal severely with those deputies, government officials, and military officers who dared oppose his accommodation policy toward the Vietnamese Communists.

The next several days proved disastrous for Sihanouk. The prince's brother-in-law, Oum Manorine, chief of Cambodia's ground defense, launched an unsuccessful military coup against Lon Nol's government. Manorine's move suggested to Lon Nol that Sihanouk was attempting to put him out of the way before his return. Compromise no longer seemed possible, and Lon Nol had no intention of accepting the kind of ruthless punishment Sihanouk had doled out in the past to others who had defied his will. So he transformed the investigation of Manorine's coup attempt and hearings in the National Assembly into a public indictment of Sihanouk, his family, and his policies. Lon Nol supporters delivered a litany of grievances against the prince: corruption, especially by his family, economic stagnation, political instability, and, most damaging of all, failure to deal with the growing North Vietnamese threat to Cambodia's survival.

On March 18 Lon Nol, convinced that Sihanouk's ability to save Cambodia had been exhausted, asked the National Assembly to vote on the prince's future as the nation's leader. The men of Sihanouk's Sangkum party filed past a table with three piles of paper. To pick up a white paper was a vote for Sihanouk, blue against him, and blue and white for abstention. By the time all the assembly members had walked by the table the entire pile of blue papers was gone. Sihanouk had been voted out of power ninety-two to zero. Sihanouk had once described his diplomacy for guiding Cambodia safely through the haz-

ards of confrontation in Southeast Asia: "I'll keep maneuvering as long as I have cards in my hand. First a little to the left, then a little to the right. And when I have no more cards to play, I'll stop." In March 1970, after fifteen years as Cambodia's chief of state, Prince Norodom Sihanouk had run out of cards.

On March 18 Prince Sihanouk heard of his downfall from Soviet premier Aleksei Kosygin, who was driving him to the Moscow airport for his flight to Peking. The Russians, offended as much as were the Americans by Sihanouk's "erratic" behavior, were unsympathetic to his plight. American CIA reports had quoted Russian officials as having called Sihanouk "a blundering fool" and "a spoiled child" who would not be able to "finagle" them into pulling Hanoi off his back. Far from being disheartened by Soviet indifference, during his flight to Peking Sihanouk vowed to fight to regain leadership of Cambodia. "We would be condemned by history," he declared, "if we permitted Cambodia to become not only a military dictatorship but once more a colony. All my life I have dreamed and fought for my country's independence. I did not win it from France in order to abandon it now."

At Peking Chinese premier Chou En-lai gave Sihanouk a cordial reception. After conferring with North Vietnam-

Students at a demonstration in Phnom Penh on April 5, 1970, hold up an anti-Communist, anti-Sihanouk poster. The poster depicts Sihanouk as the beast of the North Vietnamese inciting hostility between Cambodians and South Vietnamese, who stand on the other side of the "border" fence.

ese prime minister Pham Van Dong, who had flown secretly to Peking, and Chou En-lai, Sihanouk assumed leadership in absentia of a Communist front to be made up of the Khmers Rouges in Cambodia and backed by the North Vietnamese, the Vietcong, and the Laotian Communists, the Pathet Lao. Its mission was to "liberate" Cambodia from Lon Nol's right-wing government.

Said Sihanouk later, "I had chosen not to be with either the Americans or the Communists, because I considered that there were two dangers, American imperialism and Asian communism. It was Lon Nol who obliged me to choose between them." It was a fateful decision for the prince, for he had no way of knowing whether he would actually be Cambodia's "liberator" or just a front man for the Communists' subjugation of his country.

Despite his misgivings, in the last week of March, Sihanouk officially pronounced the government in Phnom Penh "dissolved" and asserted he would soon organize an administration in exile. He also established the National United Front of Kampuchea (FUNK) "to liberate our motherland" and called Cambodians to arms "to engage in guerrilla warfare in the jungles against our enemies." Sihanouk may have expected his appeal to have an explosive effect. It was in fact a dud. In cities like Phnom Penh the middle and upper classes, fed up with economic stagnation, felt no regrets about his removal. One well-to-do young man applauded the change: "We were bored with him and humiliated by him. His damn film shows and endless radio speeches in that singsong voice. If he tries to come back I hope they shoot him at the airport." The army, loyal to Lon Nol in his forthright stand against the Communists, also read his pro-American leanings as a sign that U.S. military aid, so sorely missed, would soon resume.

Campaign of death

In the countryside, the ground swell of peasant support Sihanouk had counted on never materialized. Although his rapport with peasants was genuine, it never evolved into a union capable of mass political action. Pro-Sihanouk riots did occur in border provinces where Vietnamese Communists had been broadcasting FUNK propaganda from loud-speakers on Jeeps and trucks, including recordings of Sihanouk's speeches on Radio Peking. But the government easily suppressed them. Elsewhere, in the market town of Kompong Cham, peasants and fishermen resisted orders to pull down their large portraits of Sihanouk. In a grisly display of hatred for Lon Nol, a frenzied mob killed his brother, Lon Nil. They tore out his liver, cooked it, and ate morsels of it. Afterward, the demonstrators marched on Phnom Penh. At an army roadblock, soldiers fired at the peasants, killing one hundred before they dispersed.

Most Cambodians, peasants and urban classes alike,

directed their anger not at Lon Nol but at the Vietnamese Communists. A government request for volunteers to bolster Cambodia's 30,000-man army received an overwhelming response. Within weeks, 70,000 volunteers, 60,000 more than called for, enlisted in the army. This surge of nationalism against the Vietnamese presence also had an ugly side to it. In late March, the Vietnamese Communists had begun sending patrols further into Cambodia to ambush and harass Cambodian units that might dare approach their sanctuaries. "The Vietcong," observed a Cambodian army officer, "want to extend their zone into Cambodia before the Cambodian army has a chance to bother them." Cambodia's outmanned and outgunned soldiers were ineffectual against them. Rumors spread of an impending Communist offensive to capture Phnom Penh itself. Frightened Cambodians succumbed to paranoia that triggered violence against the country's nearly 400,000 ethnic Vietnamese, many of whom were suspected of being Communist agents, supporters, and saboteurs. In Phnom Penh and other towns, Cambodian mobs looted and destroyed Vietnamese shops and businesses.

Lon Nol saw that he might use ethnic Vietnamese as hostages to prevent more Vietnamese Communist attacks on Cambodians. The government also capitalized on the Cambodian people's hysteria to whip up support for action against the Communists. Government aircraft dropped leaflets on Phnom Penh recalling a historic massacre "when the Khmers once rose up and killed all Annamese [Vietnamese] on Cambodian territory in one night." A 6:00 P.M. to 6:00 A.M. curfew was imposed on the capital's 120,000 Vietnamese residents to preclude "subversive activities." A government official there remarked, "We hate all Vietnamese."

Frustrated at being bullied by NVA and VC soldiers, Cambodia's army unleashed a reign of terror against its Vietnamese "hostages." Across the country Cambodian soldiers rounded up Vietnamese into makeshift detention camps. Then the killing began. In the village of Prasaut near the South Vietnamese border, after a brief skirmish with a Communist unit on April 10, Cambodian troops went on a shooting spree in a warehouse jammed with terrified Vietnamese, half of them women and children. Ninety Vietnamese died. The next day at the town of Takeo, Cambodian soldiers fired into a group of Vietnamese huddled in a schoolhouse. The death count was over a hundred. "They shot and shot and shot," said a weeping teen-aged survivor.

On April 15, the bodies of 800 Vietnamese men came floating down the Mekong River past the ferry crossing at Neak Luong. The Cambodian army had arrested the men at their village of Chrui Changwar, tied their hands behind their backs, executed them, and tossed their bodies into the river. For days bloated bodies flowed slowly by the ferry, staining the water. The Associated Press re-

Ethnic Vietnamese huddle together in a Cambodian internment camp in April 1970 after Lon Nol ordered the roundup of all Vietnamese living in Cambodia.

The bodies of Vietnamese men killed by Cambodian soldiers float down the Mekong, April 15, 1970.

145

Lon Nol, Cambodia's new premier, shortly after he seized power in March 1970.

ported, "The stench swept across the broad waters and ferry passengers gagged as the ferry churned through the bodies bobbing in the river." Many uprooted Vietnamese sought relief and protection in Phnom Penh but all they got were overcrowded "refugee" camps. Others tried to cross over the border into South Vietnam.

The South Vietnamese government excoriated Cambodia for the slaughter and internment of Vietnamese. On April 20 Saigon appealed to "all nations in the world and all international organizations . . . to prevent renewed massacres of Vietnamese." The North Vietnamese and National Liberation Front also denounced Cambodia. As a precaution, Vietcong soldiers living in Cambodia began sending their accompanying families back to South Vietnam. An American official noted, "The Vietcong feel their

families are safer in South Vietnam—the land of the enemy—than in Cambodia where they have been living." Lon Nol defended his troops for whom, he said, "it was difficult to distinguish between Vietnamese citizens who were Vietcong and those who were not. So it is quite normal that the reaction of Cambodian troops, who feel themselves betrayed, is difficult to control."

While the Cambodian army hounded civilians, the NVA and VC consolidated their twenty-four-kilometer swath of border territory. Hem Heth Sana, province chief of Svay Rieng, informed Phnom Penh that for the first time Vietnamese Communists were attacking district towns and blocking roads. Their goal, Sana said, was "to isolate the province from the rest of Cambodia." Similar assessments came from other border provinces. On March 27 a "sizable" Communist force bloodied a Cambodian patrol near Prekchrieu, Kratie Province. A 3,000-man Communist unit occupied the town of Svayandong eight kilometers from the border in Prey Veng Province, surrounding a nearby Cambodian army post. Just weeks after the coup, one could hardly discern who were the hostages, the Vietnamese or the Cambodians.

Cambodia reassessed

In meeting the emergency facing his country, Lon Nol did not act like the warmonger Sihanouk's invective made him out to be. He showed no intention of stampeding Cambodians into the Vietnam War. Lon Nol's policies, like those of Sihanouk, went in many directions and he kept his options open. On March 19, he notified foreign governments that Sihanouk's departure would not alter Cambodia's policy of "independence, sovereignty, peace, strict neutrality and territorial neutrality." He also condemned "all violations of Cambodian territory by foreign forces, whatever camp they come from."

Lon Nol's maneuvering to avoid an irreversible confrontation with the Communists availed him no more than it had Sihanouk. By mid-April, a peaceful solution seemed unattainable, and time was running out on a military one, Lon Nol's last resort. Lon Nol made a worldwide plea for arms to help Cambodia thwart "an escalation of systematic acts of aggression" by the Communists. "The government" he advised his people, "has the duty to inform the nation that in view of the present situation, it finds it necessary to accept all unconditioned foreign aid, wherever it may come from, for the salvation of the nation." From most countries Lon Nol would receive little. From the United States, he would get both less and more than he wanted.

Sihanouk's downfall had startled Washington as much as it had Peking and Hanoi. Winston Lord, at the time Kissinger's special assistant on the National Security Council, recollects, "There was considerable surprise that Sihanouk had been overthrown—he was generally seen as a force for stability—we had nothing to do with it." Sihanouk's postcoup harangues charged otherwise, but his scathing accusations of CIA intrigue against him were unfounded. The prince could simply not believe that his own political and economic policies had been his undoing.

Among Washington decision makers, initial surprise about the coup quickly gave way to intensive discussions of how the U.S. should respond to the change in Cambodia. There was "disagreement," Winston Lord recalls, "among various advisers on whether you try to bring Sihanouk back or whether you throw some support to Lon Nol." President Nixon almost immediately settled the issue in Lon Nol's favor. "From day one," said Marshall Green, the assistant secretary of state for East Asian and Pacific Affairs and State's representative on the White House's crisis management group, "Nixon was insistent on building up Lon Nol." In a memo analyzing the probable amount of U.S. aid required to prop up Lon Nol, Green concluded, "Without massive U.S. support the government of Cambodia cannot rebuild its position." But this was not 1965. The president, even had he wished to, could not have the United States spring into the breach with a long-term commitment of money, arms, and troops, as in Vietnam, to save Cambodia from the Communists. His withdrawal policy, and the de-escalatory disposition of Congress and the public, militated against it.

For the Nixon administration, therefore, "building up" Lon Nol was restricted to aid provided on a limited scale and short-term basis. Unknown to Congress, in April the White House, while publicly disclaiming involvement in Cambodia, ordered General Creighton Abrams in Saigon to ship all captured AK47 rifles to Phnom Penh. "I don't want to see any [AK47s] hanging on officers' club walls," Abrams told his subordinates. General William Westmoreland now cabled Abrams "that we might consider delivering arms by sea to Vung Tau [in South Vietnam] and then by air to Phnom Penh. We would want delivery to be covert if possible." Also made available to Lon Nol were U.S.-trained ethnic Cambodian units in South Vietnam. Despite all the secrecy, news of U.S. deliveries to Lon Nol leaked out. On April 22 the *New York Times* broke the story. The administration, however, reassured the Senate Foreign Relations Committee that the amount was minimal and did not signal a trend toward increased political commitment.

If its response to events in Cambodia confronted long-term political obstacles, the White House also detected a short-term military opportunity: the possibility of disabling the Communists' sanctuaries along the Cambodian border. Nixon's approval of the Menu bombings in 1969 had demonstrated his willingness to take offensive measures against the sanctuaries of a sort that President Johnson had prohibited. Now that Sihanouk was gone conditions were ripe for stronger actions. The White House thought so. General Westmoreland has written that "following [the] overthrow of Prince Sihanouk in March 1970 and the emergence of the Lon Nol government in Cambodia, it was Henry Kissinger who raised the possibility of at last invading Cambodia to attack North Vietnamese sanctuaries." The military in South Vietnam agreed. James Lowenstein and Richard Moose, Senate Foreign Relations Committee investigators, reported in April 1970: "From our conversations in Saigon, it appeared to us that the United States and South Vietnam military regarded Sihanouk's fall as an opportunity to strike at enemy sanctuaries along the border . . . many U.S. military officers in Vietnam used this very [phrase]."

A new ball game

President Nixon solicited proposals to deal with the sanctuaries from the Joint Chiefs in Washington and from MACV in Saigon. They presented him with several tactical options: quarantine of the Cambodian coast; South Vietnamese and American air strikes; expansion of hot pursuit by ARVN; and a ground invasion by ARVN, U.S. forces, or both. The unstable state of Cambodia imposed time limits on the president's decision making. The Communists were moving westward in Cambodia to enlarge their already bulging stretch of territory. A CIA intelligence summary in mid-April suggested to Nixon that the Communists might upend the Lon Nol government, thus making Cambodia enemy territory and outflanking South Vietnam. It also gloomily predicted "if the president doesn't act, a domino is going to fall." This dire forecast troubled Nixon, emphasizing as it did the need for a timely response. "The only government in Cambodia in the last twenty-five years that had the guts to take a pro-Western stand," he asserted, "is ready to fall." The president therefore felt he had to act, first and quickly. Nixon wanted a decisive stroke, "a bold move." The last option suggested by the Pentagon—a ground invasion—fit the bill.

The Joint Chiefs began working on contingency plans. The prospective Cambodian sanctuary targets were located in areas the Americans had named the Parrot's Beak and the Fishhook. The Parrot's Beak is a sliver of land that protrudes into South Vietnam within fifty kilometers of Saigon. The area of heaviest enemy concentration was the Fishhook, a thin arc of Cambodian territory jutting into South Vietnam about ninety kilometers northwest of Saigon. There, American intelligence speculated, might be a precious target: COSVN, the Communists' southern military headquarters and their logistical nerve center. An American officer noted, "As long as they [the sanctuaries] remained off limits to allied forces it was as if a loaded and cocked pistol was being held to the head of South Vietnam."

From the beginning, possible U.S. military involvement in Cambodia, whether by ARVN or American forces, was a subject of heated debate in Washington. On March 31 Secretary of Defense Melvin Laird wrote to Secretary of

Springtime in Phnom Penh

by Don Kirk

Prince Norodom Sihanouk called his land an "oasis of peace" in the halcyon years before the war overflowed across the border from Vietnam after his overthrow in March of 1970. In fact, even while the North Vietnamese were extending their control of the countryside and encircling Cambodia's capital city, Phnom Penh retained the graceful atmosphere of French colonial charm and ease that seemed to drug all those who sojourned there. The broad avenues, the pleasant restaurants, the tree-shaded side streets running through rich residential areas, the shops crowded with little silver animals and jade carvings—they were all there when I first visited in late 1966 on my way to Angkor Wat, and they were still flourishing when I arrived during the turbulent spring of 1970.

For all the horror stories about what was happening in Cambodia—the Communist attacks, the massacres of ethnic Vietnamese by the Cambodians, and the upheaval throughout the country—Phnom Penh was like a dream world for the foreigners who trickled in while the United States sought to prop up the regime of General Lon Nol. The American mission, expelled by Sihanouk in 1965, quickly expanded in 1970 after its return, and foreign service officers moved into plush homes and apartments in the center of Phnom Penh. Along with arms and advice, they dispensed liquor and good cheer—and delighted in showing off the latest American movies for carefully screened audiences of the local elite. Free-wheeling contractors arrived in pursuit of contracts to support the American aid effort, and a fleet of decrepit aircraft piloted by globetrotting adventurers flew in and out of the Phnom Penh airport amid intermittent shelling. They ferried arms and other supplies for the Cambodian forces at the behest of the U.S. government. Young men and women set up schools and classes to teach English to the Cambodian upper crust, educated in French, and salesmen poured in with pitches for everything from the latest electronic equipment to perfume and shaving cream.

For the foreign correspondents, perhaps more than most of the others, Cambodia's entry into what was now an Indochina war was both an opportunity—and a hazard. You could rent a room for the equivalent in riel—the Cambodian currency—of $10 a day at the Hotel Royal, eat a leisurely breakfast of croissants and café filtre in the dining room beside the pool, and hire a chauffeured Mercedes-Benz for less than $20 a day, and roar down a paved road to get your story within an hour's drive. It didn't matter a great deal in which direction you chose to go. The seemingly placid peasants whispered stories of fearful encounters with a foe that threatened to destroy them. You could count on garrulous old crones to pass on rumors picked up from farmers and woodsmen falling back on the main roads and towns.

Yet, danger always lurked around the next seemingly innocent bend in the road. Shortly after Sihanouk's fall, soldiers carrying Chinese-made AK47 rifles stopped me as I drove southeast near the Vietnam border with two Canadian correspondents, Bill Cunningham and Maurice Embre. Their leader gave us some propaganda material and accepted our assurance that we were all Canadian—without forcing me to pull my U.S. passport from my pocket. In the ensuing weeks, twenty-seven journalists left Phnom Penh on similar expeditions, never to return alive.

For those who stayed in the city the greatest danger was overindulgence in the nocturnal delights of a society accustomed for more than a century to catering to the whims of foreign interlopers, not to mention its own unabashedly corrupt leaders. Those who tired of the cuisine at the Royal or the Monorom, a distinctly second-ranked hotel, could dine in splendor at any of half a dozen first-class places. One of the favorites was La Taverne, reputed for the best in cheeses and pâtés, swilled down with local Angkor or Bayon beer. The poshest restaurant was the Café de Paris, beside a verdant park near the Royal. There a rotund French Corsican manager ministered personally to the needs of his honored guests. Then there was La Venise, with red-checked tablecloths and fine pastas along with all the wine you needed to wash it down.

But your night had only begun. Always, there were the women. They were in brothels on property owned by the Queen mother on the road leading east from the city. They were on houseboats on the Tonle Sap. They were in hotels and restaurants, on the streets and in the bars. Among the most delectable were the Vietnamese who hung out at Le Grand Lac, named for the lake in Hanoi when the French ruled the region. They all fled during the general exodus of the Vietnamese minority that began soon after the coup, but the numbers of Khmer women, available at prices ranging from the equivalent of fifty cents to several dollars, shot up as the war engulfed the country. Then, too, there were the pleasures of Mère Shum's opium den, in a ramshackle house in a residential neighborhood. Business was so good that one of her protégés, Chantal, opened a rival den.

For those who weren't fighting and dying, it was an absurdly easy life. The laconic gaiety of the capital shielded all who went there from the tragedy and suffering just a few miles away. The poor of the city shared in the mood. They too believed in the "salvation" of American aid and bombing. The central market, in a great sprawling structure in the heart of the city, was stacked high with black market products from the great U.S. military post exchange system—all smuggled in from Vietnam. Sidewalk stalls overflowed with everything from stereo sets to fountain pens marked "U.S. Government."

In that portentous spring and summer of 1970, Phnom Penh remained a fantasy land into which the sobering realities of the war around it barely intruded. Among most of the city's residents the warnings of worse to come—the bombings, the casualties, the refugees, and the sheer terror—went unheeded. Their hope was that the "good life" would continue as usual, that it couldn't happen here.

Don Kirk covered the Vietnam War for the Chicago Tribune *and the Washington* Star, *traveling to Cambodia for the* Star. *Currently, he is World Editor for* USA Today.

State William Rogers, "We will be in a difficult position if Cambodia asks the U.S. government to become militarily involved in that country." Laird did advocate shallow pursuit by ARVN, while Rogers became an outspoken opponent of substantial border operations even by the South Vietnamese. At the State Department, Marshall Green cautioned, "It would be very risky to try to solve the North Vietnamese problem in Cambodia by force. I would consider our best action to be to wait on events." But in the urgent atmosphere of Cambodian deliberations, "to wait" was not what the president wanted to do. Nixon declared, "I want to make sure that Cambodia does not go down the drain without doing something. Everybody always comes to my office with suggestions on how to lose. No one ever comes in here with a suggestion on how to win."

Action-oriented advisers, therefore, were the ones who caught the president's ear. At Honolulu on April 19 Nixon received a briefing from the CINCPAC, Admiral John D. McCain, Jr. McCain was renowned among journalists for his doom-laden sermons on the Communist threat to Southeast Asia. They called him the "Big Red Arrow Man" because of his maps, which had giant red arrows pointing southward from China. McCain unfurled a map of Cambodia with his big red arrows, like giant claws grasping south and west toward Phnom Penh. He then proffered a plan for a major Cambodian incursion, including a strongly favored option for using American troops against the Fishhook. Nixon was impressed but noncommital. A White House aide termed McCain's briefing "one more input, not pivotal."

The next day, President Nixon addressed the nation on the situation in Vietnam. His speech, "Progress Toward Peace in Vietnam," contained an announcement of a further troop withdrawal of 150,000 Americans. "We have now reached a point," he said, "where we can confidently move from a period of 'cut and try' to a longer range program for the replacement of Americans by South Vietnamese troops." Cambodia was also on his mind. He reminded "the leaders of North Vietnam that while we are taking these risks for peace, they will be taking grave risks should they attempt to use the occasion to jeopardize the security of our remaining forces in South Vietnam by increased military action in South Vietnam, in Cambodia, or in Laos. . . . I shall not hesitate to take strong and effective measures to deal with that situation."

Over the following two days it appeared to Nixon that the Communists were cunningly taunting him. On April 21, Le Duan, first secretary of the North Vietnamese Communist party, announced from Moscow that Hanoi was considering the formation of a "united front" in Indochina to oppose the United States. Communist actions in Cambodia seemed to underscore Hanoi's bellicose intentions. There were stepped-up assaults on towns during which the Communists seized the border town of Snuol, thirty kilometers from the tip of the Fishhook. President Nixon, according to Henry Kissinger, fell into an "increasingly agitated frame of mind," and concluded that the moment for direct allied intervention had come.

On the evening of April 22, while presiding over a lengthy National Security Council meeting, Nixon authorized the planning of a South Vietnamese invasion of the Parrot's Beak. "Giving the South Vietnamese an operation of their own," the president reasoned, "would be a major boost to their morale as well as provide a practical demonstration of the success of Vietnamization." Joint Chiefs Chairman General Earle Wheeler notified General Abrams that the South Vietnamese invasion was to begin on April 29. "Our objective," Wheeler said "is to make maximum use of ARVN assets so as to minimize U.S. involvement, and maintain lowest possible U.S. profile." The order to prepare for an incursion was welcomed in Saigon—by MACV, by the American embassy, and by the South Vietnamese government. Since arriving in Saigon General Abrams had been keen on slamming the sanctuaries. He was "enthusiastic," he confided to an American journalist, "about carefully timed and planned incursions to clean out the sanctuaries." U.S. Ambassador Ellsworth Bunker was of a like mind: "I think we should have gone into the sanctuaries before we did, because having the sanctuaries gave the enemy the opportunity to raise or lower the level of combat at will. They could retreat to the sanctuaries, reinforce, re-equip, come back and attack. And we couldn't do anything about it."

Winners and losers

President Thieu had no reservations about an incursion to "drive the enemy out." South Vietnamese troops had been rehearsing for it since late March. On March 27 and 28, an ARVN Ranger Battalion with air and artillery support had gone three kilometers into Kandal Province to destroy a Communist base. Four days later ARVN troops went in sixteen kilometers. ARVN ventured its biggest cross-border plunge on April 20. Two thousand troops hit the Parrot's Beak area, killing 144 of the enemy. A keyed-up ARVN officer told his U.S. adviser: "You Americans think the North Vietnamese are gods. You should give us the chance to fight as they do—on someone else's land. We would amaze you."

While the South Vietnamese prepared to assault the Parrot's Beak, Laird and Rogers sought to put strict limits on American support. But the president was not receptive to exhortations for restraint. He was wondering how much more—not how little—the U.S. could throw against the sanctuaries. Vice President Spiro Agnew, though little regarded as a policy maker, supplied the rationale for "more." Agnew, according to Kissinger's memoirs, "thought the whole debate irrelevant. Either the sanctuaries were a danger or they were not. If it was worth cleaning them out, he did not understand all the pussyfoot-

The battle of Prey Veng in Cambodia in April 1970 pitted Cambodian and South Vietnamese soldiers against an entrenched VC force. Here, a group of Cambodian troops counterattack after having been ambushed.

South Vietnamese marines run for cover during the fighting near Prey Veng.

The Vanishing Border

At the town of Saang twelve kilometers southeast of Phnom Penh, Cambodian troops fire at suspected VC positions on April 23.

ing about the American role or what we accomplished by attacking only one. He favored an attack on both Fishhook and Parrot's Beak, including American forces." The president, on April 22, authorized American air support for the Parrot's Beak "on the basis of demonstrated necessity." He did not commit himself to attacking the Fishhook. Kissinger, however, had "no doubt that Agnew's intervention accelerated Nixon's ultimate decision to order an attack on all the sanctuaries and use American forces."

Again Rogers and Laird argued against involvement by Americans. On April 23 Rogers testified before the House Appropriations Subcommittee that the administration had "no intentions to escalate the war. . . . We recognize that if we escalate and get involved in Cambodia with our ground troops that our whole [Vietnamization] program is defeated." Laird told Nixon that "I didn't think Americans should go over there [Cambodia]. I was against using American ground forces." The president sought other counsel. On the morning of April 24 he summoned Admiral Thomas Moorer, who had just replaced General Earle Wheeler as chairman of the Joint Chiefs of Staff, and Richard Helms, director of the CIA, to "discuss the feasibility of a combined U.S.–South Vietnamese operation against Fishhook, in parallel with the Parrot's Beak operation." Rogers and Laird were excluded from the discussion.

Moorer and Helms "were both strongly in favor of an attack on the Fishhook sanctuary. They felt it would force the North Vietnamese to abandon their effort to . . . terrorize Phnom Penh." The president's response was emphatic: "Ike lost Cuba but I won't lose Cambodia." Nixon authorized planning for the Fishhook but withheld a final decision. The White House called General Abrams, who instructed Lieutenant General Michael Davison, commanding general of II Field Force, to devise plans. Seventy-two hours later, Davison's Fishhook plans were submitted to the White House. When Kissinger asked his aide Larry Lynn to review them on April 26, Lynn said he was appalled by their "sloppiness." General Westmoreland thought them "very hastily thrown together."

The planning suffered from the pressure of time and the desire of the White House for secrecy. The Cambodian monsoon was only two months away. After the news leak about the shipment of AK47s to Cambodia, Nixon had exploded and demanded even more stringent secrecy. Thus, the Cambodian desk in Saigon was not consulted about the Fishhook plan nor the embassy in Phnom Penh nor even Lon Nol, who consistently opposed all foreign incursions and wanted only money and arms. Nevertheless, while receiving less from the U.S. in arms and dollars, he was about to get more than he requested in the form of unwanted troops.

On Saturday, April 25, Nixon was still ruminating. The probability of public and Congressional revulsion against the Fishhook attack made him hesitate. "I never had any

illusions about the shattering effect a decision to go into Cambodia would have on public opinion," he wrote. "I recognized that it would mean personal and political catastrophe for me and my administration." That evening the president dined with his friend, Bebe Rebozo, and Henry Kissinger. Afterward, they viewed the president's favorite movie, *Patton*. Nixon, who admired its portrayal of the "blood and guts" tank commander, had seen it five times. Commented Kissinger, "When he was pressed to the wall, his romantic streak surfaced and he would see himself as a beleaguered military commander in the tradition of Patton." The next night, April 26, Nixon ended his "agonizing." "We would go for broke," he announced, "for the big play. . . . A joint ARVN-U.S. Force would go into the Fishhook [on May 1st]."

The time for action

The president disregarded General Abrams's suggestion for a routine announcement from Saigon of the Fishhook invasion. Abrams and his staff envisioned the operation's objective as "getting into the enemy's system," not to engage and destroy the enemy itself. This would disrupt the enemy's supply lines, thereby decreasing his ability to operate offensively in South Vietnam and giving Vietnamization a little breathing room. "For the generals," as one observer put it, "the Cambodian invasion wasn't an important strategic event. Generals thought it was good tactics, nothing more."

For President Nixon the Cambodian invasion had a strategic, political, and even moral import that dwarfed "good tactics." In the struggle between Communist and "Free World" nations, Nixon saw the Parrot's Beak and the Fishhook as crucial tests of both America's mettle and moral character and of his own as its leader. While he drafted his speech for delivery on April 30, it was this broader perspective that dominated his thoughts. On April 29, news of the South Vietnamese Parrot's Beak attack came over the wire. Except for small revisions, Nixon finished his speech at five the next morning. "Now that we have made the decision," he said to Kissinger, "there must be no recrimination among us—not even if the whole thing goes wrong."

On Thursday, April 30, at 9:00 P.M., millions of Americans were flicking on televisions to watch their favorite programs. For Americans, the war seemed to be winding down. In the last week they had heard that another 150,000 more troops were coming home. Now President Nixon appeared on the screen, speaking from the Oval Office at the White House. In front of a large map of Cambodia, he said,

After final consultation with the National Security Council, Ambassador Bunker, General Abrams, and my other advisers, I have concluded that the actions of the enemy in the last ten days

Pointing to the Fishhook on a map, President Nixon describes the U.S. invasion of Cambodia on national television on April 30.

clearly endangers [sic] the lives of Americans who are in Vietnam now and would constitute an unacceptable risk to those who will be there after withdrawal of another 150,000. To protect our men . . . and to guarantee the continued success of the withdrawal and Vietnamization programs, I have concluded that the time has come for action.

"The enemy," he explained . . . "is concentrating his main forces in their sanctuaries . . . to launch massive attacks on our forces and those of South Vietnam." The president emphasized that America's policy "has been to scrupulously observe the neutrality of the Cambodian people [who] sent out a call to the United States . . . for assistance." In addition to hitting the sanctuaries, the American attack on the Fishhook had the special objective of capturing "The headquarters for the entire Communist military operation in South Vietnam."

President Nixon denied any intentions of widening the war or making Cambodia "an active belligerent on one side or the other." Yet he accentuated the wider strategic and political ramifications of his decision: breaking the deadlock at the peace talks, continuing the American withdrawal, and upholding the credibility of the president and even of the United States. "I would rather be a one-term president," he stated, "than to be a two-term president at the cost of seeing America . . . accept the first defeat in its sound 190-years' history." The world, he reminded his viewers, was watching America:

It is not our power but our will and character that is being tested tonight. The question all Americans must ask and answer tonight is this: Does the richest and strongest nation in the history of the world have the character to meet a direct challenge by a group which rejects every effort to win a just peace.

Prince Sihanouk had once described Cambodia as "the last haven of peace . . . caught between the hammer and the anvil." On April 30, 1970, the hammer was about to strike the anvil.

Life at a Firebase

The fire support base was one of the many innovations in the deployment of arms and men that accompanied American search and destroy tactics in South Vietnam. For the U.S. troops assigned to a firebase—artillerymen, logistical personnel, and clerical staff—it was home for part or all of their year-long tour in South Vietnam. Life there included some of the comforts of home: hot meals, cold drinks, radios, regular mail, a change of clothes, and maybe even a movie, as well as bunkers or hootches to sleep in. But the fire support base was not by any means an oasis, insulated from the daily round of combat in the countryside around it. The depressing routine of outgoing artillery fire and incoming dead and wounded infantrymen helicoptered from the field was sometimes interrupted by enemy mortar strikes, sapper attacks, and full-scale assaults. Amid all this, men serving at a fire support base encountered another enemy: the tedium of heat and humidity, dust and mud, loneliness and isolation. These photographs taken by Mark Jury in 1970 provide a glimpse of what it was like for American soldiers stationed at fire support bases in South Vietnam.

Fire Support Base Fuller, the northernmost U.S. base in South Vietnam. Sitting atop a pile of rocks 600 meters high and less than 40 meters at its widest point, FSB Fuller could be supplied only by air.

Above. A sketch of life at the fictional "Firebase Bundy" from the Gary Trudeau comic strip, Doonesbury.

Soldiers from the 6th Battalion, 33d Artillery, pose before a 105MM howitzer at FSB Fuller in January 1970. The small group of GIs stationed there became as close knit as a family.

Right. An artilleryman at FSB Fuller reads a letter from home, January 1970.

A latrine at Fire Support Base Fuller in January 1970.

Soldiers of the 6th Battalion, 33d Artillery, polish brass shell casings that they will fashion into souvenir ashtrays. Once each month one of the soldiers would take all the finished ashtrays from FSB Fuller to Dong Ha to get them engraved.

Chow time at FSB Wood, home of the 5th Battalion, 7th Cavalry, 1st Air Cavalry Division, in April 1970.

To raise morale at FSB Wood after a fierce firefight in April 1970, the 1st Air Cav commander has sent in the division band, along with hot food, beer and soda, and newspapers and mail.

Now the Indochina War

Even as the president put the finishing touches to his speech, a joint American-South Vietnamese task force poised to lunge into the Fishhook. The operation mobilized 10,000 Americans—primarily the 1st Air Cavalry Division and 11th Armored Cavalry Regiment—and nearly 5,000 men from the 1st ARVN Armored Cavalry Regiment and the 3d ARVN Airborne Brigade. This made it the largest allied operation since Junction City in 1967. The Fishhook attack plan entailed a pincer maneuver to trap elements of the 7th NVA Division and a Vietcong unit operating there. The 3d ARVN Airborne was to be inserted into three landing zones north of the Fishhook to block enemy escape routes and then move south to link up with the American task force swinging northward—the 1st Air Cav from the west and the 11th Armored Cav from the east and southeast. American and ARVN troops would then comb the area for bases, fortifications, and supply caches. Another important objective was the town of Snuol,

strategically located at the junction of Routes 7 and 13. Snuol served as the distribution point into South Vietnam for Communist supplies shipped through Sihanoukville. The operation commander was Brigadier General Robert Shoemaker, affectionately referred to by his men as "Handsome Bob."

Despite the official secrecy, American soldiers participating in the incursion had seen Fishhook coming. Mark Pritchard, an aviation technician in the 1st Air Cav, recalls how at Quan Loi, headquarters for the operation, in late April "a plane flew in, and a bunch of generals got out— we don't usually get generals up in that area. I knew something was up. . . . Every helicopter we had was being made ready . . . hundreds more than I've ever seen in one place in my life."

"I figured we'd be going sooner or later," said another GI. "Guys were taking bets on it." For Warrant Officer Geoffrey Boehm, a 1st Air Cav helicopter pilot, it was a chance to avenge fallen comrades: "We had lost many men in combat assaults near the Cambodian border while the gooks would go back into Cambodia, sit there and laugh at us so we were all together for going in." For Scott Gauthier, a medic, the incursion "was going to make the war that much shorter."

Before dawn on May 1 the Fishhook invasion got underway. After preparatory strikes by artillery and air, two columns of tanks and APCs of the 11th Armored Cavalry rumbled into Cambodia, followed by Sheridan reconnaissance vehicles and M48 Patton tanks. An armada of helicopters carried the troopers of the 1st Air Cav into battle. The pilots and men were both exhilarated and scared. Pilot Geoffrey Boehm remembers, "we were all hyped up and scared because flying over the border we faced enemy radar-controlled machine guns. Once they lock onto you it's like taking a fly out of the air with a fly swatter." A senior U.S. officer told a reporter, "This Cambodian operation is pure blitzkrieg, like something from a World War II Panzer division's book of tactics."

While they hoped to surprise the enemy, the invading troops expected a hard fight against large numbers of well-fortified enemy troops. "We were all a little apprehensive at first," said Brigadier General Donn Starry, commander of the 11th Armored Cavalry Regiment. "We had reports of extensive bunker systems, antitank weapons, antiaircraft guns . . . we knew that there were two NVA regiments right astride the border in the area we had to go through." Enemy resistance, however, turned out to be remarkably light. The enemy had anticipated the assault and had beat a hasty retreat westward away from the sanctuaries. "God only knows where they went after

spotting all the tracks [armored personnel carriers] and tanks we brought up for this operation," said an American officer. "I don't see how they could have missed all the commotion, and if I were them, I'd get lost." Casualty statistics for the first two days reflected the fact that the bulk of enemy troops, despite scattered contact with U.S. forces, had evaded the American encirclement. By May 3, MACV reported only 8 Americans killed and 32 wounded—a low number for such a large operation. Enemy losses were 476 killed, of which 160 were victims of tactical air and helicopter gunship attacks.

Despite the light resistance, the American assault force did not breeze through the Fishhook. Besides danger from mines and booby traps, Americans endured delaying attacks by small enemy units. Units of the 11th Armored Cav took small-arms and rocket fire three kilometers inside Cambodia. In return, they blasted the enemy's position with machine guns and tank cannons, while tactical bombers pounded it from the air. When the smoke cleared, fifty dead Communists lay sprawled on the ground. This type of brief skirmish was typical of combat throughout the operation. Only on rare occasions, as at Snuol, would a sizable Communist unit be found entrenched and unwilling to yield without a fight.

Snuol

Brigadier General Starry's armored cavalry was ordered on May 1 to proceed to Snuol, where a battalion or more of NVA regulars was reported to be dug in for a "big battle." Starry began deploying his men around the town. As a column of his tanks traversed a nearby plantation, the NVA's guns began booming. NVA antiaircraft fire from an airstrip on Snuol's outskirts peppered American helicopters circling above the American tanks. Starry's column sped toward the airstrip. Said Starry, "We almost ran into a gun pit with our track during the attack on the airfield. The sergeant major, myself, and the crew dismounted, captured the gun and the people in the pit, and then they opened up on us from the town."

A grenade thrown from another nearby bunker wounded Starry, and he was medevacked. Lieutenant Colonel Grail Brookshire assumed command. Brookshire sent a reconnaissance unit of armored assault vehicles and Sheridan reconnaissance vehicles into the southern portion of Snuol. He said to his men, "This is a reconnaissance mission in force to find out what's in there and . . . to take the town without destroying it." Brookshire added, "Now if you take heavy fire and look like you've got prepared positions, back 'em out—shoot and back out." As nearly one hundred armored vehicles entered Snuol, they met a hail of small-arms, automatic-weapons, and mortar fire. The Americans backed off and fired their cannons, volley after volley. Buildings crumbled or burned. After two days, incessant American bombardment, including

Preceding page. At a rubber plantation near the town of Snuol, seven kilometers inside the Cambodian border, smoke from a Communist rocket-propelled grenade rises in front of a tank from the U.S. 11th Armored Cavalry Regiment.

napalm and rocket fire from jets screeching overhead, reduced Snuol to rubble.

During the previous night most of the enemy had slipped out. There was no way of ascertaining casualties, since the enemy had carried away all of its dead and wounded. A captured NVA antiaircraft machine gunner who was there said he was ordered to stand and fight off the tank force to the last. The only bodies in the streets were those of four dead civilians, a young girl among them. No Americans were killed but five were wounded. "We didn't want to blow this town away," said Brookshire. "But it was a hub of North Vietnamese activity and we had no choice but to take it." American troops used a new term after that engagement—"to snuol" meant to obliterate.

The City

On D-day for the Fishhook assault, Major General Elvy Roberts, commander of the 1st Air Cavalry Division, had been optimistic. "We think we have them in a bag," he assured reporters. "In a day or two we'll reach inside the bag and see what we have." After two days of sporadic contact, Roberts realized the bag would not contain many NVA and VC soldiers. But it did contain a large hoard of Communist supplies and materiel. From day one American troops uncovered scattered enemy weapons and ammunition caches. Along Route 7, a platoon from the 1st Air Cav found a stash of 2,000 rifles wrapped in plastic and packed in boxes. An American officer noted that this was a pittance compared to the amount of materiel that intelligence had indicated was stored throughout the Fishhook: "Things are happening so fast around here that we just haven't had the time or the manpower available to go in and clean all these caches out. We've gone in here so fast that we know we've passed a lot of stuff up."

American search methods resembled those used in Vietnam. Fire support bases were established throughout the Fishhook, each of them used as a center of operations by exploring infantry units supported by artillery. In Cambodia, however, the emphasis of search and destroy was on caches, not enemy troops. "We're not body counters on this operation," said Colonel Carter Clarke, commander of the 2d Brigade, 1st Air Cavalry. "We're cache counters." Seeking out caches required aerial and ground

American troops of the U.S. 9th Infantry Division, exchange fire with enemy soldiers during the U.S. incursion into Cambodia.

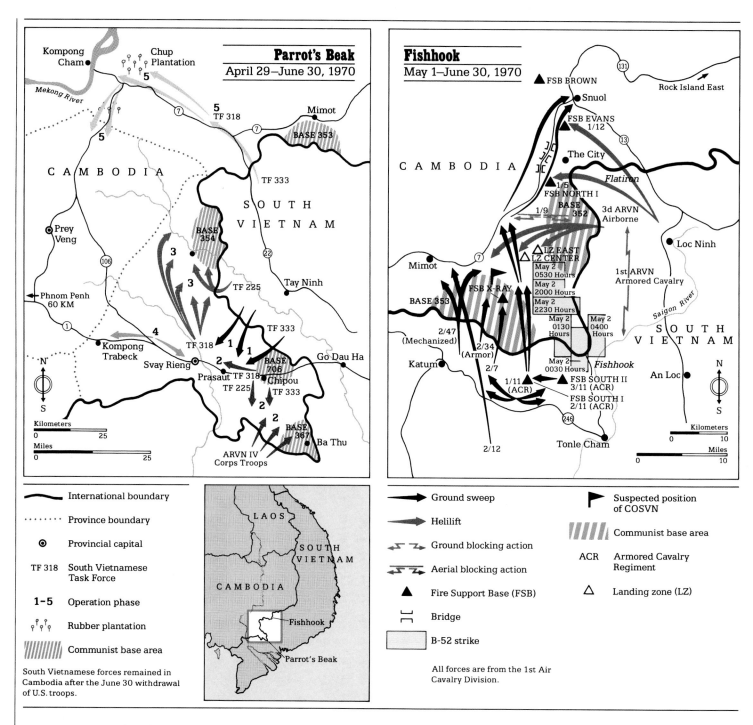

Parrot's Beak
April 29–June 30, 1970

Kompong Cham
Chup Plantation
Mekong River
5
TF 318
Mimot
BASE 353
CAMBODIA
TF 333
SOUTH VIETNAM
Prey Veng
BASE 354
3
3
TF 225
Tay Ninh
Phnom Penh 60 KM
4
TF 318
1
1
TF 333
Kompong Trabeck
2
Svay Rieng
BASE 706
Go Dau Ha
Prasaut TF 318 Chipou
TF 225
TF 333
2
2
BASE 367
Ba Thu
ARVN IV Corps Troops

Kilometers 0 25
Miles 0 25

Fishhook
May 1–June 30, 1970

FSB BROWN
Snuol
Rock Island East
FSB EVANS 1/12
CAMBODIA
The City
Flatiron
1/5
FSB NORTH I
1/9
BASE 352
3d ARVN Airborne
LZ EAST
LZ CENTER
May 2 0530 Hours
Loc Ninh
Mimot
May 2 2000 Hours
1st ARVN Armored Cavalry
FSB X-RAY
BASE 353
May 2 2230 Hours
May 2 0130 Hours
May 2 0400 Hours
2/47 (Mechanized)
2/34 (Armor)
May 2 0030 Hours
Fishhook
SOUTH VIETNAM
Katum
2/7
An Loc
1/11 (ACR)
FSB SOUTH II 3/11 (ACR)
FSB SOUTH I 2/11 (ACR)
Tonle Cham
2/12

Kilometers 0 10
Miles 0 10

International boundary
.... Province boundary
◉ Provincial capital
TF 318 South Vietnamese Task Force
1–5 Operation phase
🌳🌳🌳 Rubber plantation
▨ Communist base area

South Vietnamese forces remained in Cambodia after the June 30 withdrawal of U.S. troops.

LAOS
SOUTH VIETNAM
CAMBODIA
Fishhook
Parrot's Beak

→ Ground sweep
➡ Helilift
Ground blocking action
Aerial blocking action
▲ Fire Support Base (FSB)
⊐ Bridge
▢ B-52 strike

⊢ Suspected position of COSVN
▨ Communist base area
ACR Armored Cavalry Regiment
△ Landing zone (LZ)

All forces are from the 1st Air Cavalry Division.

reconnaissance. "Pink teams," each consisting of a light observation helicopter—an LOH or "Loach"—and an AH-1G Cobra gunship surveyed an area. The Loach skimmed low over the jungle with the Cobra flying above it for fire protection. If the Loach spied a cache it radioed a firebase for a ground reconnaissance unit. If a ground recon unit had trouble reaching the site, round-the-clock artillery strikes hit the area to prevent the enemy from removing the cache before it could be captured.

While the 11th Armored Cavalry was leveling Snuol, a battalion of the 1st Air Cavalry, led by Lieutenant Colonel James Anderson, was set down on Highway 7 to prowl for caches reported to be in the area. Anderson sent GIs with interpreters to question local Cambodian villagers about

Communist activity. "Shortly after," said Anderson, "they told us there was a large facility to the north about one kilometer. It turned out to be about three or four kilometers from where we landed and in dense jungle." Anderson called in air force jets to carve away at the jungle cover. The Loaches then flew in low to look for clues. A sharp-eyed pilot, Warrant Officer James Cyrus, finally spotted it: "We didn't see anything at first. Then I spotted one hootch well camouflaged. Unless you were at tree-top level, it would be invisible."

Anderson dispatched a company to the sighting. Loach pilots guided it. Slashing through the thick jungle the company reached the cache late that afternoon. This time there were many enemy troops on guard. But they seemed in no mood to fight. "That first night we set up ambushes," recalls Anderson. "There was all kinds of movement—men just trying to get out of the area. I remember one case when an ambush on a trail caught five NVA, killing three. . . . Two ran into another ambush a little further up the trail and a fourth one was killed. A little further on, the last guy ran into another ambush and just said the hell with it and surrendered."

When Anderson's men started poking around the tangled thickets the next day, they traced the outlines of an elaborate camp. Concealed under three layers of jungle foliage was a trail connecting clumps of lean-to huts. Outside these log huts, three-foot-deep trench lines led to bunkers. Further exploration down neatly laid out bamboo walkways and bicycle paths revealed that this was no ordinary cache site. Following the street signs, crossing bridges, the soldiers uncovered truck repair facilities, a lumber yard, recreation halls, and even a swimming pool. More extensive searching over the next week unearthed 182 separate stocks of weapons and ammunition, 18 mess halls, a firing range, a chicken and pig farm, and cavernous, log-covered bunkers. "This area is for the people who support the liberation of South Vietnam," read a sign over one bunker. After counting at least 400 thatched huts, storage sheds, and bunkers, each packed with medical supplies, foodstuffs, and clothing, the soldiers dubbed the two-square-mile complex "The City." In one hut were 480 rifles, in another 120,000 rounds of ammunition. A delighted Anderson remarked, "We are just beginning to scratch the surface."

Rock Island East

U.S. intelligence analysts at first thought The City was the largest base and supply complex along the Cambodian frontier. But a thorough search of another area showed them wrong. Some forty kilometers to the northeast a battalion of the 1st Air Cav, under Lieutenant Colonel Francis Ianni, discovered an installation that made The City "look like a suburb," according to one American. This cache also had numerous NVA defenders, and they were in a fighting temper.

On the morning of May 6 Ianni ordered Captain James Johnson's Company D down a jungle trail where helicopters had seen four trucks and thirty to forty NVA. As Company D scouted the trail, the NVA ambushed it and pinned it down. "We hit them with everything we had," said Lieutenant Timothy Holden, "[but] I had seven men killed and twenty wounded." Finally, just before dusk, Johnson rallied his men to their feet for an assault against the enemy's position. Taken by surprise the NVA scattered, leaving Company D a splendid trophy: the biggest cache ever captured in the war. The soldiers named it "Rock Island East" after Rock Island Arsenal in Illinois. It contained more than 6.5 million rounds of antiaircraft am-

munition, a half million rifle rounds, thousands of rockets, several GM trucks, and even telephone switchboards.

While many caches could be spotted from the air, others were hidden so well it was difficult even for ground reconnaissance to find them. A U.S. commander explained: "North Vietnamese soldiers took extreme pains in hiding large quantities of supplies in heavily jungled areas. American troops in some cases have actually found caches only by stumbling over them. A 140-ton arms and ammunition depot, for example, was found when a soldier tripped over a piece of metal covered with dirt. The metal covered a hole, an entrance to a mammoth cavern." Whether by detective work or sheer luck, American soldiers uncovered caches of everything imaginable from Soviet and Chinese weapons to Japanese textiles to British shovels, even Porsche and Mercedes Benz automobiles. A GI said, "I thought that the North Vietnamese were hurting until I saw all these supplies." To Captain William Paris, "it was kind of like Christmas."

One trophy the Americans did not capture was the legendary COSVN. For years COSVN had conjured among Americans visions of an enemy Pentagon. It was difficult to conceive of such an important command and logistical operation as anything but a large, fortified, stationary structure manned by military brass, intelligence units, and a variety of support personnel. President Nixon and other military and civilian officials conveyed this "Pentagon East" notion to the press and public. *Newsweek*, for instance, described COSVN as a "fortified, reinforced concrete bunker with a staff of 2,300 organized into an elaborate series of bureaucratic sections." Skeptics in the CIA and MACV repeatedly challenged this conception. An intelligence analyst, ridiculing the idea of a discrete, consolidated headquarters, described COSVN as "a kind of permanent floating crap game of Communist leaders," a highly mobile, widely dispersed operation.

On the eve of the incursion some MACV officers still thought they had pinpointed COSVN's location in the Fishhook at the precise map coordinates "X-ray Tango Four Four Nine Six." It was a false lead. Later, at The City, General Shoemaker affirmed "It [COSVN] is here, and we are in the heart of it." Neither bunkers nor documents nor equipment could be found to prove it. Probing elsewhere turned up no COSVN either. After weeks of tracking the Communists' elusive headquarters, an American intelligence analyst deadpanned, "We're still looking for the guy in the COSVN T-shirt."

A race against time

The magnitude of the booty bagged by Americans elated Washington. An inventory taken just two weeks into the operation listed 4,793 small arms; 730 mortars and other crew-served weapons; 3,254,963 rounds of rifle ammunition; 7,285 rockets; 124 trucks; and 2,182,000 pounds of rice.

And the welter of other Communist depots promised to yield much more. President Nixon was ecstatic from the very first day's reports of the operation's success. On May 1, at a Pentagon meeting, he made what he has described as an "uncharacteristic on-the-spot decision . . . to take out all of those sanctuaries." "Make whatever plans are necessary," Nixon ordered the Pentagon, "and then just do it. Knock them all out so that they can't be used against us. Ever." Soon American troops were opening up new fronts all along the Cambodian border. In the second week of May, units of the 25th Infantry Division invaded an area forty-eight kilometers southwest of the Fishhook known as Dog's Head. To the north in the Se San region that same week, sixty kilometers west of Pleiku, two brigades of the U.S. 4th Division killed 184 enemy soldiers in eight days of contact. Fresh incursions gradually raised the American troop level in Cambodia to a peak of 30,000, involving most of the major units stationed in the western provinces of South Vietnam—the 1st Air Cavalry, the 25th Infantry, and the 9th Infantry divisions.

Cleaning up the caches

While expanding the Cambodian front, President Nixon stipulated that there should be no U.S. penetration on the ground in Cambodia beyond thirty-five kilometers. This constraint angered American commanders. They worried that the Communists, who had retreated westward, would use the space beyond the limit to organize counterattacks. The president also imposed a deadline of June 30 for pulling all U.S. forces out of Cambodia. This frustrated American commanders even more than the thirty-five-kilometer limit. Field commanders charged with extracting thousands of tons of Communist materiel needed either more time or additional troops to do the job. They got neither. Resigned to their deadline, American units began cleaning out and devastating as much of the sanctuaries as possible. CIDG troops, Regional Forces, and special stevedore companies were brought in to assist in shipping Communist supplies back to South Vietnam. A steady stream of ground vehicles moved in and out of Cambodia. Company B of the 20th Engineer Brigade's 588th Battalion, 79th Engineer Group, kept Highway 4, one of two major routes into Cambodia, clear of obstructions. Bulldozers cut more than twenty kilometers of jungle trail and cleared almost 2,000 acres of jungle, including landing zones for the nonstop helicopter traffic flying captured materiel to South Vietnam. In two months, division support command for the 1st Air Cavalry alone had flown out by helicopter the highest tonnage in the unit's history, over 24,933 tons in 6,436 sorties.

What could not be transported had to be destroyed. The engineers, besides bulldozing thousands of reinforced bunkers, performed extensive demolitions operations. Here, too, time could be a crucial factor. Helicopter pilot

Geoffrey Boehm remembers working with an eleven-man demolitions team on a huge cache: "We had two ships to pull the demolitions team out after they set all the dynamite to blow it up. Because it had a weak engine, the first ship only picked up four men, leaving seven for me. There was no way I could pull seven out. The detonation had already been timed, so I couldn't just take out five and leave two." Boehm chose to wait for the other helicopter to drop off its four men and return, then both helicopters went in "to pick up the remaining members of the demolitions crew. We made it by four minutes. We finally got some altitude when the whole thing blew up like an atom bomb."

For American combat troops-turned-stevedores the task of emptying the sanctuaries was backbreaking. After the first discovery of major caches, American soldiers had exulted and, amid an almost festival atmosphere, conducted souvenir hunts and swapped prizes. "When they fight and find it," observed a colonel, "it's rightfully theirs. It's morale boosting." At The City a brisk souvenir trade developed among soldiers, helicopter pilots, and truck drivers: a case of beer for a Soviet rifle. A news correspondent wrote that it was not long before The City had "a surplus of beer." The Americans joked about invading at last the long forbidden sanctuaries. One grunt remarked to his sergeant, "I am not supposed to be here sarge, I forgot my passport." Another inscribed on the brim of his boonie hat, "Ohio, Vietnam, Cambodia."

After their euphoria wore off, the soldiers faced the drudgery of packing and loading in the stifling heat. At The City beneath a makeshift sign reading "Your tax dollars at work," soldiers labored daily until dark. "Here these guys were gripin' every five minutes about wantin' to get out of Vietnam," said Sergeant Lee Broome. "Now we're in Cambodia and they're gripin' every five minutes about wantin' to get back to Vietnam." One weary GI consoled himself by pointing out that, while "they're just like the same bunkers we've been finding for months [in Vietnam], over here they're full of equipment."

The soldiers could be thankful for one other thing. The enemy's abandonment of the sanctuaries had held combat—and therefore casualties—to a minimum. Yet, though relieved of battlefield pressure, the toiling soldiers worried about security at night. American perimeter security and night ambushes aside, it was eerie after dark amid the sprawling enemy installations. Soldiers had the nagging feeling that at any moment the enemy would pop out of bunkers, huts, or tunnels in ambush. A 1st Air Cavalry trooper complained, "There are too many gooks in Cambodia. I just didn't feel right there; it gave me a kind of spooky feeling, especially since we found all that stuff in the caches. They'll be coming back to find out what's left and they'll be coming in mad!"

Throughout the Cambodian incursion the performance of U.S. forces in the Fishhook grabbed most of the headlines in American newspapers. The Parrot's Beak in-

"The City." Troops from the 1st Air Cav haul away some of the thousands of weapons captured at the huge enemy cache using carts and bamboo sidewalks constructed by the enemy.

Soldiers of the 1st Air Cav examine a few of the 165 crates of 51MM and 57MM recoilless rifle ammunition found in this bunker at The City.

A soldier from the 11th Armored Cavalry Regiment holds up his "trophy" of the U.S. invasion into the Fishhook, a Cambodian flag.

vasion, which except for about one hundred U.S. advisers was a South Vietnamese show, attracted much less media attention. Official eyes in Washington and Saigon, however, were closely monitoring the South Vietnamese. They had their orders from President Nixon: "bite off" the Parrot's Beak.

The assault into the Parrot's Beak on April 29 marked the first major incursion into Cambodia. The tactics were designed to envelop the Parrot's Beak and the adjacent Angel's Wing area, which knifes into South Vietnam and had served as a principal enemy staging area for the 1968 Tet offensive. The 8,700-man ARVN assault force was formed from many of South Vietnam's finest units including two armored cavalry squadrons from III Corps and two from the 25th and 5th Infantry divisions, an infantry regiment from the 25th Infantry Division, and four Ranger Battalions of the 2d Ranger Group. Crossing into the Parrot's Beak from III Corps and from IV Corps, the ARVN task force had three objectives in the Parrot's Beak: to engage in battle the estimated 10,000 to 20,000 enemy troops operating there; to search and destroy base facilities and

caches; and to sweep and clear Highway 1 and the Mekong River, the main land and water routes between Phnom Penh and South Vietnam.

Lieutenant General Do Cao Tri, commanding general of III Corps, commanded the ARVN invasion force. Tri cut a dashing figure in camouflage suit, a black-starred cap and sunglasses, and a shiny snub-nosed Smith and Wesson .38-caliber revolver in a glossy leather shoulder holster. Rarely without his pipe and swagger stick, Tri fancied himself immune to death on the battlefield. American officers liked the brash, aggressive style that made him so capable a combat leader and a symbol of ARVN's new spirit. "Before, if the enemy is in South Vietnam, we destroyed them," General Tri said. "Now, if they are in Cambodian territory, we strike them also," he added. His élan affected his officers too. When told of their Parrot's Beak assignment, an ARVN general remarked, "I could see the delight in their eyes."

When Tri's task force swooped down by helicopter and columns of ARVN tanks and armored cars tore into the Parrot's Beak, they found enemy troops waiting for them.

WELCOME TO CAMBODIA

COURTESY OF

A 588TH ENGR BN

95 ENGR CO

A column of the 1st Squadron, 11th Armored Cavalry Division, rumbles back toward South Vietnam past a sign posted by the 588th Engineering Battalion at the beginning of the incursion.

During their first two days in Cambodia, the ARVN units had several sharp encounters with Communist troops entrenched in bunkers. The enemy had foreseen the attack and conducted a stubborn delaying action. After Tri's tanks had rolled within forty-five meters of a VC bunker complex, his troops, according to the general, engaged in "one of the most exciting battles I have ever seen. Our men fought the Communists in hand-to-hand combat, using rifles, knives, and bayonets. When it was over, we had killed more than fifty of the enemy, while we suffered only five wounded."

Despite its opening flurry of stiff combat, the operation soon became a replay of the Fishhook. The mass of enemy troops had been evacuated only two days after the operation began. Of the 375 enemy deaths by May 1, 300 of them were from tactical air strikes. ARVN casualties were put at 30 killed and 70 wounded. Against generally soft resistance, ARVN met its first objective swiftly, advancing west toward the provincial capital of Svay Rieng and opening Highway 1. Directed by U.S. advisers, U.S. artillery firing from inside South Vietnam and fire from American helicopter gunships patrolling overhead enabled the

South Vietnamese to occupy speedily the lower half of Parrot's Beak.

Soon after its initiation, the operation settled into a search and destroy mode. ARVN units forayed into fortified enemy bases and caches. An additional 4,300 ARVN troops of the 9th Infantry Division, five armored cavalry squadrons, and one Ranger group arrived to assist them. Although their cache and base finds did not rival those found in the Fishhook, ARVN troops claimed an impressive tally of supplies and equipment. At Ba Thu, fifty kilometers west of Saigon, ARVN troops seized the center for outfitting and retraining NVA/VC units. The base complex covered ten square kilometers with hundreds of houses and bunkers connected by dozens of roads. There were numerous cafés, shops, and refreshment stands to serve enemy troops. An astonished American officer who flew over Ba Thu likened it to the U.S. Army headquarters base at Long Binh in South Vietnam.

As ARVN troops razed enemy houses, bunkers, and warehouses, they savored one of the sweetest victories in their now-twenty-year-old war. The Communists, as one American put it, "had bugged out." A smiling General Tri,

Near the town of Svay Rieng in the Parrot's Beak, a South Vietnamese troop column (center) heads past a U.S. heavy artillery emplacement.

South Vietnamese lieutenant general Do Cao Tri, the "Patton of Parrot's Beak," confers with South Vietnamese officers and two American advisers at the town of Kompong Chak in the Parrot's Beak.

praised by *Time* magazine as the "Patton of Parrot's Beak," told an American journalist the operation was "going very well." And "if the VC get too close," he threatened, waving his swagger stick, "I use my stick on them." Tri's men were also triumphant and lighthearted as they freely plundered the enemy's stores of goods. Men of the 10th ARVN Armored Cavalry Regiment decked themselves in baby-blue hats lifted from a cache along with several tons of rice and medicine. They strutted about mocking the Vietcong. Others gleefully loaded their trucks and tanks with formerly "Communist" chickens, motorbikes, and bicycles.

Nevertheless South Vietnamese soldiers experienced some somber, even anguished moments. At the little town of Prasaut they found themselves in the place where on April 10 Cambodian soldiers had murdered ninety Vietnamese civilians. The soldiers gathered in the center of Prasaut. No Cambodian voices could be heard. Not even an animal moved about. "Where were they killed? I would like to see the place," asked a distraught ARVN soldier. Some soldiers viewed the scene in a nearby field with mournful respect for their fellow Vietnamese. "I am proud to be here," murmured one. Others expressed hatred for Cambodians. A few swore revenge. "Now is the time for the killers to pay in blood," an angry soldier scrawled on the walls of a shattered store. This scene was repeated in other towns where Cambodian soldiers had earlier mistreated or killed ethnic Vietnamese civilians or sent them to internment camps along the Mekong.

Downstream to safety

Revenge could not help Vietnamese already killed by Cambodian persecution, but there were those tens of thousands of Vietnamese living in Cambodia who could now be evacuated to safety. Previously Saigon had been unable to do anything but protest the mistreatment of its compatriots. Now, with his task force in Cambodia, President Thieu arranged with Cambodia's Lon Nol to repatriate as many Vietnamese as were willing to leave. On May 8 a South Vietnamese rescue flotilla of one hundred vessels sailed up the Mekong to Phnom Penh. There and at other pickup points on the river they intended to take on board as many refugees as possible. In addition to its humanitarian aspect, the operation was to clear the upper Mekong of Communist troops and to retake a ferry crossing at Neak Luong the Communists had overrun on May 3. Accompanying the flotilla were 3,200 South Vietnamese sailors and marines and thirty U.S. riverine patrol boats in support.

The mission encountered little resistance. At various points South Vietnamese Marines landed to sweep the banks. In a combined assault with a brigade of Cambodians, the town of Neak Luong, from which NVA troops fled, was easily occupied. Meanwhile tattered hordes of

Vietnamese, clinging to what few belongings they could carry, anxiously awaited the boats. The Vietnamese farmers and fishermen of Lo Gach, for example, stood on a muddy Mekong beach, their wives wailing in sorrow to have to leave their village. At Phnom Penh, over 50,000 Vietnamese, crammed in "regroupment" camps, sought passage on the flotilla. Mostly craftsmen and shopkeepers, they were forbidden by the Cambodian government to sell their homes or cars, which were seized for distribution to "needy and deserving Cambodian families." Those Vietnamese who preferred not to repatriate were forcibly expelled by the Cambodians. Cambodian soldiers gave Vietnamese residents at the town of Miche only two hours to pack.

When the flotilla reached Phnom Penh on May 11, every vessel quickly filled with refugees. The *Vung Tau* and her sister ship, the *Cam Ranh*, carried 1,700 apiece. South Vietnamese officers were fearful that Communist soldiers would fire upon the overcrowded vessels. "If fighting starts, we'll have to shoot back," fretted an officer. "Heaven help the people on the deck. One rocket and we'll have a hundred people lying dead. . . ." Once, at the halfway mark of the return journey, the *Vung Tau* sounded general quarters. Sailors rushed to their guns, pointing them toward enemy troops sighted on shore. But the enemy did not shoot, and the flotilla safely reached Saigon. A South Vietnamese sailor commented, "This is a tragedy for all Vietnamese. Even the Vietcong must be thinking this is about the saddest thing that has happened to our nation, even after twenty years of war."

Ironically, after rescuing Vietnamese from the Cambodians, the South Vietnamese were asked by Phnom Penh to rescue Cambodians from the Vietnamese Communists. The NVA had surrounded Kompong Cham, a market town 70 kilometers northwest of Phnom Penh and the site of the Cambodian Military Region I headquarters. Cambodian troops alone were unable to reinforce or relieve Kompong Cham's 1,000-man garrison. South Vietnam's General Tri took on the job. On May 23 his column of 10,000 ARVN troops with tanks and APCs roared west on Route 7 and southwest on Route 15 to Kompong Cham. Their first obstacle was the Chup rubber plantation southwest of the city. According to intelligence, a Vietcong regiment had been occupying the 180-square-kilometer plantation as a base. Anticipating a battle, Tri asserted, "This is a hunting game between my forces and the Communists. If the Communists stand and fight, we will destroy them."

Preparatory air strikes left the Chup plantation in flames. When Tri's column moved in on May 24, there was no VC resistance. The familiar pattern of Communist evasion continued. General Tri informed Chup's French managers he would have to confiscate all materials the enemy might subsequently find useful. The indiscriminate confiscation by ARVN soldiers verged on looting. They

Vietnamese refugees rescued from Cambodia by a U.S. and South Vietnamese flotilla arrive in South Vietnam.

Captured Vietcong soldiers await their fate at an ARVN fire support base in the Parrot's Beak area in May 1970.

stripped air conditioners, refrigerators, and personal possessions from the plantation houses, then moved on. Two days later the ARVN lifted the siege of Kompong Cham, having killed ninety-eight of the enemy.

The Communists menaced other strategic Cambodian cities. On June 13 they overran Kompong Speu. Along Highway 4 southwest of Phnom Penh, Kompong Speu overlooked the only route from the capital to Sihanoukville. All of Cambodia's petroleum came through the port, so the loss of Kompong Speu would enable the Lon Nol regime's Communist opponents to squeeze dry Phnom Penh's fuel supply.

Lon Nol asked the ARVN forces to reclaim Kompong Speu. A 4,000-man ARVN tank force sped to the aid of 2,000 Cambodian assault troops. This time it looked as if the Communists would be encircled and trapped, but when the allies drove into the city, they found it deserted. The enemy forces had wriggled free to the south. Again denied their prey, South Vietnamese troops fell to vandalizing and looting shops. They shot off locks, stealing whatever they could from flashlights to sewing machines. Some even forced civilians at gunpoint to empty their pockets and hand over jewelry and watches. The ARVN commander Tran Ba Di later compelled his troops to restore much of what they had stolen.

These were but the highlights of ARVN's varied mobile operations in Cambodia during May and June. South Vietnamese forces there had swollen to more than 48,000. Their offensive kept the Communists off balance and forced them out of their sanctuaries. A few small Communist units did filter back into the Parrot's Beak, but their harassment attacks did not interfere with ARVN's search and destruction of the sanctuaries. Instead, drenching monsoon rains caused the winding down of the ARVN offensive in mid-June. President Thieu in May had affirmed his forces would not be bound by the June 30 deadline Washington had imposed on American forces. "We have no deadline, no limits, when there is a target we will strike it." For now, as General Tri stated, "the North Vietnamese are going to have a hell of a time" trying to recover from the damage inflicted on their sanctuaries.

The Americans, who because of President Nixon's thirty-five-kilometer limit could not penetrate as deeply as the ARVN, spent much of May and June clearing border sanctuaries. In mid-May the enemy had made some pretense of counterattack. At Firebase Brown in the northern Fishhook, NVA troops launched a night attack with a large-scale charge. The Americans killed fifty-two of them, many at close range. Other firebases reported similar incidents. "For weeks, we really had them going," an American observed. "But now it looks like the units we haven't messed with are beginning to pull themselves together. There's going to be more fighting, you can bet on that." But the monsoon rains brought offensive activity by both sides to a standstill in early June. On June 28 the last

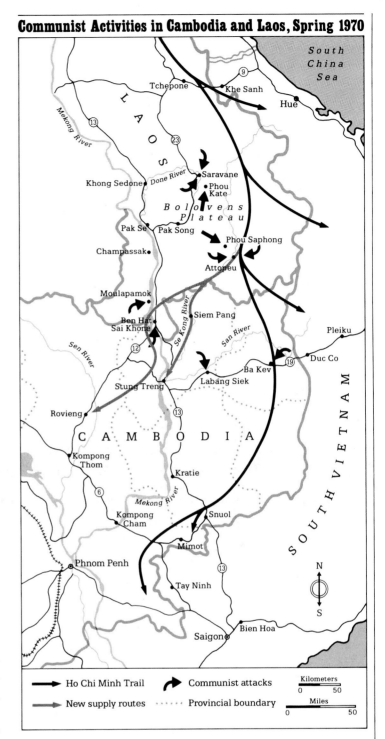

Communist Activities in Cambodia and Laos, Spring 1970

American armored vehicles churned down the Fishhook's muddy roads toward South Vietnam. The U.S. bid farewell with a hammering air and artillery strike against the enemy's sanctuaries.

Mixed results

The incursion by 30,000 American and 48,000 ARVN troops was a highly successful maneuver. Using the usual means of measurement—enemy casualties and captured material—U.S. officials estimated the results were ten times greater than the preceding twelve months of operations in

Vietnam itself. The allies captured enemy ammunition—15 million rounds and 143,000 rockets—that could have supplied all NVA and VC in II, III, and IV Corps for more than ten months. The other statistics were equally spectacular: 14 million pounds of rice, enough to feed all enemy combat battalions in South Vietnam for four months; 22,892 individual weapons, sufficient to equip seventy-four NVA infantry battalions; 435 vehicles and 11,700 bunkers destroyed; and 199,552 antiaircraft rounds, 5,487 mines, and 62,000 grenades. Although the enemy for the most part had retreated, the allies still claimed 11,349 Communists killed. The CIA, however, called the body count "highly suspect." "Many of the alleged casualties," it stated, "were the result of air and artillery strikes, [making] a precise body count so difficult [and resulting] in civilian and non-combatants . . . being included in the loss figure."

The failure to find COSVN was something of an embarrassment for the Americans. It was President Nixon, not the military, who designated COSVN as a key objective of the Cambodian incursion. Defense Secretary Laird recalls, "Right up to the time he gave that speech I was pleading to have that out because COSVN was never a single headquarters . . . . So again the American people were misled by not having a real understanding of what it was about. But the speech was made and COSVN was listed as a major military target."

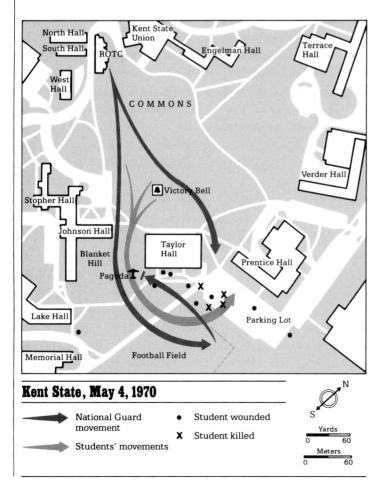

Kent State, May 4, 1970

→ National Guard movement
→ Students' movements
● Student wounded
X Student killed

Yards
0 — 60

Meters
0 — 60

If the Parrot's Beak was a test of the feasibility of America's Vietnamization policy, the ARVN's aggressive mobility and thorough searching was an encouraging sign. Looting at the Chup plantation and Kompong Speu, however, did somewhat mar their record.

The political controversy generated at home and abroad by the Cambodian incursion quickly overshadowed its impressive military results. The day after President Nixon's televised announcement of the invasion on April 30, public protests disrupted colleges throughout the country. In Schenectady, New York, Union College students burned Richard Nixon in effigy, then blocked downtown traffic. One thousand University of Cincinnati students marched downtown and staged a ninety-minute demonstration. Similar outbursts occurred at colleges in Georgia, Wisconsin, Texas, California, and almost every other state. At President Nixon's alma mater, Whittier College, at least a third of the student body denounced him. Before May was over, 57 percent of the country's 1,350 campuses experienced strikes against classes and protests involving 4.5 million students.

Nixon's resumption of the bombing of North Vietnam, simultaneous with the Fishhook operation, appeared to confirm for critics a pattern of escalation, perhaps even an attempt to win a military victory the president had repeatedly foresworn. Republican Senator George Aiken of Vermont said he "did not think the president would do [it]." Democratic Senator Lee Metcalf of Montana declared, "Nixon has made it his war." After the bombing of North Vietnam, Senate Majority Leader Mike Mansfield asserted that "there is without question a step-up in the fighting, which means in plain English, an escalation of the war."

Tragedy at Kent State

May 1 was Derby Day at the sprawling, modern campus of Ohio's Kent State University. For the 21,000 students there the annual observance was one of the highlights of springtime. Members of the university's many fraternities traditionally walked about campus wearing derbies, challenging sorority girls to chase and catch them. The girls' reward for their efforts was a kiss.

This Derby Day was unlike any before. Although fraternity men were out in their derbies, the atmosphere at Kent State was tense, anxious. Most students were caught up in the controversy generated by the U.S. Cambodian invasion and the demonstrations being organized to protest it. Until now Kent State had been described as an apathetic, basically conservative campus. Its student body had generally remained aloof from the antiwar dissent that had disrupted so many college campuses in the 1960s. Events of the first week of May 1970, however, were transforming Kent State's formerly placid campus into a tragic symbol of the nationwide rebellion against the Nixon administration and its handling of the war in Southeast Asia.

A Kent State student hurls a tear gas canister back toward National Guardsmen on May 4, 1970.

On Derby Day 300 students held a rally at noon to condemn the invasion and decided to organize a larger demonstration for the following Monday. Their hope for planning orderly, peaceful demonstrations ended over the weekend when a series of spontaneous riots broke out. Rampaging students tossed bottles and smashed windows in downtown Kent, then scuffled with police. The police quickly dispersed them with tear gas, but Kent city authorities and university administrators braced for further outbreaks of violence.

On Saturday night the university's ROTC facility was torched with the apparent approval of a large crowd that gathered to watch the fire and deliberately hampered fire fighters trying to extinguish it. Ohio's governor James Rhodes immediately dispatched National Guard troops to protect the fire fighters and confine the students to campus. Enraged by the students' wanton destruction, he also declared martial law. Rhodes decried Kent State's protesters as "worse than the Brown Shirts and the Communist element and also the night-riders and the vigilantes. They're the worst type that we harbor in America."

On Monday morning calm seemed to settle over the campus, even though an antiwar rally was planned for noon in defiance of the ban on student assemblies. Kent State administrators were relieved as students returned to classes and resumed normal activities. The sun shone brightly as the 900 tired National Guardsmen rested in the shade of tall oak and maple trees. At noon, about 1,000 students assembled on the commons, as planned. Another 2,000 students ringed the nearby sidewalks and buildings to observe them. When warned he was violating the martial law, a student replied, "We just couldn't believe they could tell us to leave. This is our campus."

The National Guard reacted quickly. From their staging area near the gutted ROTC building, officers in Jeeps approached the commons, ordering the students to "evacuate the commons area. You have no right to assemble." But the students refused and shouted back, "Pigs off campus! We don't want your war." Then, armed with loaded M1 rifles, .45-caliber pistols, and machine guns, detachments of guardsmen advanced toward the crowd. Jeering students hurled rocks and chunks of concrete at them. After the guardsmen fired a couple of rounds of tear gas into the crowd, some students fled toward Johnson Hall, a men's dormitory, and others to an area between Johnson Hall and Taylor Hall, the school's architecture building.

A detachment of about one hundred guardsmen from the 107th Armored Cavalry and the 145th Infantry Regiment pursued the students to the grounds between Johnson and Taylor halls. The detachment soon found itself backed against a chain-link fence and flanked by rock-throwing students cheered on by spectators. After exhausting their supply of tear gas against the students, these guardsmen retreated slowly up a hill toward Taylor Hall, most of them walking backward to face their pursuers. "Hot, angry, and disgusted at having been pinned against the fence," some of the beleaguered guardsmen knelt and aimed their rifles at students following them up the hill. A few moments later, one guardsman fired, then sixteen or seventeen more. Professor Charles Brill, standing nearby, recalls thinking "They're shooting blanks, they're shooting blanks. . . . Then I heard a chipping sound and a ping and I thought, my God, this is for real."

Terrified students flung themselves to the ground or ran for cover behind buildings or parked cars. A few just froze where they were standing. Amid the screams of fright one girl cried "My God, they're killing us!" The thirteen-second burst of bullets left four dead and ten wounded. Only two of the dead, Jeffrey Miller and Alison Krause, were demonstrators. William Schroeder, an ROTC enrollee, and Sandy Scheur were passers-by who had paused to watch the rally on their way to a class. One of the wounded, Dean Kahler of Canton, Ohio, was shot in the spine and paralyzed below the waist.

After ambulances had borne away the casualties, angry groups of students began massing to attack the guardsmen. A professor, Glenn Frank, pleaded with the troops to hold their fire and then urged the students to disperse: "I am begging you, if you don't disperse right now they're going to move in and it can only be a slaughter." The students acquiesced and pulled back. The confrontation was over.

There was considerable confusion over how and why the shootings had occurred, and many recriminations and accusations were investigated by the Ohio State Police, the National Guard, and the FBI. But it would take years to ascertain the details and determine the responsibility for the tragedy that sunny Monday afternoon at Kent State University.

The commander in chief

To many Americans the victims at Kent State became martyrs, galvanizing opposition to the war among the formerly undecided. On May 8 over 100,000 Americans, including thousands of recent converts to the protest movement, invaded Washington, D.C. Explained Michigan law

Nearing Taylor Hall, a group of guardsmen spin around, aim their guns, and begin firing into the crowd of students. Guardsmen later defended their action as self-defense.

student Carter Kethley, "My conscience wouldn't let me sit back knowing someone else was protesting for me . . . . I had to come. What has happened last week was kind of the last straw." The deaths at Kent State also engendered an "it's us or them" attitude, opening the way for more confrontation, more violence. At the University of Buffalo on May 7, police wounded four protesting students with buckshot. At Jackson State College in Mississippi, highway patrolmen shot two black student protesters. Thirty ROTC buildings were burned or bombed. Twenty-six schools witnessed clashes between students and police. At twenty-one universities, in California, Ohio, Illinois, and elsewhere, a state of emergency was declared and the National Guard ordered in to quell disturbances. A Kent State student rationalized the protesters' militant perspectives: "If . . . the governor thinks I'm a Nazi, what does it matter how I act."

Dramatic and widespread as the antiwar violence and turmoil were, a sizable portion of Americans voiced both their support for the president's decision to invade Cambodia and their anger toward antiwar protesters. A *Newsweek* poll of the second week of May showed 50 percent approval of President Nixon's decision. Those polled also deplored the protesters' tumultuous behavior. Fifty-eight percent blamed students for what happened at Kent State.

This backlash against antiwar activism had been building since 1967 and in the spring of 1970 finally made itself felt. The "silent majority" was no longer silent.

The Wisconsin legislature slashed half a billion dollars from the university budget because of upheaval on its Madison campus. California voters defeated a bond issue for the University of California medical schools. "I'm for education," said one voter, "but I won't vote bonds for the university. Until they get the campuses free from the infiltration by Red elements, you're wasting your money."

On May 20, 100,000 construction workers, stevedores, tradesmen, and office clerks marched through Manhattan to City Hall in a display of support for President Nixon. Although more than 4,000 police were on hand to prevent violence, the mood of the march was festive, much like a Fourth of July celebration. Hard-hats chanted "All the way U.S.A." or "America, love it or leave it." Banners proclaimed "God Bless America" and tens of thousands of people waved American flags. Bands kept them in step as the marchers sang "Those Caissons Go Rolling Along." Peter Brennan, head of the New York Building and Construction Trades Council, explained the marchers' show of solidarity with President Nixon: "Not because he's for labor, because he isn't, but because he's our president and we're hoping that he's right."

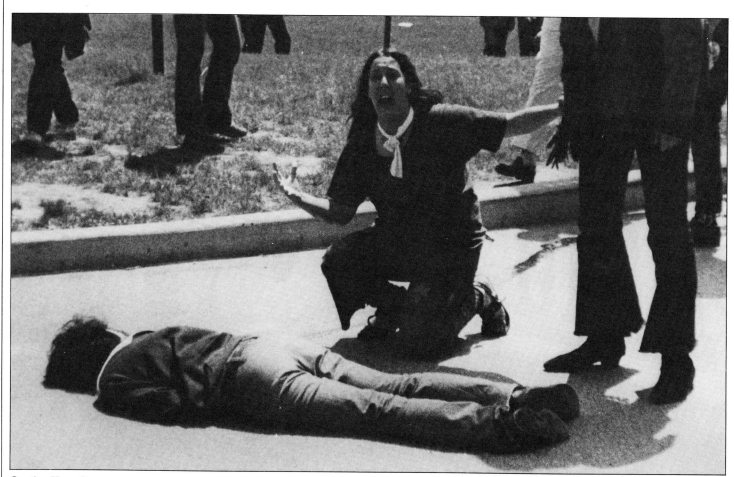

On the Kent State campus, a young woman looks up from the body of Jeffrey Glen Miller, a victim of a National Guardsman's bullet.

Even the GIs far away in Vietnam and Cambodia made their voices of support heard. Sergeant Paul Hodge, who had fought in Cambodia with Company B, 2d Battalion, 8th Cavalry, 1st Air Cavalry Division, told a *New York Times* correspondent, "I feel it was definitely worthwhile to do it. It kind of made me happy to capture weapons and ammunition that could be used against us." Sergeant Martin Cacioppo, who entered Cambodia on May 15 with Company D, 4th Battalion, 23d Mechanized Infantry, 25th Infantry Division, could not understand the demonstrations at home against the incursion: "We had been told by intelligence that there were big enemy troop build-ups in Cambodia and that they could come across the border anytime. So we really felt good, if you can describe it that way, about going across the border. I couldn't understand the protests. There were a lot of people who felt that way."

Helicopter pilot Geoffrey Boehm spoke for many of his comrades when he commended the president's Cambodian decision in a letter to his hometown newspaper: "I have personally extracted or witnessed the destruction of thousands of weapons, medical supplies, and tons of rice, along with millions of ammunition rounds. . . . We have definitely placed them [the enemy] in a bind and for every weapon and bullet we destroyed, these can no longer be used to destroy our men."

A president on trial

The issue of the rising violence and tension afflicting the country swiftly superceded the political and moral questions of who or what was right or wrong. America was being rent once more by the war in Southeast Asia. And the turmoil seemed a more immediate danger than the sanctuaries. Old wounds the president had promised to heal were reopening. Both the "silent majority" and those demonstrating against the Cambodian incursion turned to him to restore the consensus that had united them behind the withdrawal. Nixon, who had seen the incursion as a demonstration of his leadership in world affairs, now found his capacity to lead at home on trial.

Reconciliation was an aspect of leadership to which Nixon was neither inclined nor well suited. He had foreseen the protest, but the range and depth of the fury jolted him. Some years later former Defense Secretary Laird disclosed that "he was surprised, [but] I'm not sure he'd tell you that." Disregarding the warning of Secretary of the Interior Walter Hickel that "history shows that youth in its protest must be heard," the president had harsh words for impassioned students. En route to a Pentagon briefing he referred to protesters as "bums . . . blowing up campuses." Such acrimony appeared to many Americans, even those who disapproved of demonstrators, as excessively provoking. The father of Alison Krause, a student killed at Kent State, assailed the president's inflammatory statements: "May her death be on Nixon's back, called a bum because she disagreed with someone else's opinion." Although the president said later he "regretted" using the word "bums," the harm was done.

The president's continuing inability to address the concerns of protesters was evident during the May march on Washington. Late on the evening of May 9, he "impulsively" decided to take a ride out to the Lincoln Memorial and chat with a group of protesters, many of them college students, who had gathered there. In his memoirs Nixon described his conversation with several of the young activists he met: "I said that since some of them had come to Washington for the first time I hoped that while they were young they would never miss an opportunity to travel. . . . I told [them] that when they went to California . . . there was the greatest surfing beach in the world." He also talked about the importance of traveling in Europe and the Soviet Union. One student told a reporter afterward, "He really wasn't concerned with why we were here." Other students complained that Nixon "rambled aimlessly from subject to subject."

The president's awkward attempt at communication did more harm than good. He himself noted, "The newspapers reported that I had been unable to communicate with the young people I met, and that I had shown my insensitivity to their concerns by talking about inconsequential subjects like sports and surfing." For most Americans whether or not they supported the incursion, that the president could not effect a conciliation gradually eroded their confidence in him and, therefore, in the wisdom of his decision.

The grandiose nature of the president's original disclosure of the Cambodian incursion had inevitably exposed his credibility to risk. Nixon had also played up the imminence of a full-scale enemy offensive against South Vietnam from the sanctuaries, even after intelligence had indicated Communist troops were moving westward—not eastward—two days before operations began in the Fishhook. The enemy's preoperation retreat and the reports that the president had been forewarned of it increased public skepticism. In addition, Prime Minister Lon Nol's indignant complaints on May 1 that he had not been consulted about the incursion—contrary to what the president had intimated in his speech—caused many Americans to feel confused or, worse, deliberately deceived. According to a Harris poll, the net effect of his contradictory and inflated claims was that "Richard Nixon had been unable to persuade Americans that his method for deciding was sound, or that his statements about the decision believable, or that his conduct of the war, wise."

Nixon's handling of the incursion and its aftermath was also damaging America's credibility abroad. In contrast to his assertion that United States influence and prestige depended on swift action against the sanctuaries, the response of America's allies, in the words of British prime minister Harold Wilson, was one of "apprehension and anxiety." In June a secret public opinion poll conducted in four European and four Asian countries by the U.S. Information Service "showed a considerable decline in U.S. prestige—apparently as a result of the May–June operations in Cambodia—in almost all of the countries sampled."

On June 30, the deadline he set for the withdrawal of all U.S. ground forces from Cambodia, President Nixon announced the completion of the Fishhook and Parrot's Beak operations. The president also urged Americans to put behind them the divisiveness arising from the incursion and to join once more in seeking a resolution to U.S. involvement in Southeast Asia. "With American ground operations in Cambodia ended," he said, "we shall move forward with our plan to end the war in Vietnam and to secure the just peace on which all Americans are united."

As for the broader strategic objectives he had attached to the mission in Cambodia, Nixon thought the incursion would have several effects. He said they "will save Americans and allied forces in the future; will assure that the withdrawal of American troops from South Vietnam can proceed on schedule; will enable our progress of Vietnamization to continue on its current timetable; and should enhance the prospects for a just peace."

The widening battlefield

Developments in Southeast Asia, however, seemed to belie the president. They indicated not just more fighting but a widened battlefield. In Cambodia the enemy was quickly returning to reclaim and rebuild its border sanctuaries. According to Lieutenant General William McCaffrey, deputy commanding general-Vietnam, "although weakened by the allied operation in Cambodia, the North Vietnamese and Viet Cong are regrouping and resupplying themselves, man by man, piece by piece." Through May and June the North Vietnamese also appeared bent on trying to seize all of eastern Cambodia, thus consolidating their supply lines to South Vietnam. Although the North Vietnamese were also steadily moving westward to encircle Phnom Penh and isolate the capital from the rest of the country, their purpose was not to control all of Cambodia but to cripple the ability of the Lon Nol government to reestablish control over the eastern half of the country.

To compensate for the damage to their Cambodian sanctuaries, in the late spring and summer of 1970 the North Vietnamese also energetically began to expand their logistical and communications lines through Laos, enabling them once more to rush men and materiel down the Ho Chi Minh Trail into South Vietnam. On April 30, as American forces were driving into Cambodia, the North Vietnamese seized the strategic Laotian town of Attopeu on the Sekong River. On June 10 they overran the key provincial capital of Saravane in southern Laos, midway between the Cambodian and South Vietnamese border. The

Royal Laotian government appeared no more capable of resisting Communist aggression than that of Lon Nol in Cambodia.

Moreover, from the sanctuary the United States forces were forbidden by Washington to invade, across the DMZ in North Vietnam, the Communists were massing to continue the struggle in South Vietnam. Throughout May and June Communist forces launched attacks against South Vietnamese and American strong points in I Corps. On May 8, Communist units shelled sixty-four South Vietnamese and American installations near the provincial capitals of Tam Ky and Hoi An. On June 3 a South Vietnamese battalion was ordered into Firebase Tun Tavern, thirty-four kilometers south of the DMZ, to relieve an ARVN garrison besieged by a large enemy force. And on July 23, U.S. paratroopers had to abandon Firebase Ripcord near the A Shau Valley after three weeks of relentless North Vietnamese attacks. At Ripcord, 61 Americans were killed and 354 wounded.

The "prospects for a just peace" President Nixon cited on June 30 appeared dim. In its assessment of the peace negotiations following the U.S. invasion of Cambodia, the CIA observed that "the talks in Paris are dead for the time being. In the aftermath of the upset in Cambodia, Hanoi is in no mood to negotiate about anything. . . . Hanoi now believes that nothing is to be gained through negotiations until the U.S. is ready to offer major concessions to the Communists."

Although a successful tactical solution to the problem of the sanctuaries, the Cambodian invasion was therefore presenting the U.S. with a host of new and unforeseen dilemmas. How much should the U.S. assist the Cambodian government to fend off the Communist attacks and retake lost territory? How deeply should the South Vietnamese, who had affirmed their intention of reentering Cambodia whenever they deemed necessary, commit themselves to the fighting between Lon Nol's troops and the Communists? What about Laos, where U.S. and South Vietnamese commanders were already proposing allied incursions to assist the Laotian government and to destroy the Communist supply lines? Would the wider war sparked by the Cambodian incursion overtax ARVN resources and lengthen the Vietnamization process? Above all, would the expanded conflict, as well as the intensified fighting in South Vietnam, produce in the long run more American casualties than the incursion might have prevented? A traumatized America, which had begun to think that its Vietnam War was almost over and the date of total withdrawal near, wondered anew if the troops would soon be coming home after all. The gloomy prospect for a still-divided nation was one of more frustrating years of trying to get out, more painful years of struggle. America was no longer embroiled in just a Vietnam War but one threatening to engulf all of Indochina.

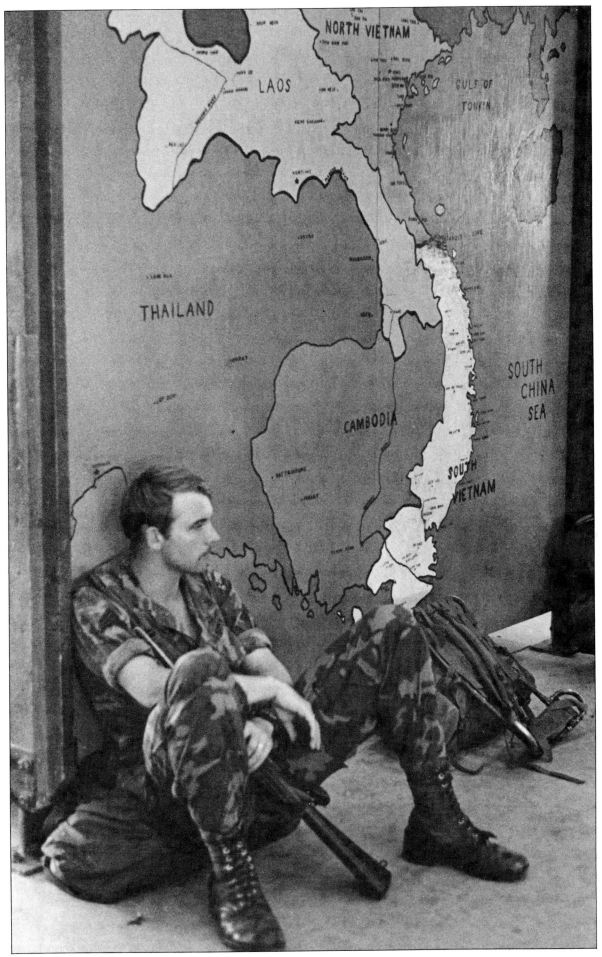

In June 1970, as the war begins to engulf all of Indochina, an American soldier awaits transport.

Bibliography

I. Books and Articles

"Air Force Air Attacks on Rise in Laos." *Air Force Times* 30 (April 29, 1970): 2.
Allman, T.D. "Cambodia: The Daring Dozen." *Far Eastern Economic Review*, August 13, 1970.
——. "The Night of the Long Knives." *Bangkok Post*, April 24, 1970.
Atwood, William. "Sihanouk Talks." *Look*, April 2, 1968.

Bailey, Tom. "The Cambodian Action: An Enemy Sanctuary Despoiled." *Soldier*, September 1971.
Baskir, Lawrence M., and William Strauss. *Chance and Circumstance*. Knopf, 1978.
Berger, Carl, ed. *The United States Air Force in Southeast Asia*. Office of Air Force History, 1977.
Blaufarb, Douglas S. *The Counterinsurgency Era*. Free Pr., 1977.
Blumenfeld, Ralph et al. *Henry Kissinger: The Public and Private Story*. NAL, 1974.
Boyle, Richard. *The Flower of the Dragon*. Ramparts Pr., 1972.
Braestrup, Peter. "New Look for Marines in Vietnam." *Navy* 12 (February 1969): 26-9.
Buckley, Tom. "The ARVN Is Bigger And Better, But—." *New York Times Magazine*, October 12, 1969.
Burchett, Wilfred. *The Second Indochina War: Cambodia and Laos Today*. Lorrimer Publishers, 1970.

Caldwell, Malcolm, and Lek Tan. *Cambodia in the Southeast Asian War*. Monthly Review Pr., 1973.
Cambodian Ministry of Information. *Documents on Viet Cong and North Vietnamese Aggression Against Cambodia*. Phnom Penh, 1970.
Cantril, Albert. 1970. "The American People, Vietnam and the Presidency." Paper delivered at the 66th Annual Meeting of American Political Science Association, September 8-12, at Los Angeles.
Carney, Timothy Michael. *Communist Party Power in Kampuchea (Cambodia): Documents and Discussion, Data Paper: no. 106*. Southeast Asia Program, Cornell University, January 1977.
Chandler, David. "Cambodia's Strategy of Survival." *Current History*, December 1969.
——. "Changing Cambodia." *Current History*, December 1970.
Chapman, Gen. Leonard. "State of the Corps." *Marine Corps Gazette* 53 (December 1969): 41-2.
Colby, William, and Peter Forbath. *Honorable Men. My Life in the CIA*. Simon & Schuster, 1978.
Collins, Lawton S. *Training and Development of the South Vietnamese Army*. Department of the Army, Vietnam Studies Series, 1978.
Cook, John L. *The Advisor*. Dorrance, 1973.
Cortright, David. *Soldiers in Revolt*. Anchor Pr., 1975.
Cosmas, Graham A. *The Marines in Vietnam, 1970-1971*. Draft manuscript, History and Museums Division, Headquarters, U.S. Marine Corps, no date.
Cossaboom, Bruce. "Hill Stirs Tempest in a Pot (on Drug Abuse in Vietnam)." *Armed Forces Journal* 107 (April 4, 1970): 9-10.

Davis, 1st Lt. Gordon M. "Dewey Canyon: All Weather Classic." *Marine Corps Gazette* 53 (July 1969): 32-40.
Dommen, Arthur J. "The Future of North Vietnam." *Current History*, April 1970.
——. "Laos in the Second Indochina War." *Current History*, December 1970.
Du Plessix Gray, Francine. "The Moratorium and the New Mobe." *New Yorker*, January 3, 1970.

Erickson, Jaci. "Withdrawal Symptoms (for U.S. Combat Troops in Vietnam)." *Armed Forces Journal* 106 (July 12, 1969): 12.

Gabriel, Richard, and Paul Savage. *Crisis in Command*. Hill & Wang, 1978.
Gallup, George, ed. *The Gallup Poll: Public Opinion 1935 to 1971*. Vol. 3, *1959-1971*, Random, 1972.
Gayn, Mark. "Domino." *New York Times Magazine*, April 22, 1973.
Gettleman, Marvin et al., eds. *Conflict in Indochina: A Reader on the Widening War in Laos and Cambodia*. Random, 1970.
Girling, J.L.S. "Crisis and Conflict in Indochina." *Orbis* 14 (Summer 1970): 349-65.
——. "The Resistance in Cambodia." *Asian Survey*, July 1972.
Gitlin, Todd. *The Whole World is Watching*. Univ. of California Pr., 1980.
Goldstein, Joseph, Burke Marshall, and Jack Schwartz, eds. *The My Lai Massacre and its Cover-up: Beyond the Reach of the Law?* Free Pr., 1976.
Goodman, Allan E. *Politics in War: The Bases of Political Community in South Vietnam*. Harvard Univ. Pr., 1973.
——. *The Lost Peace*. Hoover Inst. Pr., 1978.
Gordon, Bernard, and Kathryn Young. "Cambodia: Following the Leader?" *Asian Survey*, February 1970.
Grant, Jonathan et al., eds. *Cambodia: The Widening War in Indochina*. Washington Sq. Pr., 1971.
Grant, Z.B. "Whites Against Blacks in Vietnam." *New Republic*, January 18, 1969.

Halstead, Fred. *Out Now!: A Participant's Account of the American Antiwar Movement*. Monad Pr., 1978.
Hanser, William. *America's Army in Crisis*. Johns Hopkins Univ. Pr., 1973.
Heinl, Robert. "The Collapse of the Armed Forces." *Armed Forces Journal* 19 (June 7, 1971): 30-8.
Herring, George C. *America's Longest War*. Wiley, 1979.
——. "The Nixon Strategy in Vietnam." Paper, no date.

Herrington, Stuart A. *Silence Was a Weapon: The Vietnam War in the Villages, A Personal Perspective*. Presidio Pr., 1982.
Hersh, Seymour. *Cover-up*. Vintage Bks., 1973.
——. "Kissinger and Nixon in the White House." *Atlantic Monthly*, May 1982.
——. *The Price of Power*. Summit Bks., 1983.
——. "The Story Everyone Ignored." *Columbia Journalism Review* (Winter 1969-1970): 55-8.
Hessmann, James. "Answer to My Lai—Vietnam: The Story of (GI Nation-Building) That Doesn't Get Told." *Armed Forces Journal* 107 (December 13, 1969): 18-23.
Hinh, Maj. Gen. Nguyen Duy. *Vietnamization and the Cease-Fire*. Indochina Monographs, U.S. Army Center for Military History, GPO, 1980.
Hurwitz, Ken. *Marching Nowhere*. Norton, 1971.
Huyen, No Khac. *Vision Accomplished*. Collier Bks., 1971.

Joiner, Charles A. *The Politics of Massacre: Political Processes in South Vietnam*. Temple Univ. Pr., 1974.
Jones, Maj. Mel. "Cambodian Blitz." *Armor* 80 (January/February 1971): 21-4.

Kaiser, Robert. "Getting Into the Enemy's System." *Interplay*, July 1970.
Kalb, Marvin, and Bernard Kalb. *Kissinger*. Little, Brown, 1974.
Kalicki, H. "Sino-American Relations After Cambodia." *The World Today*, September 1970.
Kendrick, Alexander. *The Wound Within*. Little, Brown, 1974.
King, Edward. *The Death of the Army*. Saturday Review Pr., 1972.
Kirk, Donald. "Presidential Campaign Politics: The Uncontested 1971 Election." In *Electoral Politics in South Vietnam*, edited by John C. Donnell and Charles A. Joiner. Temple Bks., 1974.
——. *Wider War*. Praeger, 1971.
Kissinger, Henry A. "The Viet Nam Negotiations." *Foreign Affairs* 47 (January 1969): 211-34.
——. *The White House Years*. Little, Brown, 1979.
——. *A World Restored*. Houghton Mifflin, 1957.
Komer, Robert W. "Clear, Hold and Rebuild." *Army* 20 (May 1970): 16-24.
——. "Pacification: A Look Back . . . and Ahead." *Army* 20 (June 1970): 20-9.
Kosut, Hal, ed. *Cambodia and the Vietnam War*. Facts on File, 1971.

Lacouture, Jean. "From the Vietnam War to an Indochina War." *Foreign Affairs* 48 (July 1970): 617-28.
Laird, Melvin R. 1969. "Vietnamization." Address, AFL-CIO Convention, October 7, at Atlantic City.
Langguth, A.J. "Dear Prince: Since You Went Away." *New York Times Magazine*, August 2, 1970.
Leifer, Michael. *Cambodia: The Search for Security*. Praeger, 1967.
——. "The Cambodian Opposition." *Asian Survey*, April 1962.
——. "Political Upheaval in Cambodia." *The World Today*, May 1970.
——. "Rebellion or Subversion in Cambodia?" *Current History*, February 1969.
Lewy, Guenter. *America in Vietnam*. Oxford Univ. Pr., 1978.
Linden, Eugene. "Fragging and Other Withdrawal Symptoms." *Saturday Review*, January 8, 1972.
Lung, Col. Hoang Ngoc. *The General Offensives of 1968-69*. Indochina Monographs, U.S. Army Center for Military History, GPO, 1981.

McCaffrey, Lt. Gen. W.J. "Vietnam in 1970: Year of Transition." *Army* 20 (October 1970): 94-109.
McCoy, Alfred. *The Politics of Heroin in Southeast Asia*. Harper & Row, 1972.
Maclear, Michael. *The Ten Thousand Day War*. St. Martin, 1981.
McMahon, Lt. Col. Richard A. "The Indirect Approach." *Army* 19 (August 1969): 56-63.
Mazlish, Bruce. *Kissinger: The European Mind in American Policy*. Basic Bks., 1976.
Michener, James. *Kent State: What Happened and Why*. Random, 1971.
Millet, Stanley, ed. *South Vietnam. U.S.-Communist Confrontation in Southeast Asia*. Vol. 4, *1969*. Facts on File, 1974.
Morgan, Thomas J. "General Zais Views 'Hamburger Hill'." *Providence Journal*, June 7, 1969.
Morris, Roger. *Uncertain Greatness*. Harper & Row, 1977.
Moskos, Charles. *The American Enlisted Man*. Russell Sage Foundation, 1970.
Mueller, John E. *War, Presidents and Public Opinion*. Wiley, 1973.
Myers, Maj. Donald J. "The Pacification of Cam Lo." *Marine Corps Gazette* 53 (October 1969): 50-1.

Neglia, Capt. Anthony V. "NVA and VC—Different Enemies, Different Tactics." *Infantry* 60 (September/October 1970): 50-5.
Nixon, Richard M. *RN: The Memoirs of Richard Nixon*. Grosset & Dunlap, 1978.
Novak, Michael. "The Battle Hymn of Lt. Calley . . . and the Republic." *Commonweal*, April 30, 1971.

O'Ballance, Edgar. *The Wars in Vietnam*. Hippocrene Bks., 1975.
Osborne, John. "Death to Gooks." *New Republic*, December 13, 1969.
Osborne, Milton. *Before Kampuchea: Preludes to Tragedy*. Allen & Unwin, 1979.
——. *Politics and Power in Cambodia*. Longman, 1973.

Palmer, David R. *Summons of the Trumpet*. Presidio Pr., 1978.
Parks, W. Hays. "Crimes in Hostilities." *Marine Corps Gazette* 60 (August-September 1976): 16-22, 33-9.
Peers, Lt. Gen. William R. (Ret.). *The My Lai Inquiry*. Norton, 1979.
Peterson, Richard E., and John Bilorsky. *May 1970: The Campus Aftermath of Cambodia and Kent State*. Carnegie Commission on Higher Education, 1971.

Pike, Douglas. *War, Peace and the Viet Cong*. MIT Pr., 1969.

Polner, Murray. *No Victory Parades*. Holt, Rinehart & Winston, 1971.

Pol Pot. "Speech at KCP Anniversary Meeting." *Daily Report: Asia and Pacific*. U.S. Foreign Broadcast Information Service, September 28, 1977.

Poole, Peter. *Expansion of the Vietnam War Into Cambodia*. Ohio University, 1970.

Popkin, Samuel L. "Pacification: Politics and the Village." *Asian Survey*, August 1970.

Saar, John. "You Just Can't Hand Out Orders." *Life*, October 23, 1970.

Safire, William. *Before the Fall: An Inside View of the Pre-Watergate White House*. Doubleday, 1975.

Sale, Kirkpatrick. *SDS*. Vintage Bks., 1973.

Salter, MacDonald. "Land Reform in South Vietnam." *Asian Survey*, August 1970.

Sanford, Nevitt, and Craig Comstock, eds. *Sanctions for Evil*. Beacon Pr., 1971.

Schell, Jonathan. *The Time of Illusion*. Knopf, 1976.

Scott, Peter Dale. *The War Conspiracy*. Bobbs-Merrill, 1972.

Shaplen, Robert. "The Challenge Ahead." *Columbia Journalism Review* (Winter 1971).

_____. "Letter From Cambodia." *New Yorker*, September 17, 1966.

_____. *The Road from War, 1965–1970*. Harper & Row, 1970.

_____. *Time Out of Hand: Revolution and Reaction in Southeast Asia*. Harper & Row, 1969.

Shaver, Maj. C.A. "Reflections of a Company Commander." *Marine Corps Gazette* 53 (November 1969): 29–34.

Shawcross, William. *Sideshow*. Simon & Schuster, 1979.

Sheehan, Neil, ed. "Letters from Hamburger Hill." *Harper's*, November 1969.

Shulimson, Jack, and Maj. Edward Wells. 1982. "First In, First Out: The Marine Experience in Vietnam, 1965–1971." Paper presented at 1982 International Military History Symposium, August 4, Pennsylvania.

Sidey, Hugh. "In the Shadow of My Lai." *Life*, December 12, 1969.

Simmons, Brig. Gen. Edwin H. "Marine Corps Operations in Vietnam." *Marines in Vietnam, 1954–1973: An Anthology and Annotated Bibliography*. U.S. Marine Corps, History and Museums Division, 1974.

Smith, Charles R. "The Marines in Vietnam, 1969." Draft manuscript, History and Museums Division, U.S. Marine Corps, no date.

Smith, Roger M. "Prince Norodom Sihanouk of Cambodia." *Asian Survey*, June 1968.

Sobel, Lester A., ed. *South Vietnam: U.S. Communist Confrontation in Southeast Asia 1970*. Vol. 5. Facts on File, 1973.

Staff of the *Infantry* Magazine, ed. *A Distant Challenge: The U.S. Infantryman in Vietnam, 1967–1970*. Birmingham Publishing, 1971.

Starry, Gen. Donn. *Mounted Combat in Vietnam*. Department of the Army, Vietnam Studies Series, 1978.

Summers, Laura. "Cambodia: Model of the Nixon Doctrine." *Current History*, December 1973.

Sutsakhan, Lt. Gen. Sak. *The Khmer Republic at War and the Final Collapse*. Indochina Monographs, U.S. Army Center for Military History, GPO, 1980.

Szulc, Ted. *The Illusion of Peace: Foreign Policy in the Nixon Years*. Viking Pr., 1978.

"Talk of the Town, Moratorium." *New Yorker*, October 25, 1969.

Thompson, W. Scott, and Donaldson D. Frizzell, eds. *The Lessons of Vietnam*. Crane, Russak & Co., 1977.

Tho, Brig. Gen. Tran Dinh. *The Cambodian Incursion*. Indochina Monographs, U.S. Army Center for Military History, 1979.

Tocci, Vincent. "Understanding the War in Indochina." *Armed Forces Journal* 108 (January 18, 1971): 37–9.

Truong, Lt. Gen. Ngo Quang. *Territorial Forces*. Indochina Monographs, U.S. Army Center for Military History, 1981.

Turner, Nicholas. "Sihanouk: Prince on a Tightrope." *Reader's Digest*, May 1969.

Turner, Robert F. *Vietnamese Communism: Its Origins and Development*. Hoover Inst. Pr., 1975.

Vien, Gen. Cao Van et al. *Reflections on the Vietnam War*. U.S. Army Center for Military History, 1980.

Westmoreland, William C. *A Soldier Reports*. Dell, 1980.

Wills, Gary. *Nixon Agonistes*. Houghton Mifflin, 1970.

Wingo, Hal. "The Vexing Peacekeeper of Cambodia." *Life*, February 16, 1968.

Wren, Christopher S. "The Vietnamese GI: Can He Win His Own War?" *Look*, August 11, 1970.

Young, Kenneth. "Thailand and the Cambodian Conflict." *Current History*, December 1970.

Zasloff, Joseph, and MacAlister Brown, eds. *Communism in Indochina: New Perspectives*. Lexington Bks., 1975.

Zasloff, Joseph, and Allan E. Goodman, eds. *Indochina in Conflict*. Lexington Bks., 1972.

Zinberg, Norman. "GIs and OJs in Vietnam." *New York Times Magazine*, December 5, 1971.

II. Government and Government-Sponsored Published Reports

BDM Corporation. *A Study of Strategic Lessons Learned in Vietnam*. National Technical Information Service, 1980.

Heiser, Lt. Gen. Joseph M., Jr. *Logistic Support*. Department of the Army, Vietnam Studies Series, 1974.

Jenkins, Brian M. *The Unchangeable War*. Rand Corporation RM-6278-1-ARPA, 1972.

Moose, Richard, and James Lowenstein. "Cambodia: May 1970." Report prepared for the Committee on Foreign Relations, U.S. Senate, 91st Congress, 2d sess., 1970.

National Security Council. "National Security Study Memorandum #1." *Congressional Record*, May 10, 1972, pp. 16749–836.

Nixon, Richard M. 1969. "Vietnam Peace Initiatives." Televised address, May 14.

Office of the Inspector General. *Inspector General History, 1964–1972*. MACV, Saigon, Vietnam, no date.

Special National Intelligence Estimate. "The Outlook from Hanoi: Factors Affecting North Vietnam's Policy on the War in Vietnam." No. 14.3-70, Carrollton Pr. Declassified Documents Reference System, February 5, 1970.

Thayer, Thomas C. "How to Analyze A War Without Fronts: Vietnam 1965–1972." *Journal of Defense Research* 7B (Fall 1975).

U.S. Congress. House. Committee on Armed Services. Armed Services Investigating Subcommittee. *Unauthorized Bombing of Military Targets in North Vietnam*. 92d Congress, 2d sess., 1972.

U.S. Congress. Senate. Committee on Armed Services. *Bombings in Cambodia*. 93d Congress, 1st sess., 1973.

_____. *Nomination of General Creighton W. Abrams for Appointment as Chief of Staff*. 92d Congress, 2d sess., 1972.

_____. *Nomination of Robert F. Froehlke for Appointment as Secretary of the Army*. 92d Congress, 1st sess., 1971.

U.S. Congress. Senate. Committee on Foreign Relations. *Vietnam: Policy and Prospects*. 91st Congress, 2d sess., 1970.

_____. *Moral and Military Aspects of the War in Southeast Asia*. 91st Congress, 2d sess., 1970.

_____. U.S. Security Agreements and Commitments Abroad Subcommittee. *U.S. Air Operations in Cambodia: April 1973*. 93d Congress, 1st sess., 1973.

U.S. Congress. Senate. Committee on Government Operations. Investigating Subcommittee. *Fraud and Corruption in Management of Military Club System*. 91st Congress, 2d sess., 1971.

U.S. Congress. Senate. Committee on the Judiciary. Subcommittee to Investigate Problems Connected with Refugees and Escapees. *Civilian Casualty, Social Welfare and Refugee Problems in South Vietnam*. 92d Congress, 1st sess., 1969.

_____. *Problems of War Victims in Indochina, Part I: Vietnam*. 92d Congress, 2d sess., 1972.

_____. *Refugee and Civilian War Casualty Problems in Indochina: A Staff Report*. 91st Congress, 2d sess., 1970.

_____. *Refugee and Civilian War Casualty Problems in Laos and Cambodia*. 91st Congress, 2d sess., 1970.

_____. *War-Related Civilian Problems in Indochina, Part I—Vietnam*. 92d Congress, 1st sess., 1971.

_____. *War-Related Civilian Problems in Indochina, Part III—Vietnam*. 92d Congress, 1st sess., 1971.

_____. *World Refugee and Humanitarian Problems*. 92d Congress, 1st sess., 1971.

U.S. Department of State. Vietnam Documents and Research Notes, 39, 46–8, 51, 64, 66, 81, 82, and 101 (part I–IV). GPO, Variously, October 1967–January 1972.

U.S. General Accounting Office. *Refugee and Civilian War Casualty Problems in Vietnam*. Report prepared for U.S. Judiciary Committee, Subcommittee to Investigate Problems Connected with Refugees and Escapees. GPO, December 14, 1970.

U.S. Naval Forces Vietnam Force Intelligence. *An Assessment of the Enemy Sapper Threat*. Carrollton Pr. Declassified Documents Reference System, October 1969.

U.S. Operations Mission, Vietnam. *The Vietcong Infrastructure, A Background Paper*. GPO, 1970.

Vietnam Documents and Research Notes. Document no. 88: *The Viet Cong's March–April, 1970 Plans for Expanding Control in Cambodia: A Documentary Record*. January 1971.

III. The authors consulted the following newspapers and periodicals:

Air Force Times, 1969–1970; *Air University Review*, 1969–1970; *Armor*, 1969–1970; *Army*, 1969–1970; *Army Times*, 1969–1970; *Infantry*, 1969–1970; *Life*, 1969–1970; *Marine Gazette*, 1969–1970; *Navy*, 1969–1970; *Newsweek*, 1969–1971; *New York Times*, 1965–1966, 1969–1970; *Time*, 1969–1971; *U.S. News and World Report*, 1969–1970; *Wall Street Journal*, 1969–1970; *Washington Post*, 1969–1970.

IV. Unpublished Documents

Department of the Army, Office of the Adjutant General

    After Action Reports

        11th Armored Cavalry Regiment. Operation Dong Tien II and Toan Thang 43, December 9, 1970.

        9th Infantry Division. August 27, 1969.

        U.S. Army Support Command. Attack on Cam Ranh Peninsula, August 13, 1969.

    Operational Reports

        101st Airborne Division. Lessons Learned, Period Ending July 31, 1969. December 9, 1969.

        _____. "Battle at Dong Ap Bia (Hamburger Hill)," no date.

        _____. 22d Military History Detachment. "'Apache Snow', May 10, 1969 to June 7, 1969." July 31, 1969.

        18th Military History Detachment. Lessons Learned, 25th Infantry Division, Period Ending July 31, 1970. March 15, 1971.

        1st Cavalry Division (Airmobile). Lessons Learned, HQ, 1st Cavalry Division (AM), Period Ending July 31, 1970. August 14, 1970.

        HQ, 6th Convalescent Center. Lessons Learned for the 6th Convalescent Center for the Period Ending October 31, 1969. November 3, 1969.

U.S. Military Assistance Command, Vietnam

    "Bi-Weekly Summary of VCI Activities," February 1–4, 1970, April 19–May 9, 1970, May 10–30, 1970, December 1–31, 1970.

"Commander's Summary of the MACV Objectives Plan." No date.
Country Logistics Improvement Plan. July 1, 1968.
Long Range Planning Task Group. "Briefing Given to COMUSMACV on November 20, 1969." No date.
RVNAF Improvement and Modernization and Management System Report. Fourth Quarter, 1969. 1970.
RVNAF Improvement and Modernization Progress Report. April 24, 1970.
Department of Defense
Secretary of Defense Melvin Laird
Memorandum for the President: "Trip to Vietnam, March 5-12, 1969." March 13, 1969.
Office of the Assistant Secretary of Defense (Comptroller). Statistics on Vietnam, 1965-1972.
Report on Selected Air and Ground Operations in Cambodia and Laos. September 10, 1973.
National Archives
National Security Study Memoranda 36 & 37. April 10, 1969.
History and Museums Division, Headquarters, U.S. Marine Corps.
Oral Histories of Capt. David Winecoff, Gen. Robert H. Barrow, and Gen. Raymond G. Davis.
2d Battalion, 9th Marines, 3d Marine Division.
Combat Operations After Action Report, Dewey Canyon. February 25, 1969.
3d Battalion, 9th Marines, 3d Marine Division.
Combat Operations After Action Report, Dewey Canyon. March 25, 1969.
Private Papers
Paul Lapointe, former 1st Lt., U.S. Army.
Dr. Donald S. Marshall, Lt. Col. U.S. Army (Ret.).

V. Interviews
Gen. Robert H. Barrow, former CO, 9th Marines, 3d Marine Division, 1969.
Geoffrey M. Boehm, former Warrant Officer, 100 Bravo, helicopter pilot, 1st Air Cavalry.
Amb. Ellsworth Bunker, former Ambassador to South Vietnam.
Marty Cacioppo, former communications NCO.
Col. Norman Camp, former member of Northern Neurological Psychiatric Team in Da Nang.
Amb. William Colby, former Deputy COMUSMACV, CORDS.
Col. Joseph B. Conmy (Ret.), former CO, 3d Brigade, 101st Airborne Division.
Maj. Gen. Raymond G. Davis (Ret.), former CG, 3d Marine Division.
Lawrence Fuller, former Captain, Advisory Team 86, Long An Province.
Scott Gauthier, former medic, 9th and 25th Infantry Divisions.
Donald Kirk, covered the Vietnam War for four years and is the author of two books on Cambodia.
Jonathan Ladd, former Political-Military Counselor, U.S. Embassy, Phnom Penh.
Melvin Laird, former Secretary of Defense.
Paul Lapointe, former 1st Lt., platoon leader, 1st Battalion, 52d Infantry, 198th Infantry Brigade, American Division.
George McArthur, former AP bureau chief and *Los Angeles Times* reporter in Saigon.
Lt. Col. Donald S. Marshall (Ret.), former head, Long Range Planning Task Force (MACV).
Keith Martin, former fire direction officer, 1st Battalion, 7th Artillery, 1st Infantry Division.
William Paris, former Capt., Aero-Scout platoon leader, 11th Armored Cavalry Regiment.
Mark Pritchard, former avionics technician, 2d Battalion, 20th Aerial Artillery, 1st Air Cavalry.
Lloyd Rives, former chargé d'affaires, U.S. Embassy, Phnom Penh.
Brig. Gen. Nathan Vail, former CO, 2d Battalion, 22d Infantry (Mechanized), 25th Infantry Division.
James Willard, former Spec 4, Mortar Co., 1st Battalion, 5th Infantry, 25th Infantry Division.
Lt. Col. David Winecoff, former CO, H Company 2d Battalion, 9th Marines.

Photography Credits

Cover Photograph
Shunsuke Akatsuka—UPI.

Chapter 1
p. 7, Elliott Erwitt—Magnum. p. 9, Mark Gibson. p. 11, U.S. Marine Corps. p. 13, UPI. p. 14, U.S. Marine Corps. p. 20, top, Wide World; bottom, Hubert Van Es—Wide World. p. 21, Hubert Van Es—Wide World.

Chapter 2
p. 25, Camera Press Ltd. p. 27, Alfred Eisenstaedt—LIFE Magazine, © 1969, Time Inc. pp. 30-1, Kent Potter—UPI. p. 34, Ngo Vinh Long Collection. pp. 38-9, Marc Riboud.

Moratoriums
p. 41, John Olson. p. 42, top, Woodfin Camp; bottom, Constantine Manos—Magnum. p. 43, Ted Streshinsky. p. 44, David Gahr. pp. 45-6, Bonnie Freer. p. 47, top, Bonnie Freer; bottom, Wide World.

Chapter 3
pp. 49, 51, Mark Gibson. p. 53, Dick Swanson—LIFE Magazine, © 1969, Time Inc. p. 55, Wallace Terry. p. 56, U.S. Army. p. 58, Co Rentmeester—LIFE Magazine, © 1972, Time Inc. p. 65, UPI. p. 66, Bob Hodierne. p. 67, Shunsuke Akatsuka—UPI.

Back to Basic
p. 68, Aldo Panzieri. p. 70, top, © Larry Burrows Collection; bottom, Mark Godfrey—Archive Pictures Inc. p. 71, top, Nik Wheeler—UPI; bottom, Mark Godfrey—Archive Pictures Inc. p. 72, Nik Wheeler—UPI. p. 73, top, Philip Jones Griffiths—Magnum; bottom, Mark Godfrey—Archive Pictures Inc.

Chapter 4
p. 75, Mark Gibson. p. 77, Philip Jones Griffiths—Magnum. pp. 78-9, U.S. Army. p. 81, © Larry Burrows Collection. p. 82, Philip Jones Griffiths—Magnum. p. 83, © Larry Burrows Collection. pp. 84-8, Larry Burrows—LIFE Magazine, © 1969, Time Inc.

Chapter 5
p. 93, Mark Jury. pp. 94-5, Dick Swanson—LIFE Magazine, © 1969, Time Inc. p. 96, Aldo Panzieri. p. 99, Dick Swanson—LIFE Magazine, © 1970, Time Inc. p. 102, Wallace Terry. p. 105, Bruno Barbey—Magnum. p. 107, Philip Jones Griffiths—Magnum. pp. 108-9, Ron Haeberle—LIFE Magazine, © 1969, Time Inc. p. 113, Bernard Edelman.

Chapter 6
p. 117, Marc Riboud. p. 119, Werner Bischof—Magnum. p. 122, Horace Bristol—LIFE Magazine, © 1955, Time Inc. p. 124, Larry Burrows—LIFE Magazine, © 1968, Time Inc. p. 125, Howard Sochurek—LIFE Magazine, © 1952, Time Inc. p. 126, top, Li Chang-yung—Eastfoto; bottom, Larry Burrows—LIFE Magazine, © 1967, Time Inc. p. 129, Pictorial Parade.

Cambodia Portraits
pp. 131-3, © Albert Kahn Collection. p. 134, top, Don McCullin—Magnum; bottom, Denis Cameron. p. 135, Larry Burrows—LIFE Magazine, © 1970, Time Inc. p. 136, top, Don McCullin—Magnum; bottom, Denis Cameron. p. 137, Don McCullin—Magnum.

Chapter 7
p. 139, Kyoichi Sawada—UPI. p. 143, Terence Khoo—Black Star. p. 145, top, John Robaton—Camera 5; bottom, Denis Cameron—NEWSWEEK. p. 146, Terence Khoo—Black Star. p. 150, Don McCullin—Magnum. p. 151, top, Don McCullin—Magnum; bottom, UPI. p. 153, The Nixon Project—National Archives.

Life at a Firebase
pp. 154-60, Mark Jury. p. 156, top, © 1972, G. B. Trudeau. Reprinted with permission of Universal Press Syndicate. All rights reserved.

Chapter 8
p. 163, Shunsuke Akatsuka—UPI. p. 165, Henri Huet—Wide World. p. 169, Larry Burrows—LIFE Magazine, © 1970, Time Inc. pp. 170-1, Philip Jones Griffiths—Magnum. pp. 172-3, Le Minh—TIME Magazine. pp. 175-6, Larry Burrows—LIFE Magazine, © 1972, Time Inc. p. 179, John Filo—UPI. p. 180, John A. Darnell, courtesy Life Picture Service. p. 182, John Filo, courtesy VALLEY NEWS DISPATCH. p. 185, Bernard Edelman.

Acknowledgments

Boston Publishing wishes to acknowledge the kind assistance of the following people: Joyce Bennett; Dr. Norman Camp; Major Edgar C. Doleman, Jr., U.S. Army (retired); Madeline Doleman; Charles Dunn, professor and chairman, Department of Celtic Languages and Literature, Harvard University; Barbara Flum; Albert Kahn Collection, Paris; Lieutenant Colonel Dr. Donald S. Marshall, U.S. Army (retired); Terry Moy; Jack Shulimson, Marine Corps Historical Center; Brigadier General E. H. Simmons, former commandant, U.S. Marine Corps (retired); Charles R. Smith; Paul Taborn, Office of the Army Adjutant General; Melissa Totten; and numerous veterans of the Vietnam War who wish to remain anonymous.

The index was prepared by Lee Carr.

Map Credits

All maps prepared by Diane McCaffery. Sources are as follows:
p. 18, top—United States Marine Corps.

p. 18, bottom—Department of the Army.

p. 52—U.S. Army Center of Military History.

p. 63—Department of the Army.

p. 166, left and right—U.S. Army Center of Military History.

p. 178—*The Kent Affair* (eds. Ottavio Casale and Louis Paskoff). Copyright 1971 by Houghton Mifflin Co. Used by permission.

p. 62. "The Boonierat Song" is from *The Thirteenth Valley* by John M. Del Vecchio. Copyright © 1982 by John M. Del Vecchio. Reprinted by permission of Bantam Books, Inc. All Rights Reserved.

Index

U.S. Military Units
see note below

Note: Military units are listed according to the general organizational structure of the U.S. Armed Forces. The following chart summarizes that structure for the U.S. Army. The principal difference between the army and the Marine Corps structures in Vietnam lay at the regimental level. The army eliminated the regimental command structure after World War II (although battalions retained a regimental designation for purposes of historical continuity, *e.g.,* 1st Battalion, 7th Cavalry [Regiment]). Marine Corps battalions were organized into regiments instead of brigades except under a few unusual circumstances. The marines, however, do not use the word "regiment" to designate their units; *e.g.,* 1st Marines refers to the 1st Marine Regiment.

U.S. Army structure
(to company level)

Unit	Size	Commanding officer
Division	12,000–18,000 troops or 3 brigades	Major General
Brigade	3,000 troops or 2–4 battalions	Colonel
Battalion*	600–1,000 troops or 3–5 companies	Lieutenant Colonel
Company	150 troops** or 3–4 platoons	Captain

* Squadron equivalent to battalion.
** Size varies based on type of unit.

Names, Acronyms, Terms

ARVN—Army of the Republic of Vietnam (South Vietnam).

Base Area—MACV designation for area used by the Communists as a base camp. Usually contained fortifications, supply depots, hospitals, and training facilities.

CAG—Combined Action Groups. Pacification teams organized by U.S. Marines. Consisted of a South Vietnamese Popular Forces battalion and a U.S. Marine Company.

CAP—Combined Action Platoons. Pacification teams organized by U.S. Marines. Consisted of a South Vietnamese Popular Forces platoon and a U.S. Marine rifle squad and a medical corpsman.

Chieu Hoi—the "open arms" program promising clemency and financial aid to guerrillas who stopped fighting and returned to live under South Vietnamese government authority.

CIA—Central Intelligence Agency.

CINCPAC—Commander in Chief, Pacific Command. Commander of American forces in the Pacific region, which includes Southeast Asia.

CIDG—Civilian Irregular Defense Group. Project devised by the CIA that combined self-defense with economic and social programs designed to raise the standard of living and win the loyalty of the mountain people. Chief work of the U.S. Special Forces.

COMUSMACV—Commander, U.S. Military Assistance Command, Vietnam. (In 1968–72, General Creighton Abrams.)

CORDS—The Civil Operations and Revolutionary Development Support was established under MACV in 1967. CORDS organized all U.S. civilian agencies in Vietnam within the military chain of command.

COSVN—Central Office for South Vietnam. Communist party headquarters in South Vietnam.

DEROS—Date eligible for return from overseas. The date a soldier's tour in Vietnam was to end.

DMZ—demilitarized zone. Established by the Geneva accords of 1954, provisionally dividing North Vietnam from South Vietnam along the seventeenth parallel.

DOD—Department of Defense.

DRV—Democratic Republic of Vietnam. The government of Ho Chi Minh, established on September 2, 1945. Provisionally confined to North Vietnam by the Geneva accords of 1954.

firebase—artillery firing position, often secured by infantry.

fire support base—semifixed artillery base established to increase indirect fire coverage of an area and provide security for the firing unit.

fragging—killing or attempting to kill a fellow soldier or officer, usually with a fragmentation grenade.

IV Corps—fourth allied military tactical zone encompassing Mekong Delta region.

FUNK—National United Front of Kampuchea. Government established by Sihanouk after he had been ousted from power and exiled from Cambodia.

GVN—U.S. abbreviation for the government of South Vietnam. Also referred to as the Republic of Vietnam.

JCS—Joint Chiefs of Staff. Consisted of chairman, U.S. Army chief of staff, chief of naval operations, U.S. Air Force chief of staff, and marine commandant (member ex officio). Advises the president, the National Security Council, and the secretary of defense.

Kalishnikov—AK47 rifle, made originally by the Kalishnikov company in Russia.

Khmers Rouges—members of the Pracheachon, the Cambodian leftist party. Named "Khmers Rouges" by Sihanouk to distinguish them from the right wing "blues."

KIA—killed in action.

LORAPL—Long Range Planning Task Group. Created in July 1968 by General Abrams to review U.S. strategy in Vietnam over the previous four years and recommend changes. Headed by Lieutenant Colonel Dr. Donald S. Marshall.

LZ—landing zone.

MACV—Military Assistance Command, Vietnam. U.S. command over all U.S. military activities in Vietnam, originated in 1962.

MAT—Mobile Advisory Team. Usually a six-member team consisting of two U.S. Army officers, three enlisted men, and an interpreter responsible for training territorial forces (RFs and PFs).

M-Day—Moratorium day.

Menu—code name for B-52s bombing operation against Communist base areas in Cambodia.

New Mobe—The New Mobilization Committee To End the War.

NLF—National Liberation Front. Officially the National Front for the Liberation of the South. Formed on December 20, 1960, it aimed to overthrow South Vietnam's government and reunite the North and the South. The NLF included Communists and non-Communists.

NSC—National Security Council.

OCS—Officers' Candidate School.

I Corps—"Eye" Corps. First allied tactical zone encompassing the five northernmost provinces of South Vietnam.

pacification—unofficial term given to various programs of the South Vietnamese and U.S. governments to provide security, destroy enemy influence in the villages, and gain support of civilians for the GVN.

PF—Popular Forces. South Vietnamese village defense units.

Phoenix—(*Phung Hoang*). A South Vietnamese intelligence-gathering program advised by CORDS, Phoenix was designed to neutralize the Vietcong infrastructure through identification and arrest of key party cadres.

PRG—People's Revolutionary Government. Established in 1969 by the NLF.

PROVN—Program for the Pacification and Long Term Development of South Vietnam.

PSDF—People's Self-Defense Force.

REMF—Rear Area Mother Fucker. Nickname given to men serving in the rear by front-line soldiers.

RF—Regional Forces. South Vietnamese provincial defense units.

ROTC—Reserve Officers' Training Corps.

RVNAF—Republic of Vietnam Armed Forces.

Sangkum Reastr Niyum—People's Socialist Community. Cambodian party formed in 1955 by Sihanouk, which espoused an ideology of Buddhist Socialism.

sapper—originally, in European wars, a soldier who built and repaired fortifications. VC sappers were commando raiders adept at penetrating allied defenses.

SDS—Students for a Democratic Society.

Tet—Lunar New Year, the most important Vietnamese holiday.

III Corps—third allied military tactical zone encompassing area from northern Mekong Delta to southern central highlands.

II Corps—second allied military tactical zone encompassing the central highlands and adjoining coastal lowlands.

USIS—United States Information Service.

VCI—Vietcong infrastructure. NLF local apparatus, responsible for overall direction of the insurgency including all political and military operations.

Vietcong—originally a derogatory reference to the NLF, a contraction of Vietnam Cong San (Vietnamese Communist).

VMC—Vietnam Moratorium Committee.

VNAF—Vietnamese Air Force (South).